Variation in Second Language Acquisition
Volume II: Psycholinguistic Issues

D0808078

Multilingual Matters

Age in Second Language Acquisition
  BIRGIT HARLEY
Bilingual Children: From Birth to Teens
  GEORGE SAUNDERS
Bilingual and Multicultural Education: Canadian Perspectives
  S. SHAPSON and V. D'OYLEY (eds)
Bilingualism and the Individual
  A. HOLMEN, E. HANSEN, J. GIMBEL and J. JØRGENSEN (eds)
Bilingualism in Society and School
  J. JØRGENSEN, E. HANSEN, A. HOLMEN and J. GIMBEL (eds)
Bilingualism and Special Education
  JIM CUMMINS
Bilingualism: Basic Principles
  HUGO BAETENS BEARDSMORE
Code-Mixing and Code Choice
  JOHN GIBBONS
Current Trends in European Second Language Acquisition Research
  HANS W. DECHERT (ed.)
The Education of Linguistic and Cultural Minorities in the OECD Countries
  STACY CHURCHILL
Introspection in Second Language Research
  C. FAERCH and G. KASPER (eds)
Key Issues in Bilingualism and Bilingual Education
  COLIN BAKER
Language Acquisition: The Age Factor
  D. M. SINGLETON
Language and Ethnicity in Minority Sociolinguistic Perspective
  JOSHUA FISHMAN
Language and Education in Multilingual Settings
  BERNARD SPOLSKY (ed.)
Learner Language and Language Learning
  C. FAERCH, K. HAASTRUP and R. PHILLIPSON (eds)
Methods in Dialectology
  ALAN R. THOMAS (ed.)
Minority Education and Ethnic Survival
  MICHAEL BYRAM
Modelling and Assessing Second Language Acquisition
  K. HYLTENSTAM and M. PIENEMANN (eds)
Oral Language Across the Curriculum
  DAVID CORSON
Papers from the Fifth Nordic Conference on Bilingualism
  J. GIMBEL, E. HANSEN, A. HOLMEN and J. JØRGENSEN (eds)
Raising Children Bilingually: The Pre-School Years
  LENORE ARNBERG
The Role of the First Language in Second Language Learning
  HÅKAN RINGBOM
Schooling in a Plural Canada
  JOHN R. MALLEA

Please contact us for the latest book information:

Multilingual Matters,
Bank House, 8a Hill Rd,
Clevedon, Avon BS21 7HH, England

Multilingual Matters 50
Series Editor: Derrick Sharp

Variation in Second Language Acquisition Volume II: Psycholinguistic Issues

Edited by
Susan Gass, Carolyn Madden,
Dennis Preston and Larry Selinker

MULTILINGUAL MATTERS LTD
Clevedon · Philadelphia

Library of Congress Cataloging in Publication Data

Variation in second language acquisition
  (Multilingual matters ; 49–50)
  Selected papers presented at the XIth Michigan
Conference in Applied Linguistics held October 7–9,
1987 at the University of Michigan in Ann Arbor—Pref.
  Includes bibliographies and indexes.
  Contents: v. 1. Discourse and pragmatics.
v. 2. Psycholinguistic issues.
  1. Second language acquisition—Congresses.
2. Language and languages—Variation—Congresses.
I. Gass, Susan M.   II. Conference on Applied
Linguistics (11th : 1987 : University of Michigan)
III. Series: Multilingual Matters (Series); 49–50.
P118.2.V37   1989   401'.9   88-25503

British Library Cataloguing in Publication Data

Variation in second language acquisition.
  (Multilingual matters; 50).
  Vol. II: Psycholinguistic issues
  1. Foreign language skills. Acquisition.
Sociolinguistic aspects
I. Gass, Susan
401'.9

ISBN 1-85359-028-2
ISBN 1-85359-027-4 Pbk

Multilingual Matters Ltd
Bank House, 8a Hill Road,   &   242 Cherry Street,
Clevedon, Avon BS21 7HH,   Philadelphia, PA 19106-1906
England   USA

Index compiled by Meg Davies (Society of Indexers)
Typeset by MCS Ltd, Salisbury, SP1 2AY
Printed and bound in Great Britain by WBC Print, Bristol

Contents

Preface

This volume is composed of selected papers presented at the XIth Michigan Conference in Applied Linguistics, 'Variation in Second Language Acquisition', held October 7–9, 1987, at the University of Michigan in Ann Arbor. There were two distinct themes which emerged from this conference: those papers which dealt primarily with psycholinguistic issues are published in this volume; those papers which have as their major theme issues of discourse and pragmatics are published in *Variation in Second Language Acquisition: Discourse and Pragmatics*, also published by Multilingual Matters.

The purpose of the conference was to bring together scholars from two related areas of research. In particular, it was our goal to create a dialogue between sociolinguistic and second language acquisition researchers in an attempt to understand precisely where their areas of concerns intersect and how those shared concerns contribute in a broader perspective to the issue of language variation. The conference succeeded in bringing together scholars from North America, Asia, Eastern Europe and Western Europe, representing a wide range of geographical and academic backgrounds.

As usual in such a large undertaking, there are many people to thank. The University of Michigan, continuing its commitment over the years to language teaching and learning, provided, through a number of resources, the principal funding and the setting for this endeavour. The English Language Institute and its Director, Professor John Swales, gave the essential financial and logistic support. The Interdisciplinary Program in Linguistics, the English Composition Board, The Department of Germanic Languages and Literatures and the Rackham School of Graduate Studies also provided financial support as did the Polish Exchange program of Eastern Michigan University and the English Language Center of Michigan State University. Many colleagues, students and staff helped with the running of the Conference, and we are grateful to them as well.

Section One:
Introduction

1 Introduction

Variation is central to the discipline of sociolinguistics. Recently, there has been a growing interest in establishing connections between sociolinguistics, on the one hand, and second language acquisition, on the other, the goal being to determine the relevance of each discipline to the concerns of the other. One can find in the literature a clear intersection of interests, yet until now there has been little mutual contact. Important advances in the study of variation have been made in both sociolinguistics and second language acquisition studies with each separate area having implications for the other (see Preston, in press). These books specifically address those areas which are of concern to both disciplines.

A primary goal of sociolinguistics is to account for the facts of variation within a theory of language. Second language acquisition researchers extend variation studies into acquisition settings. This book and the accompanying volume provide an initial impetus for understanding the range of phenomena to be considered and, consequently, for reformulating models of variation.

Two basic connections between these two fields of inquiry form the framework for these two books: variation external to the learner and variation internal to the learner. The first provides the basis for Volume I; the second the basis for Volume II. The decision to include a particular chapter in Volume I or Volume II is intended to highlight that chapter's major contribution rather than imply a limitation of its scope.

The focus of this volume is on variation of linguistic form in the developing grammars of second language learners. In an attempt to align second language acquisition research with a linguistic model of inquiry, early research emphasised the systematicity of learners' grammars with little mention or recognition of variation. Evidence, however, soon emerged which indicated the importance of variation within the context of a theory of second language acquisition. Dickerson (1975) and Dickerson & Dickerson (1977) demonstrated convincingly that a learner's interlanguage phonology 'varies systematically' both in response to the degree of 'formality' of the elicitation task and to varying phonological environments. Tarone *et al.* (1976) presented variable interlanguage data on several linguistic levels (morphological, syntactic and semantic) relating these to learner communication strategies. Tarone integrated the work of Labov (1966) by making the claim that variation takes place along a 'style-shifting continuum' with 'attention to form' being the key determinant. Ellis (1985), building on Tarone's work and drawing on Bickerton's account of variation, suggested that there is non-systematic variation in learner-language. He further claimed that this type of variation is a 'necessary condition' for the continuous development of a learner's language and that the variation of form/function relationships is necessary for the enhancement of the communicative effectiveness of the learner's language system.

From the perspective of researchers such as Ellis and Tarone, the study of interlanguage variation of linguistic form and function has emerged as an essential area of investigation. This volume brings together the concerns of psycholinguistics and sociolinguistics in attempting to find a methodological and theoretical framework on which a theory of second language acquisition can be built. The chapters vary in their approach to the essential issues of variation and interlanguage development, but provide cohesion in their attention to the developing forms and functions of second language learners.

Section Two provides a comprehensive overview of current theoretical models of second language acquisition and how these models can and should account for interlanguage variation.

Tarone's chapter provides an account of proposed theories of interlanguage variation and a critique of how each fails to meet the criteria of an adequate theory. She discusses the characteristics and weaknesses of both 'inner processing theories' and 'sociolinguistic and discourse theories' and thus provides a basis for the evaluation and interpretation of the psycholinguistic issues of this volume and the discourse and pragmatic research of Volume I.

Ellis' chapter elaborates on the notions and sources of interlanguage variability as he develops a coherent and dynamic model of second language acquisition. Ellis defines and explores the dichotomous concepts of free and systematic variation, horizontal and vertical variation, and development-as-sequence and development-as-growth. Throughout, Ellis emphasises the need for a model which not only recognises and accounts for emerging forms of second language learners but one which integrates the social uses of language as a major source of language variation and language development.

In Chapter 3 Andersen sets about the task of providing a framework for explaining variation within a theory of second language acquisition. Andersen takes a cognitive view of variation in the developing grammars of individual learners over time. Within the framework of a Cognitive–Interactionist Theory, Andersen applies a Nativisation Model and twelve Slobin-like operating principles to learner data. His analysis of how the operating principles apply to these data provides a convincing account of variation in the developing grammars of English, Spanish and Japanese second language learners. He concludes with directions for further research within this framework over a broader base of linguistic data, across different styles, registers and tasks.

In the final chapter in Section Two, Young criticises previous studies in second language acquisition variation for their use of such unsubstantiated independent variables as 'attention to form' and 'formality', noting, in particular, that a large number of sociolinguistic components are allowed to vary even under experimental conditions. He suggests that such research might make use of a more comprehensive model of components (Hymes' SPEAKING) and of multivariate statistical analysis (VARBRUL) to determine their influence on interlanguage performance.

In studying the variation in noun plural marking by Chinese learners of English, Young holds the variables suggested by Hymes' mnemonic constant, altering only 'participants' by having the respondents in his study interviewed by a native and non-native speaker. In addition, two levels of proficiency were selected to provide a cross-sectional analysis of the developing interlanguage in terms of plural marking.

Young shows how VARBRUL analysis allows identification of a number of influences on plural marking and notes that these influences derive from the linguistic as well as the social and interactional environment. Particularly noteworthy is the fact that phonological environments emerge as a strong factor in determining plural marking for low proficiency respondents but are not a factor at all for the high proficiency group. Similarly, the degree of identification with the interlocutor has a significant influence on the high proficiency respondents but none on those with low proficiency, suggesting that social contexts replace linguistic ones as the more powerful influences on variation in the development of learner language.

In Section Three attention is given to the topic of conversation as a source of variation in learner's intralanguage/interlanguage. Lantolf & Ahmed investigate a language learner's performance across tasks and demonstrate how a change in task, from interview to conversation, elicits a shift from syntactic to pragmatic speech, the former evidenced by morphological accuracy and subject–predicate utterances and the latter by less accuracy and topic–comment utterances. Lantolf & Ahmed, like Ellis, argue against a linear model of language development exemplified by a focus on formal analysis of morphological accuracy and suggest, rather, a dynamic model of interlanguage development inclusive of co-existing patterns of syntactic and pragmatic speech determined by the social and psychological context of the language tasks.

In Chapter 7 Bailey attempts to reconcile the apparently divergent explanations of form versus function in accounting for variation in developing interlanguages. Taking the progressive as a test case, she distinguishes the functional uses of the present and past progressives, noting that they have often been conflated by earlier researchers. Her claim is that the simplicity of form of the progressive cannot fully account for the fact that it is learned early in the present tense but late in the past. In imitation and production tasks she shows that the simple past is generally acquired earlier than the past progressive, confirming the idea that the functional priority of the simple past gives it greater prominence, although analogy with the simple form of the functionally more salient present progressive may cause the past progressive to occur more frequently in the earliest stages of acquisition. Eventual accuracy in the use of past progressives by more advanced learners is found to be related specifically to the discourse function of narrative backgrounding. Variation in accuracy was also based on irregular versus regular past tense forms. Bailey concludes that considerable interlanguage variation is due to a complex interplay between the influences of form and function.

Eisenstein & Starbuck explore the effects that emotional investment in topic has on learners' accuracy in extended conversation. Ten second language learners were engaged in two interviews each, one on a predetermined topic of low interest and the other of high interest. As in the Lantolf & Ahmed study, an investment in topic resulted in less morphological accuracy and more variation in discourse patterns, suggesting once again the need to look beyond the development-as-sequence approach to account for variation in second language learning.

Section Four emphasises individual learner differences. Obler's chapter is both a comprehensive study of neuropsychological factors associated with language learning abilities and an investigation of particular language learners' performance on a battery of neuropsychological tests. Results of a talented second language learner's performance indicate, not surprisingly, the learner's exceptional verbal memory and ability to extract patterns from complex input. Other results of unsuccessful learners' performance, however, challenge some of the accepted lore of second language acquisition theories.

Ioup in her chapter presents an in-depth investigation of selected unsuccessful young adult language learners who arrived in the United States as children (aged 6 to 9). Ioup examines their knowledge of English from various perspectives, including facts derived from Universal Grammar, language particular aspects of English grammar and pronunciation abilities. She then administers a series of neuropsychological tests to one of the unsuccessful learners and compares the result with those of a successful language learner.

In Chapter 11 Wode uses second language data to support his contentions concerning early phonological representations of monolingual children. An important assumption underlying Wode's research is that learning abilities change as a function of age. His emphasis in this chapter is on phonological learning, focusing on the ways in which the phonological components of lexical items are encoded in memory. He specifically argues that early phonological representations are holistic rather than segment-based. Wode's evidence comes not only from the behaviour of young children, but more importantly for our concerns, from the phonology of bilingual children. He reports no evidence of phonological transfer (of the sort reported for second language acquisition) in early bilinguals, suggesting a non-segment based internalisation of the phonologies of the two languages. Wode's analysis provides a principled basis for the explanation of the sudden burst of L1 vocabulary growth in young children. Wode proposes that processing mechanisms which depend on holistic storage and retrieval are much less efficient than those based on the storage and retrieval of segments. Thus, when new organisational principles develop for coding phonological information (i.e. segment-based representational strategies), the child is equipped to deal more effectively with new words.

Unlike the other chapters in this volume, Section Five is concerned with situations of language loss. In Chapter 12 Fakhri describes the effect that interruption in foreign language study has on the means by which reference is encoded. His study focuses on the language of native speakers of English who had studied French as a foreign language and who had terminated their study of French with varying degrees of recency. Considering the form of reference (full noun phrases or pronominalisations) to a previously mentioned noun phrase in the discourse, Fakhri argues that one has to consider the linguistic environment in which reference takes place. Whether learners use full noun phrases or pronominalisation is dependent on the number of referents in the discourse and the grammatical function of the referential form. Fakhri suggests that, as in acquisition, loss is observed in one linguistic context before spreading to others.

In Chapter 13 Kaufman & Aronoff show how typological differences play a role in variable language attrition. Their particular emphasis is on the way *code-blending* at the morphological level in Hebrew and English can be used to account for a child's productivity in the two language systems. Hebrew verbs have a rich system of internal modification for various functions, but the nominal system, though open to some internal variation, is principally affixation-based, like English. The child persists in the use of internal modification of verbs, even inventing a Hebrew-like system for L2 (English) verbs, but her nominal system becomes rapidly and exclusively affixal. Kaufman & Aronoff conclude, therefore, that some variable features of a developing interlanguage may be attributed to typological divergence between the L1 and the L2.

Finally, Section Six illustrates applications of a variety of approaches from general linguistics to variable data in both second language acquisition and inter—intralingual contact situations. Adamson suggests that some variation in a developing interlanguage has its source in the degree to which learners move from least to most marked members of prototypical grammatical configurations. He notes that animate subjects of transitive verbs, more prototypical and less marked than inanimate ones, are more likely to show other features of nouns, e.g. plural marking. Such degrees of markedness may be expressed in variable rules, and a psycholinguistic implicational hierarchy may be deduced for learners from marked forms. That is, knowledge of such marked passives as 'the entrance was blocked by the chair', in which the 'agent' is inanimate, implies knowledge of such unmarked strings as 'the entrance was blocked by the workers', but not vice versa. Adamson concludes that the variables of prototypical forms constitute just the sorts of features which profit from explicit teaching/monitoring in second language acquisition, in contrast to so-called developmental features which follow a natural order of acquisition sequence.

In Chapter 15 Bartelt, after providing the linguistic and cultural setting for south-west Amerindian varieties of English, distinguishes interlanguage variation due to cross-linguistic influences from that due to the emergence of deeper, cognitive (bioprogram) features of the sort discussed by Bickerton. For example, the persistence of Navajo L1 input causes Navajo English to have a predictable number of transfer features rather than the structure typical of pidgins (e.g. CV syllable structure). On the other hand, native language versus target language contrast will not account for a number of grammatical features of Navajo English. Bartelt concludes that bioprogram grammatical and semantic priorities (e.g. state/nonstate and punctual/ nonpunctual) may be observed. He also notes the social function ('not trying to sound like a white man') served by various levels of the continuum between, for example, Navajo and English in many Amerindian speech communities.

The final chapter in this volume is that of Trudgill. In his far-reaching discussion he seeks to establish common elements in two distinct linguistic contact situations—dialect and language. Trudgill argues that *koinéisation* (or levelling and simplification) play a role. Levelling is a loss of marked forms in favour of unmarked ones, but simplification is the invention of new (*interdialect*) forms which arise from interaction and are more regular than the originals, due perhaps in part to the greater 'learnability' of such varieties. In low-contact situations, however, Trudgill suggests that the opposite process is at work; such varieties *complicate* rather than simplify, and he cites the introduction of consonants in place of the second elements of a diphthong in a number of isolated European language varieties. Trudgill is quick to point out, however, that the claim that levelled and simplified varieties are 'normal' is questionable. Many students of language are from high-contact areas and are speakers of Western European languages; those norms may not be universal. Regardless of that caveat, he still recommends the koinéised varieties of languages as models for adult learners. Perhaps a great deal of simplification in historical change is due to pressure from non-native speaker adult learners. The term *creoloid* refers to varieties which have had a particular history of such simplification, but Trudgill is especially interested in the study of the reverse trend in low-contact languages, that of complication. From these perspectives *interlanguage* and *interdialect* forms are natural consequences of and contributors to developments in language contact situations. Trudgill's work informs us that these terms do not necessarily refer to distinct phenomena.

Of course, not every theme in language variation that is of importance to second language acquisition is taken up in this and the accompanying volume, but we do hope that the chapters summarise much important work which has been done, reveal current interests and point out likely directions. More abstractly, but no less sanguinely, we hope they serve also to place second language studies solidly within the concerns of general linguistics.

Second language acquisition scholars, while recognising the importance of variation to their own interests, need to establish even more firmly the centrality of the study of developing second language systems to general linguistics, particularly in showing how such work entails modification and re-evaluation of sociolinguistic claims formulated in a more limited setting. We will also be pleased if these volumes do something to help realise that position.

References

DICKERSON, L., 1975, Interlanguage as a system of variable rules, *TESOL Quarterly*, 9, 401–7.

DICKERSON, L. and DICKERSON, W., 1977, Interlanguage phonology: Current research and future directions. In S. P. CORDER & E. ROULET (eds), *The Notions of Simplification, Interlanguages and Pidgins and their Relation to Second Language Pedagogy*. Geneva: Droz.

ELLIS, R., 1985, *Understanding Second Language Acquisition*. Oxford: Oxford University Press.

LABOV, W., 1966, *The Social Stratification of English in New York City*. Arlington, VA: Center for Applied Linguistics.

PRESTON, D. (in press), *Sociolinguistics and Second Language Acquisition*. Oxford: Basil Blackwell.

TARONE, E., FRAUENFELDER, U. and SELINKER, L., 1976, Systematicity/variability and stability/instability in interlanguage systems. In H. D. BROWN (ed.), *Papers in Second Language Acquisition* (Special Issue *Language Learning*), 4, 93–104.

Section Two:
Theoretical and
Methodological Foundations

2 Accounting for style-shifting in interlanguage

ELAINE E. TARONE
University of Minnesota

Empirical and theoretical work on variation in interlanguage have been growing in both volume and sophistication over the last ten years. There can be no doubt now that the linguistic forms produced by second language learners vary markedly as those learners move from one situation to another, and one task to another. Empirical data documenting this phenomenon in more than 80 studies completed in the last 15 years or so have been summarised in Tarone (1988); many of the chapters in this volume have documented this variation. This is clearly a phenomenon which exists and which must be explained.

A variety of theoretical models has been proposed to account for these patterns of variation in interlanguage (IL). These models, also described and evaluated in detail in Tarone (1988), will be presented in brief here, and their relative effectiveness in accounting for the known facts of IL variation will be assessed.

Before describing the theories which have been proposed to account for IL variation, it is important to establish some criteria that we may use in evaluating these theories. Only in this way will there be a basis for comparison among the different theories.

The first criterion which any adequate theory on IL variation must meet is that those causes of systematic variation which are proposed must be empirically verifiable, in the sense that the observable phenomena which support (or fail to support) that theory are agreed by all observers to exist and to support (or fail to support) that theory. A theory which proposes that IL variation is caused by gremlins in the cortex may be quite simple, elegant and even aesthetically pleasing in some sense—but it is not empirically verifiable, and thus cannot be an adequate theory of IL variation.

A second criterion is that an adequate theory must be able to explain and ultimately predict all the known facts of IL variation. For example, empirical evidence has accumulated showing that all of the following factors can cause such variation:

1. the linguistic context of the varying forms (and here, 'linguistic context' refers to the phonetic, phonological, morphological and syntactic context);

2. the 'function' performed by the linguistic form in different sorts of discourse;

3. psychological processing factors, identified variously as 'attention to form', 'automaticity', and 'Monitoring';

4. social factors, such as the speaker's relationship to the interlocutor, the topic of conversation and the social norms activated in the social setting;

5. miscellaneous task-related factors, such as the form of the instructions given the speaker.

Evidence has been presented which shows that each of the five general factors described above can cause shifts in accuracy of interlanguage forms. Further, there is some evidence that these different causes of IL variation may interact in any given elicitation situation; so, the speaker's relation to the interlocutor may lead to one accuracy level in the production of a particular IL form, while at the same time the function of that form in the particular discourse being produced may lead to another. An adequate theory of variation in interlanguage will have to account for the existence of all the causes of variation which have been shown to exist, and for the possibility of this sort of interaction among these causes in any given language production situation.

While these first two criteria have dealt with the theory's relation to the empirical evidence, the last criterion focuses upon the theory itself: its internal consistency, parsimony and elegance. In cases where empirical data are lacking, or when the same empirical data seem compatible with two different theories, we may need to evaluate those theories in the light of what Schumann (1983) terms 'aesthetic' standards. Examples of such standards are listed by Schumann as:

'X's hypothesis has to be rejected because it is clearly less beautiful than Y's'

'X's position is ineffective because it unconsciously adopts the metaphor it seeks to discredit'

'X's position is less appealing because he fails to recognize the partial validity of his claim'

'X's position must be doubted because it forces me to deny my experience'

(Schumann, 1983:67)

The three criteria just discussed, and represented in Table 1, can be used to assess the relative effectiveness of the various theories of IL variation which have been proposed.

The major theories which have been proposed to account for interlanguage variation may be usefully divided into two types. These theories are listed in Table 2.

TABLE 1. *Criteria to be used in evaluating theories of IL variation*

1	Proposed causes of systematic variation must be empirically verifiable.
2	All known facts of IL variation (effect of linguistic context, function of forms, psychological processing factors, social factors and task-related factors) must be explained and ultimately predicted.
3	Theory must meet aesthetic standards: be internally consistent, parsimonious and elegant.

TABLE 2. *Major theories proposed to account for IL variation*

I. *'Inner Processing' Theories*
   A 'Chomskyan' models (Adjémian, 1982; Liceras, 1985)
   B Monitor Model (Krashen, 1981, 1982)
   C Cognitive models (Bialystok, 1982; Ellis, 1985)
   D 'Labovian' models (Dickerson 1974, 1975; Tarone, 1983)

II. *'Sociolinguistic and Discourse' Theories*
   A 'Social psychological' models
      1. Multidimensional model (Meisel *et al.*, 1981)
      2. Littlewood's (1981) model
      3. Speech Accommodation Theory (Beebe & Giles, 1984)
      4. 'Discourse Domains' Model (Selinker & Douglas, 1985)
   B 'Function−Form Model (Hakuta, 1976; Huebner, 1983; Tarone, 1985; Schachter, 1986)

The first group of theories consists of what I have called 'inner processing theories'. These theories tend to trace the causes of IL variation to psychological processes of various kinds: the setting of parameters of core grammar; the focus of attention on language form as opposed to language content; the degree to which one's knowledge of the language has been 'analysed', and so on. Examples of these theories are the Monitor Model (Krashen, 1981) and Bialystok's (1982) cognitive model.

I have called the second group of theories 'sociolinguistic and discourse theories'. In this group of theories, the causes of IL variation are usually traced to external, social constraints such as the identity of the interlocutor, the topic of discussion, or the semantic and pragmatic functions of the IL form in discourse. Two of these theories are the Speech Accommodation Theory of Beebe & Giles (1984) and the 'function–form' model of Huebner (1983).

There are four major 'inner processing' theories.

1. The Chomskyan models of Adjémian (1982) and Liceras (1985) suggest that permeable intuitions about IL result from the 'fact that there may be rules of parameters of core grammar that will be fixed in a variety of ways or not fixed at all' (Liceras, 1985:355).

2. The Monitor Model of Krashen (1981, 1982) traces differences in accuracy of performance on different tasks to the learner's use or non-use of the Monitor: *learned* (as opposed to *acquired*) language.

3. The cognitive models of Bialystok (1982), Bialystok & Sharwood-Smith (1985) and Ellis (1985) explain task-related variation in IL performance as a result of the learner's use of 'controlled' vs. 'automatic' psychological processes.

4. The extensions of the 'Labovian' model of Dickerson (1974, 1975) and Tarone (1983) suggest that IL variation results from the differing degrees of attention paid to language form by the learner on different tasks.

One point should be clear at the outset: all the theories in the 'inner processing' group will have the same problem in meeting our first criterion: namely, it is virtually impossible to obtain empirical evidence to prove that the processes of the mind operate in this way rather than that way. There is no direct window on the workings of the mind which will provide evidence beyond a reasonable doubt that it is, for example, one mental process (e.g. attention paid to language form) rather than another (e.g. degree of analysis of knowledge) which causes a shift in accuracy of a particular IL form. The best we can hope for is that the two theories which propose the existence of these two different mental processes will be precise enough to be able to make clearly different predictions about the IL data. For example, if a 'Labovian' theory predicted increased accuracy in article use from Task A to Task B due to a postulated shift in degree of attention to speech, while a cognitive theory predicted (on the basis of postulated degree of analysis of IL knowledge about articles) a different accuracy pattern on the same tasks, we might then be able to indirectly evaluate these theories in the light of criterion 1. In fact, none of the 'inner processing' theories have been precisely enough formulated for us to be able to make such precise predictions. Typically, these theories all make the same general predictions about patterns of IL variation in the data, on the basis of very different assumptions about underlying psychological processes. Consequently, all of these inner processing theories must be viewed as inadequate in the light of our first criterion: the causes they propose for IL style-shifting are not specified clearly enough to be empirically verifiable. (For reasons of space, it will not be possible to show that this claim is true for all the theories listed above; Tarone (1988) evaluates them in detail.)

But surely it should be possible to formulate these 'inner processing' theories precisely enough to be able to make clear predictions about interlanguage outcomes on various tasks. Such predictions, where they propose different patterns of variation, should make it possible for us to evaluate them in light of criterion 1. But if more precise formulation of these theories does not result in the prediction of different patterns of variation, it seems to me that the value of the different psychological processes they postulate is minimal: aesthetically interesting, perhaps, but not very useful.

As a consequence of their common weakness in predicting empirical outcomes, these theories are usually evaluated by researchers in our field, not in the light of our first criterion, but rather of our third: their aesthetic qualities. When different theories make the same empirical predictions, one must then differentiate among them on the basis of their internal consistency, their consistency with our own experience, their parsimony and elegance and so on. This is in fact the point of Schumann's (1983) comparison between the positions of Krashen and McLaughlin on the acquisition/learning distinction: the differing positions are best understood as aesthetic statements rather than scientific ones.

However, even on 'aesthetic' grounds, many of these 'inner processing' theories must be faulted. Several of them fail to maintain consistently the very distinctions they seek to make. The lack of clarity of Krashen's distinction between acquisition and learning has been pointed out by several authors (e.g. McLaughlin, 1978, 1987), and both Liceras (1985) and

Bialystok & Sharwood-Smith (1985) fail to maintain clear distinctions among the various theoretical constructs they propose (cf. Tarone, 1988).

Thus, the 'inner processing' theories can be faulted because of their violation of both criteria 1 and 3. Nevertheless, empirical results of studies conducted by researchers in this group have produced results which are difficult to explain in any other terms than those of psychological processing. For example, the amount of time a subject is allowed to spend on a task clearly affects IL variation in major ways, and cannot be due to social constraints. The sequence of task types used by Labov and others elicits a very consistent pattern of variation across studies and across time. Such data must, it seems, be explained in terms of psychological processes of some sort.

An adequate theory of IL variation must contain a component which clearly identifies some psychological process as an important cause of IL variation, but specifying the nature of that psychological process in a way that is empirically verifiable and theoretically clear promises to be a very difficult task.

Among the 'sociolinguistic and discourse' theories, in contrast to the theories just presented, the causes of interlanguage variation are viewed as more external to the learner him/herself.

1. The multidimensional model (Meisel *et al.*, 1981) attempts to show that a kind of variation related to the influence of linguistic environment is tied to the socio-psychological characteristics of certain types of learners.

2. Littlewood (1981) argues that there are three causes of IL variation: influence of linguistic environment, functions of linguistic forms, and social–situational factors.

3. Speech Accommodation Theorists (e.g. Beebe & Giles, 1984) tie IL variation to the learner's convergence or divergence from the speech patterns of the interlocutor, and appeal to constructs like identity assertion and group membership as end causes of variation.

4. The 'Discourse Domains' model (Selinker & Douglas, 1985) suggests that IL develops differentially in different contexts which are defined by the learner, and shifts in accuracy occur as the learner moves from one such discourse domain to another.

5. The 'function–form' model (Huebner, 1983) proposes that accuracy of

a given linguistic form varies as that form performs different pragmatic functions in discourse.

In the 'sociolinguistic and discourse theories', the cause of IL variation is traced to external, social constraints—proposed causes of variation for which, on the face of it, empirical data would seem to be more readily available.

However, these theories tend to originate in the disciplines of socio-linguistics, social psychology and discourse analysis/pragmatics; the experi-mental design used in these theories, and the sort of data considered, are heavily influenced by these disciplines. For example, anecdotal evidence rather than data obtained in controlled studies is often presented in support of the claims of theories rooted in social psychology, and case studies of the second language acquisition of single individuals are often presented in support of theories rooted in discourse analysis. This tendency to rely upon case studies and anecdotal evidence in support of theories in this second group is unfortunate, in view of the fact that the external, social constraints which are claimed to cause IL variation would seem to be more readily suited to our first criterion, that the proposed causes of IL variation should be empirically verifiable. In the case of all the theories in this group, there is some relatively objective data base which all researchers could appeal to in their efforts to find support for putative causes of variation.

So, for example, if the identity of the interlocutor is supposed to be a cause of IL variation, it would seem to be relatively easy to conduct studies in which the physical characteristics and social role of the interlocutor are controlled, and their effect upon the IL of the learner observed.

The relationship between pragmatic function and linguistic form is possibly less amenable to objective empirical verification since the analysis of this relationship can often be as much a matter of art as of science. Nevertheless, even here all analysts are working with the same transcribed language data and not with completely hypothetical constructs; there may be differences of opinion as to how those data should be interpreted, but at least there are transcriptions and agreed-upon procedures of analysis to help in the attempt to resolve those differences. Thus, the theories in this group would seem to be empirically verifiable, and thus to fulfil criterion 1— although for the most part, empirical evidence supporting most of these theories has not in fact been systematically presented.

However, most of the theories in this group have not yet been thoroughly developed, and thus they lack the required clarity of definition we have required in criterion 3. The Littlewood and 'discourse domains' theories, for example, have been presented in only the barest of outlines, and require a great deal more consistency in maintaining the key distinctions proposed (see Tarone, 1988, for details). The most thoroughly developed of these theories, and the one which best meets our third criterion, is Speech Accommodation Theory.

Thus, the 'sociolinguistic and discourse' theories fall short because they violate criterion 3: they are unclear and lack consistency. Also, these theories, while they seem in principle to fulfil criterion 1, apparently being empirically *verifiable*, do not in fact seem to have been empirically *verified* in any systematic way.

We see, then, that the theories in the second group come slightly closer to fulfilling our criteria for an adequate theory of IL variation than do those in the first group, particularly on the score of empirical verifiability, but they still fall short on the score of theoretical clarity and consistency.

It should be clear as well that none of the theories in either group succeeds in meeting our second criterion: none can explain all the known facts of IL variation. None accounts for all the causes of IL variation for which there is empirical evidence.

Conclusion

It has been argued that an adequate theory of interlanguage variation will have to be empirically verifiable, account for the existence of all the causes of variation which have been shown to exist, and be clear and consistent in maintaining key theoretical distinctions. What is needed is a theory of interlanguage variation which is empirically verifiable, like the theories in the second group we have examined, but which is more comprehensive than these, providing a role for each of the constraints for which there is empirical evidence: linguistic context, psychological processing factors, interlocutor, topic and social norm, and function–form relationships. While all these factors seem to play a role in causing interlanguage variation, no single theory we have examined here provides a role for all these factors. What is needed is a clear, consistent theory which ties all these causal factors together in a single coherent framework—not simply listing them, but showing their interrelationships—a theory which makes empirically verifiable claims. The development of such a theory should be our goal in the next few years.

References

ADJÉMIAN, C., 1982, La spécificité de l'interlanguage et l'idéalisation des langues secondes. In J. GUERON & S. SOWLEY (eds), *Grammaire Transformationelle: Théorie et Méthodologies*. Vincennes: Universite de Paris VIII.

BEEBE, L. and GILES, H. 1984, Speech accommodation theories: A discussion in terms of second language acquisition, *International Journal of the Sociology of Language*, 46, 5–32.

BIALYSTOK, E., 1982, On the relationship between knowing and using linguistic forms, *Applied Linguistics*, 3(3), 181–206.

BIALYSTOK, E., and SHARWOOD-SMITH, M. 1985, Interlanguage is not a state of mind, *Applied Linguistics*, 6(2), 101–17.

DICKERSON, L., 1974, 'Internal and external patterning of phonological variability in the speech of Japanese learners of English: toward a theory of second-language acquisition.' Doctoral dissertation, University of Illinois.

——, 1975, The learner's interlanguage as a system of variable rules, *TESOL Quarterly*, 9, 401–7.

ELLIS, R., 1985, *Understanding Second Language Acquisition*. Oxford: Oxford University Press.

HAKUTA, K., 1976, A case study of a Japanese child learning ESL, *Language Learning*, 26(2), 321–52.

HUEBNER, T., 1983, *A Longitudinal Analysis of the Acquisition of English*. Ann Arbor: Karoma.

KRASHEN, S., 1981, *Second Language Acquisition and Learning*. Oxford: Pergamon.

——, 1982, *Principles and Practice in Second Language Acquisition*. Oxford: Pergamon.

LICERAS, J., 1985, The role of intake in the determination of learners' competence. In S. GASS & C. MADDEN (eds), *Input in Second Language Acquisition*. Cambridge, MA: Newbury House.

LITTLEWOOD, W., 1981, Language variation and second language acquisition theory, *Applied Linguistics*, 2(2), 150–8.

MCLAUGHLIN, B., 1978, The Monitor Model: Some methodological considerations, *Language Learning*, 28(2), 309–32.

——, 1987, *Theories of Second-Language Learning*. London: Edward Arnold.

MEISEL, J., CLAHSEN, H. and PIENEMANN, M., 1981, On determining developmental stages in natural second language acquisition, *Studies in Second Language Acquisition*, 3(2), 109–35.

SCHACHTER, J., 1986, In search of systematicity in interlanguage production, *Studies in Second Language Acquisition*, 8, 119–34.

SCHUMANN, J., 1983, Art and science in second language acquisition research, *Language Learning*, 33(5), 49–76.

SELINKER, L. and DOUGLAS, D. 1985, Wrestling with 'context' in interlanguage theory, *Applied Linguistics*, 6(2), 190–204.

TARONE, E., 1983, On the variability of interlanguage systems, *Applied Linguistics*, 4(2), 143–63.

——, 1985, Variability in interlanguage use: A study of style-shifting in morphology and syntax, *Language Learning*, 35(3), 373–404.

——, (1988), *Variation in Interlanguage*. London: Edward Arnold.

3 Sources of intra-learner variability in language use and their relationship to second language acquisition

ROD ELLIS
Ealing College of Higher Education

The existence of variability within the second language use of a single learner is acknowledged by all researchers, irrespective of their theoretical standpoint. Researchers differ, however, in the importance which they attach to variability. Those researchers who adhere to what Tarone (1983) calls the 'homogeneous competence paradigm' treat variability as an aspect of performance or 'control', while researchers—such as Tarone herself —who argue for a 'capability continuum paradigm' see variability as an integrative characteristic of the learner's competence. In this chapter I will argue for the second of these two positions.

The main purpose of this chapter is to develop a framework for understanding the role that variability plays in the process of second language acquisition (SLA). I intend to focus on *linguistic* aspects of SLA, although in order to do so I shall argue that pragmatic factors cannot be ignored. The chapter divides into two principal sections. In the first section I will examine a number of *sources* of intra-learner variability in order to answer the question 'Why and in what ways is language learner language variable?' This section will consider *horizontal* variability, i.e. the variability that is evident in language use at a given point in time. In the second section I shall try to relate the different sources of variation to the process of SLA by examining what is sometimes called *vertical variation*. My overall aim is to argue that variability is an integral characteristic of interlanguage and that in order to understand how SLA proceeds it is necessary to recognise this and to build explanatory models that take account of it.

PART ONE:
Sources of intra-learner variability in language use

Variability in language use is the result of a complex set of interrelating factors. Following previous work by Ellis (1985a, 1985b), a basic distinction is drawn between free and systematic variation. The latter is the product of a number of sources—linguistic, sociolinguistic and psycholinguistic. Some confusion in SLA research has arisen because of the failure to separate these sources of systematic variation. The general aim of this section, therefore, is to present a clear and coherent account of the different sources, identifying and discussing some of the methodological and theoretical problems which have arisen in previous research. The section concludes with a schematic framework for describing the different sources of variability.

Free variation

According to Ellis (1985b), free variation is of two kinds. The first type, manifest as false starts, changes of plan, etc., is the result of performance lapses. The second type consists of competing rules in the learner's competence, rules which are acted on quite haphazardly. It is this second type that will concern us here; performance variability will be considered later when psycholinguistic sources of variability are discussed.

Ellis' claims for the existence of free variation draw on the work of Bickerton (1975). Bickerton envisages two types of variability: variability that is random and variability that is the consequence of using different grammars on different occasions. Bickerton argues that linguistic change is not motivated by situational factors. Rather, linguistic change occurs and is then utilised for social purposes. He is sceptical of what he calls the 'contextual' theory of linguistic variation:

> While, with the help of a little hindsight, a plausible contextual explanation can be given for many stylistic shifts, there are many more that operate in quite unpredictable ways. (Bickerton, 1975: 183)

Ellis (1985b) provides an example of free variation in the speech of J, a Portuguese learner of L2 English. J produced two variants of negation contiguously (i.e. in an identical context):

> No look my card.
> Don't look my card.

The 'don't' variant was the single example out of 18 spontaneous negative utterances produced during the first month of the study. Only in the second month do 'no' negatives start to give way regularly to 'don't' negatives. Ellis suggests that Gatbonton's (1978) diffusion model, adapted to describe the shifting pattern of form–function relationships, can account for J's use of negative variants. Initially, J uses the two variants to express both commands and statements. Subsequently, he learns to use 'don't' for commands while maintaining 'no' for statements. In other words, free variation provides the basis upon which reorganisation can take place.

A further example of free variation comes from the work of the ZISA researchers on German word order rules. Meisel (1983) provides data to show that, although word order rules such as PARTICLE, INVERSION and VERB-END are themselves developmentally ordered, there is no sequencing of the different linguistic contexts to which the rules apply. For example, INVERSION applies in a number of linguistic contexts: in WH interrogatives, after a sentence initial adverbial or direct object and in a complex sentence after an adverbial clause. When INVERSION first appears in a learner's interlanguage it does not do so in all these contexts at once. There is an initial period of free variation, when the rule is applied in one or more of these contexts but not in the others. For some learners this period can be quite lengthy.

However, not all investigators are prepared to recognise free variation. Downes (1984) views free variation simply as a way of excluding variability from the object of inquiry. Schachter (1986) suggests that what has been identified as free variation may well turn out to be systematic. Indeterminancy is only apparent because the analyst has failed to probe in sufficient depth to identify the underlying systematicity. Schachter supports her arguments with a subtle re-analysis of the data collected by Cazden et al. (1975). She shows that one learner's use of negative variants (no V, don't V, aux-neg, analysed don't) is far less random than the original researchers had supposed. What appeared to be free variation was in fact functionally determined. Although two variants occurred at the same developmental point, they were used to perform different language functions (e.g. no information vs. denial).

In fact, Ellis' and Schachter's positions are not as incompatible as they seem. Schachter acknowledges that a structure appears occasionally 'before onset of the productive use of that form' (Schachter, 1986:127). It is when 'onset' (i.e. 'productive use' in Schachter's definition) occurs that the systematic distribution of variants becomes evident. Prior to that, however, there is the 'occasional' occurrence of forms that are presumably in free variation. If there is any difference in the positions taken up by Ellis and Schachter, then, it is only a matter of emphasis. For Ellis, free variation is significant because it provides the resources for later systematicity. For Schachter, it is the systematicity of productive use that is important.

It is possible that free variation is evident in some structures but not in others. Sato (1985) could find no patterning in a 12-year-old Vietnamese learner's production of target final consonants, but did find consistency in the production of target final clusters. She suggests that the choice of feature for study may influence the degree and consistency of the variation found. Not all variables yield similar patterns.

If, as I have argued, free variation is a characteristic of language-learner language in at least some structures, we need to establish what the cause of such variation is. Following Valdman (1987) I would like to suggest that there are both learner internal and environmental (i.e. input) sources. Free variation can occur when the learner attends to internally generated language norms which result in simplification of the input while at the same time responding to target norms present in the input. In other words, a conflict arises between those forms which are 'natural' for the learner and those forms which constitute the target norms. A form may be considered 'natural' in different ways. Features that are unmarked in terms of a theory of universal grammar might be considered 'natural' in the sense that they are available to the learner with minimal triggering from the input. Alternatively, a form that is not subject to complex cognitive processing might also be considered 'natural'. The strength of internally generated norms is considerable so that when the learner begins to attend to external, target norms, free variation arises. A good example can be found in the acquisition of English copula. Typically learners first produce utterances with zero copula before going through a stage of development when zero alternates randomly with full copula. Such a pattern of development was found in J, the Portuguese child learner referred to above.

Free variation can also arise when the learner recognises that a target language feature is itself variable (cf. Ellis, 1988). Variable rules exist within a given target variety—for example, English copula which can be realised as a full or contracted form. The 'onset' of the acquisition of such rules can again be marked by free variation before the learner begins the process of mastering the distributional pattern described by the target rule. J displayed initial free variation in the use of 'is' and '-s'.

Finally, the target variety or varieties which the learner selects as the model of acquisition can result in free variation. Some learners expand their repertoire by changing their model during the course of SLA. Thus, J began by orienting solely to the pedagogic norms of the classroom, but in the middle of his second year of learning English gave evidence of responding to the dialectal forms of the London region. This is reflected in the sudden appearance of a new copula form—'ain't'—which is initially used with existing copula forms (i.e. 'is not' and 'isn't') in apparent free variation.

If the presence of two or more variants used randomly is to be treated as a source of interlanguage development, as I strongly maintain, then it is important to establish a clear operational definition of 'free variation'. Ellis (1985b) attempts such a definition. Free variation can be held to exist when:

1. the two forms occur in the same situational context;
2. the two forms perform the same illocutionary meaning;
3. the two forms occur in the same linguistic context;
4. they occur in the same discourse context;
5. there is, in the manner of their production, no evidence of any difference in the amount of attention paid to the form of the utterances.

Systematic variability

I turn now to consider the sources of systematic variability. It is these that have figured the most strongly in studies of SLA.

Linguistic sources

The first source is the linguistic context of a structure. This can have an always–never effect or an often–seldom effect (Fasold, 1984). An example of the former in native-speaker speech is aspiration of voiceless stops in English, which occurs in word initial positions but never occurs after /s/. An example of the latter is the copula in Black English Vernacular. The three variants (zero, contracted and full) are influenced by aspects of both the preceding and following linguistic environments (Labov, 1969). Hudson (1980) notes that the effects of linguistic context are typically probabilistic rather than categorical.

There are a number of L2 studies that have investigated the effects of linguistic context on choice of variant (see Ellis, 1988, for a review). These studies provide ample evidence to demonstrate the presence of substantial systematic variation according to linguistic environment in language-learner language. These effects are evident in phonological, lexical and morpho-syntactic variables and are, in turn, induced by phonological, lexical and morphosyntactic properties of the linguistic context. In passing, it is worth noting that one aspect that has been poorly explored in SLA research is variation according to lexical context. It would seem likely that the acquisition of L2 features is closely linked to the specific lexical items in which they first appear.

We are a long way from having a clear and convincing explanation of the effects brought about by linguistic context. Fasold (1984), drawing on the work of Bailey (1973) proposes that linguistic contexts can be ordered according to 'environment weight', such that the 'heavier' the context, the greater the frequency of occurrence of a given variant. However, it is not clear what determines environment weight. There is a danger of circularity; a context is heavy or light according to whether the use of the variant under consideration is heavy or light. If the notion of environmental weight is to have any explanatory value, it is necessary to identify independent means for establishing which context is heavy and which is light. One promising candidate for providing such means is typological markedness. Hyltenstam (1984) has shown that the variation in the deletion and retention of pronominal copies in L2 Swedish relative clauses can be accounted for in terms of Comrie's accessibility hierarchy. An interesting possibility, there-fore, is that the heavy–light distinction can be determined with reference to the unmarked–marked distinction.

The linguistic context is an important source of systematic variability in L2 use and one that sheds light on the relationship between synchronic variability and interlanguage development, as we shall see later.

Sociolinguistic sources

Under this general heading we look at a number of sources of systematic variation that derive from the social uses of interlanguage.

Discourse context

Variation according to register is a well-documented phenomenon (cf. Halliday et al., 1964). In SLA research, Selinker & Douglas (1985) provide evidence to suggest that what they call 'discourse domains' influence L2 performance. They define discourse domain as 'a personally and internally created area of one's life that has importance' but in the empirical research they report, it appears to involve chiefly discourse content or topic. Systematic variation in linguistic behaviour occurs, depending on whether the subject of their study is talking about 'critical path schedules' (a technical engineering topic) or telling his life-story.

It is not clear, however, to what extent the discourse content constitutes a separate source of systematic variability. Bell (1984) argues that the effect of topic is related to the interlocutor effect (see below under 'Social context'), because the speaker associates classes of topics with particular audiences. However, the results of Selinker & Douglas' study, in which the subject addressed the same interlocutor for both topics, suggest that Bell may be wrong. As Tarone (1987) concludes, the topic may be considered a significant determinant of systematic variability.

The effects of discourse topic on linguistic choice are likely to attract considerable research interest in the future. The 'genre' studies currently undertaken in the field of English for Specific Purposes (e.g. Cornu & Delahaye, 1987) show us the way forward. A full framework for describing SLA variability will need to incorporate discourse content—together with related notions such as user investment and expertness—as a major source of variation.

Social context

The second source of sociolinguistic variation—the social context in which communication takes place—is the one that has attracted the closest attention in SLA research. The social context, of course, comprises not a single source but rather multiple sources in the form of the different situational determinants of language use. They are considered together, however, as they derive from the same, rather static view of 'context' and have given rise to a well-defined and popular methodology for the quantitative study of interlanguage use. Later I will approach 'context' from a different perspective, treating it as a dynamic phenomenon that unfolds through interaction.

According to the static view of context, which is our concern here, situational factors, which are taken to be independent of language, correlate with the use of specific linguistic features. Thus language use is seen as determined by situational factors. It is customary to distinguish two sets of extralinguistic factors: social and stylistic (Bell, 1984). The former indicate differences between speakers and result, therefore, in inter-speaker variation. Typical social factors are social class, age, sex and ethnic origin. Stylistic factors, on the other hand, mark the level of formality required by a particular situation and result in intra-speaker variation.

Most of the studies of stylistic variation in SLA have taken place within the methodological framework developed by Labov. According to the Labovian paradigm, language users possess a variable competence that enables them to perform in different styles which can be ranged along a single dimension according to the amount of attention paid to linguistic form. Labov argues that when speakers pay little attention to speech this shows a lack of concern with whether the hearers are assessing their social status. Conversely, a focus on form indicates sensitivity to social status. 'Attention to form', then, is the central construct in the Labovian approach to stylistic variation. It constitutes the pyscholinguistic mechanism for socially motivated style-shifting. It also provides a methodology for investigating style-shifting: different styles can be elicited by instruments permitting varying degrees of attention to form. This is not the place to review the ample research that has followed the Labovian paradigm (see, Tarone, 1983; Ellis & Roberts, 1987, for surveys of this research). Here we will summarise the main conclusions reached:

1. In general, the research supports the view that learner competence comprises a continuum of styles ranging from the vernacular (least attention to form) to the careful (most attention to form).

2. In general, target language variants (i.e. variants that correspond to target language norms) occur more regularly in styles near the careful end of the continuum. As Tarone (1979) puts it, the careful style is more easily influenced by the target language.

3. The careful style is also influenced by the learner's L1; that is, transfer is more evident in this style than in the vernacular.

4. The vernacular style is considered primary in the sense that it is the most stable and the most internally consistent (Tarone, 1983).

It is important to note, however, that for each of these generalisations there are a number of significant exceptions.

Recently, the Labovian paradigm has come in for substantial criticism. The main target of attack has been the 'attention to form' construct. Bell (1984) notes that there is no empirical foundation for attention as a variable, that there are cases where attention increases rather than decreases as a speaker shifts to less formal speech and that the techniques used to elicit speech at successive points on the style continuum have been mistaken for factors which actually account for variation. Other criticisms include the difficulty of measuring how much attention to speech learners are actually paying (Sato, 1985) and, more significantly, that the attention-to-speech model focuses only on the private status of the individual and ignores social context.

This is the crux of the problem. Attention to speech is a psycholinguistic construct as it deals with how production is planned. However, it purports to inform about social factors. The weakness of the Labovian model is that it fails to identify what social factors motivate style-shifting. This is a serious omission for, as Bell observes:

> To say that an individual speaker's language varies according to style ... is to say merely that a speaker's language varies.

Thus, unless it is possible to relate the attention mechanism to the social factors that power it, the model is of little explanatory value.

In order to overcome this problem, Bell proposes the 'style axiom', which states:

> Variation on the style dimension within the speech of a single speaker derives from and echoes the variation which exists between speakers on the 'social' dimension. (Bell, 1984:151)

In other words, the distinction between social and stylistic factors with which we began this section is far from clear-cut. Bell goes on to reinterpret stylistic variation in terms of audience design, developing a convincing framework for examining the accommodations that speakers make when influenced by different audience roles. Speakers' perceptions of their addressees' educational level, social class, gender, ethnicity, etc. affect the linguistic choices they make.

A number of studies of addressee-factors in SLA have been carried out within the methodological framework of accommodation theory proposed by Giles (1977, 1980). Beebe (1981) and Beebe & Zuengler (1983) have shown, for instance, that the ethnicity of the interlocutor can influence interlanguage use. Beebe & Zuengler found that Chinese-Thai children displayed phonological variation according to whether they were addressing a person from their own ethnic group or someone outside. The children converged in the direction of their interlocutor's pronunciation. Beebe (1981) found a similar effect on amount of talk by Puerto-Rican learners of English. To date, studies of this kind have concentrated on only limited types of linguistic behaviour—phonological variables and certain higher-order variables such as amount of speech. There is a need for detailed studies that explore other types of linguistic behaviour, in particular morphosyntactic variables. Research within the framework of accommodation theory, however, promises to increase our understanding of how different social factors (status, social background, ethnicity, etc.) result in systematic variation in language-learner language.

Where does this leave Tarone's 'stylistic continuum', based, as it is, on the Labovian model? We suggest that the drift of Tarone's arguments is essentially a psycholinguistic rather than a sociolinguistic one. Attention to form is an important source of variability but needs to be considered within a psycholinguistic theory of language production. Unfortunately most of the stylistic studies undertaken to date have failed to recognise this and as a result the pyscholinguistic process of attending to form has been confounded with other factors which constitute potential sources of variability. The tasks used in a typical Labovian-type study differ on far too many dimensions to enable potentially independent sources of variation to be identified. For example, it is difficult to make any meaningful comparison of performance on a grammaticality judgement task and an interview task, given the obvious situational and psycholinguistic differences.

This is not to say that 'attention-to-form' is a worthless construct. Later I shall argue that it does indeed constitute an important source of variability. First, however, I want to take a more dynamic view of 'context' and explore how this can contribute to our understanding of synchronic variability.

Interactional context

When participants take part in a communicative event they actively and dynamically create the context in the process of discourse construction. As Roberts & Simonot (1987) put it, context in this sense is *accomplished* through communication.

How does the interactional context constitute a source of systematic variability? It does so in two related ways. First, the process of constructing context through discourse leads language users to exploit whatever linguistic means they possess in the performance of the communicative functions that make up the discourse. According to this view of language, the grammar of a human language is the way it is because of the discourse functions it must serve. Givón (1979) writes: '... syntax cannot be explained or understood without reference to its use in communication.'

Thus, what may appear random behaviour from the standpoint of a purely formal analysis, can be shown to be highly systematic when a functional analysis is applied. The second way in which the interactional context serves as a source of systematic variation is through *impression management*—the negotiation of face in interpersonal communication. Brown & Levinson (1978) note:

> ... there will be correlations between overall levels and kinds of face redress in a culture and the special elaboration of grammatical devices for achieving that redress. (Brown & Levinson, 1978:262)

An examination of politeness phenomena in L2 communication can reveal hidden systematicity.

The application of functional models of language of the kind proposed by Givón and Brown & Levinson opens up new possibilities for the study of variability in SLA. Huebner (1979, 1983) has been able to show how a Laotian learner's use of English articles was highly systematic once a functional analysis was used. He examines this learner's use of English articles ('da' = 'the'; 'a'; zero) in terms of whether they were marked by the presence or absence of two binary features, $+/-$ specific referent and $+/-$ assumed hearer's knowledge. What appeared to be initially a random distribution of articles was shown to be probabilistically systematic. Tarone (1985) employs a Labovian approach in an investigation of a number of morphological features of L2 English. One of these features, articles, behaved contrary to the stylistic hypothesis, displaying higher levels of accuracy in the task that required least attention to speech (oral narrative) than in the task requiring the most (grammaticality judgement). Tarone speculates that this occurred because in the narrative task articles were needed for purposes of reference, whereas in the grammaticality judgement task they were not. Parrish & Tarone (1986) have re-examined the same data and applied Huebner's typology of noun phrase types. The analysis shows that the task did indeed affect the frequency of the type of noun phrases produced and, in this way, influenced the articles the learners selected. Accuracy of article usage in noun phrases characterised by $+$ specific referent $/+$ hearer knowledge was dramatically higher on the narrative task. These studies suggest that a 'functional–typological syntactic analysis' of the kind advocated by Givón (1979) may be essential if the true systematicity of interlanguage use is to be identified.

There has been little research into the role played by impression management in interlanguage performance. In one interesting study, Rampton (1987) has analysed a limited corpus of speech data collected from ESL learners in a Local Education Authority language unit in England. Rampton considers utterances of the 'me no like' and 'me too clever' type, noting that these appeared regularly in a variety of different contexts and with different addressees. The learners were not beginners, however, and certainly possessed the 'core competence' to perform a more standard version of these structures. Rampton suggests that the learners deliberately exploited the Broken English associations of such structures in order to mitigate the force of potentially face-threatening speech acts (i.e. boasts and refusals). The 'me' constructions cannot be explained away as 'backsliding', which might be the conclusion of a purely formal analysis; rather they reflect the careful exploitation of remembered interlanguage structures for impression management.

The requirements of communication are such that learners will always seek to maximise their formal knowledge in the performance of meanings that are important to them. Thus, learners create their own form–function arrangements to meet their communicative needs. This being so, we need to heed what Bley-Vroman (1983) has called 'the comparative fallacy of interlanguage studies'. Instead of measuring interlanguage using the yard-stick provided by the target language—as in obligatory occasion analysis —we need to illuminate the inner logic of learner systems by examining how they operate in the 'pragmatic mode'.

Psycholinguistic sources

So far I have considered linguistic and sociolinguistic sources of systematic variability in language-learner language. I now turn to psycho-linguistic sources, taking a closer look at the attention-to-form construct.

Irrespective of whether there is a social or communicative motivation for language choice, users will perform variably according to the amount of effort required to process one variant of a structure as opposed to another. All language production is constrained to a greater or lesser extent by the facility with which the user's linguistic resources can be accessed and processed. Contrary to Chomsky's early assumption that the resulting performance is random, it can be shown to be highly systematic, reflecting regularities in the way that the language processing mechanisms operate.

The crucial factors appear to be the amount of time for planning an utterance and the degree to which the user is attending to form. We will consider briefly two studies which have investigated the effects of these factors on L2 performance.

Ellis (1987a) asked 17 adult learners of L2 English to perform three tasks that were chosen to allow different amounts of planning time. Task 1 consisted of a written composition for which one hour was allowed; Task 2 was an oral reproduction of the same composition (without recourse to the written version); Task 3 consisted of a different composition which the subjects were required to relate orally without any advance planning. Ellis compared the learners' accuracy in the use of three past tense morphemes: regular -ed, irregular and copula. In the case of the regular past tense, a clear pattern was evident; learners performed most accurately in Task 1 and least accurately in Task 3, with Task 2 intermediate. The results for one of the learners were particularly striking (see Figure 1) as they revealed a completely uniform pattern. It would appear from Ellis' study that for some structures at least, the availability or non-availability of planning time systematically affects the accuracy with which target variants are produced.

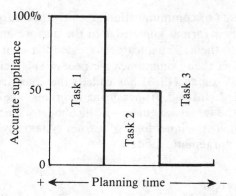

FIGURE 1. *Accurate suppliance of -ed by one learner in three tasks varying in planning time*

The second study of interest to us is that carried out by Hulstijn & Hulstijn (1984). They investigated the effects of time pressure, focus of attention (i.e. whether on information or on form) and metalingual knowledge on the accuracy with which INVERSION and VERB-END were performed in L2 Dutch. The results indicated that time pressure by itself had no effect, but that focus of attention on form increased accuracy in both structures. Also learners with explicit knowledge applied the two rules more frequently than learners without such knowledge. The authors concluded that 'performance can be influenced by task constraints and that it can be manipulated'.

The results of these two studies appear to be contradictory, but, in fact, need not be so. Clearly time pressure by itself need not result in systematic variation, but planning time that is used to focus attention on form may well do so. Skehan (1987) suggests that speech planning involves assembling units or chunks of language in short-term memory. These are then accessed with different time delays. Skehan seeks to account for the systematic effects of psycholinguistic factors on production in terms of the co-ordinated functioning of short-term memory and access processes. Speech that uses extensive memory space limits the operational flexibility of control processes; conversely, speech requiring complex control decisions restricts the space available for memory. Production involves a constant trade-off between the competing demands on memory and control mechanisms. Thus attention-to-form is only possible when there are no other demands on short-term memory, as in Ellis' Task 1. In such cases the learner may be able to access metalingual knowledge. If memory space is taken up with other planning operations, such as discourse content or organisation, as in Ellis' Task 3, the learner can only access those resources over which he has automatic control (Atkinson & Schriffin, 1968).

There is sufficient evidence from both the Labovian studies of style-shifting and the studies referred to above to show that language planning in relation to attention-to-form produces systematic effects on L2 production. Patterned variability is the product of psycholinguistic as well as socio-linguistic and linguistic factors, the three interacting in ways that are not yet clear.

Summary

In this section a number of different sources of intra-learner variability in L2 use have been discussed. These are summarised in schematic form in Figure 2. My concern has been with horizontal variability, i.e. variability

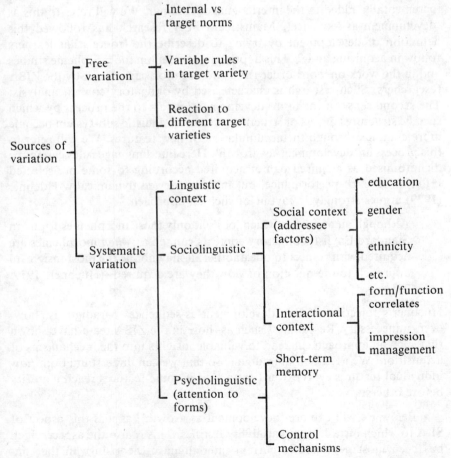

FIGURE 2. *A framework of sources of intra-learner variation*

that occurs synchronically in interlanguage. In the next section I turn to consider vertical variation—the changes that take place over time as the learner revises some interlanguage rules in the direction of the chosen target language norms. The principal thesis which will be explored is that horizontal variability is not only a window for viewing the process of L2 development but is a concomitant of this process.

PART TWO: Vertical variation

In order to understand the nature of vertical variation it is necessary to recognise two separate meanings of the term 'development' in interlanguage studies. First, development can refer to the process by which rules are incrementally added to the interlanguage grammar. We will refer to this as 'development-as-sequence'. Mainstream SLA research has followed this definition of development by trying to describe the 'route' that learners follow in acquiring an L2. This approach is evident in the morpheme studies and in the work on word-order rules and negation carried out by the ZISA researchers. Such research is characterised by obligatory context analysis. The second sense of the term 'development' refers to the process by which specific structures or sets of structures within a linguistic sub-system become more complex through the accumulation of new features. We will refer to this process as 'development-as-growth'. Here interlanguage rules cannot be dichotomised as acquired or not acquired according to some pre-selected criterion level of performance, but must be viewed dynamically. Huebner (1979) argues strongly in favour of such an approach:

> Although an approach which looks at only those morphemes found in Standard English obligatory contexts can tell us *when* morphemes are acquired with respect to one another, it may not be the most insightful approach to the question of *how* they are acquired. (Huebner, 1979: 22)

Huebner's rejection of the 'development-as-sequence' paradigm is, however, unnecessary. Researchers such as those in the ZISA team have shown that such an approach can lead to valuable insights into the mechanisms of acquisition. We need both paradigms, so that we can understand both *how* individual features evolve over time and *why* some features reach maturity before others.

Below we will explore 'development-as-growth', as it is this aspect of SLA to which intra-learner variability testifies. This is also the aspect which has been most neglected in current interlanguage theorising. In the conclusion to this chapter we will consider the relationship between sequence and growth in interlanguage systems.

Development-as-growth and intra-learner variation

In order to understand the relationship between horizontal and vertical variation, it is necessary to distinguish two aspects of development-as-growth: *knowledge* and *control*. This distinction has been proposed in a series of articles by Bialystok and Sharwood-Smith (e.g. Bialystok, 1981; Bialystok, 1982; Bialystok & Sharwood-Smith, 1985) in the process of developing a modular theory of SLA. As proposed by these authors, 'knowledge' concerns the way language is represented in the mind of the learner and is analogous with linguistic competence. The authors recognise variability in 'knowledge', but only according to how 'analysed' it is. The concept of analycity is not entirely clear to me. Bialystok defines it as referring to the extent to which the learner has formed a 'mental represent-ation' of the structures which have been internalised. It is a psycholinguistic construct. 'Control' concerns the processing of knowledge in actual per-formance; this, too, manifests variability according to how automatic language use is. The distinction between 'knowledge' and 'control' will be maintained in the following discussion. However, the concept of 'know-ledge' will be redefined: competence will be viewed sociolinguistically rather than linguistically. The reasons for this will become clearer as the discussion proceeds and will be made explicit in the conclusion to this chapter.

The acquisition of sociolinguistic knowledge

The acquisition of sociolinguistic knowledge is characterised by three major processes:

1. innovation, i.e. the introduction of new forms into the interlanguage system;

2. elaboration, i.e. the extension of the sociolinguistic base of the new form;

3. revision, i.e. the adjustments to the entire interlanguage system resulting from innovation and elaboration.

These processes are not stages; they are overlapping and continuous, not consecutive. Thus, while form x is entering the learner's interlanguage, forms y and z are in the process of becoming elaborated. Similarly, as the introduction of x and the elaboration of x and z take place, so internal pressure is created necessitating the revision of the entire interlanguage system.

Little is known about how new forms enter linguistic systems. As we have already noted, Bickerton (1975) argues that linguistic change is not situationally determined. Rather it happens and is then utilised for social purposes. Labov (1980) takes a different viewpoint, arguing that the mechanism of change is located in social structures. I have followed Bickerton. In the case of L2 systems we can speculate that 'openness' to new linguistic forms is the product of two factors: (1) the desire for communicative choice and (2) the recognition of target language norms.

The desire for communicative choice arises as a result of the speaker's need to be fully expressive in order to encode a complex range of notions in a variety of ways. It is reflected in the seeking out of formal options for performing speech acts which are already part of the learner's pragmatic range. Nicholas (1986) describes how a $3\frac{1}{2}$-year-old learner of L2 German comes to recognise that the same function can be expressed by more than one form and so becomes motivated to explore the potential of this kind of variation. Nicholas sees this as an essential characteristic of the successful language learner: '... the successful language learner is one who can adequately correlate a range of forms with a range of functions' (p. 6). It is this that motivates the acquisition of new forms which in turn leads to free variation.

Learners are also potentially sensitive to target language norms; Færch (1980) points out that SLA differs from historical change in that it is 'targeted'. The motivation to incorporate target language norms is partly the need to improve communicative efficiency; simplified interlanguage systems cannot easily cope with communication relating to displaced activity and abstract topics. However, the main reason why learners pay attention to target language norms is because they acknowledge the legitimacy of such norms and wish to conform.

Learners may lose their desire for communicative choice and their sensitivity to target language norms. *Fossilisation* (see Selinker, 1972) can be explained as the absence of any desire for communicative choice and of recognition of target language norms. The learner is closed off from new forms. Such learners are likely to manifest far lower levels of free variation than learners who remain open to input.

If we accept that communicative choice and recognition of target language norms are the necessary conditions for the introduction of new linguistic features, we can go on to consider what happens when a new form enters interlanguage. I have argued that the immediate result is free variation. The arguments for and against this position have already been discussed. There is sufficient evidence (Wagner-Gough, 1975; Eisenstein *et al.*, 1982; Ellis, 1985b; Schachter, 1986) to justify the claims I have made for free variation. It is possible, however, that for many learners and many structures the stage in which free variation occurs is a very brief one (cf. Schachter, 1986).

The process of elaboration begins almost immediately a new form enters interlanguage. It occurs as the learner gathers information about the new structure. When a new form is internalised it can be thought of as a proto-form. The introduction of the form, however, sensitises the learner to its existence in different contexts provided by the input. As a result, the learner attends to its various occurrences, accumulating various kinds of sociolinguistic information about its use in communication. This accretion of information occurs in different ways.

1. *Linguistic context*, i.e. the learner gradually learns which contexts the new form can be used in. As suggested earlier this process may be regulated by purely linguistic factors to do with the degree of markedness inherent in different contexts.

2. *Discourse context*, i.e. the learner learns which topics or genres the new form belongs to. Initially, knowledge of a form is restricted to that discourse content in which it was acquired. Subsequently the learner begins to discover the discourse range of the new form. The evidence for this form of accretion is however, more limited (cf. earlier accounts of Selinker & Douglas, 1985).

3. *Social context*, i.e. the learner discovers what social meanings the new form carries and learns how to use it with the appropriate addressee.

4. *Interactional context*, i.e. the learner learns to use the new form to perform an increasing range of communicative functions (not necessarily in accord with native-speaker use).

In other words, the process of elaboration accounts for the different sources of variability described in Section One. The process is never-ending as it is the same process by which forms achieve 'value' through communication in native-speaker use. As Widdowson (1978) has pointed out, language forms do not just possess 'signification' (a defined and static meaning content) but 'value' (potential meaning that is realised in communication). 'Value' is created and recreated through acts of use, the only constraint on maverick extensions being social convention. Seen in this light, the process of interlanguage elaboration is the result of the process of communication itself.

The third process is that of revision. This occurs as a result of the internal pressures that arise in the learner's interlanguage when new forms enter and old forms are elaborated. We assume that learners are guided by certain efficiency principles such as Andersen's (1984) one-to-one principle. When such principles are broken, the learner attempts to reconstruct the system. Thus, for instance, if the introduction of a new form results in two forms serving a single function (free variation) the learner will endeavour to establish new form–function correlates so that one form serves one function and maximal communicative efficiency is maintained. The need for communicative expressiveness induces the learner to acquire new forms and to use old forms in new functions, but their acquisition in turn obliges him to reorganise in order to follow other ground rules—the need for language to be semantically transparent and humanly processible (cf. Slobin, 1977).

In this way the learner's sociolinguistic competence is constructed—a slow, incremental process involving concurrent innovation, elaboration and revision. The process is potentially without end, just as native-speaker systems are eternally subject to the same mechanisms of change.

The acquisition of control

In addition to the slow process of building sociolinguistic knowledge, the learner also has to learn how to control the knowledge he possesses, so that it is available for use under different processing conditions. Again, we can anticipate that horizontal variability will mirror vertical growth, although as yet there are no longitudinal empirical studies of the acquisition of control. I hypothesise that there will be progress towards categoricality as the learner acquires the capacity to perform in increasingly unplanned discourse (see Figure 3).

A bidimensional model of L2 proficiency

The development of sociolinguistic knowledge and channel control take place simultaneously. The proficiency attained by a learner at any stage of development can be represented in terms of the points reached on these two dimensions, as shown in Figure 4. Ellis (1987b) has shown that learners vary in the extent to which they orientate towards one or the other dimension. It was found that gains in fluency in an oral narrative (measured

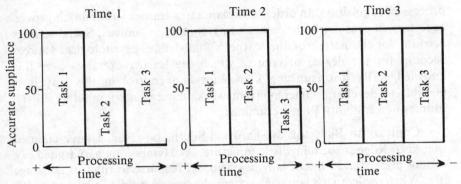

FIGURE 3. *The acquisition of control*

in terms of number of syllables per minute) correlated inversely with gains in the accuracy of production of three word order rules by 37 adult learners of L2 German. We can expect to find three broad types of learner. Type A learner develops a high level of control but fails to advance sociolinguistic knowledge to any extent. Type B learner is the opposite; considerable sociolinguistic competence is developed but there is little control over this (i.e. the learner can act on this competence only in planned discourse). The Type C learner is more balanced, progressing equally on both dimensions.

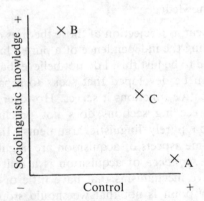

FIGURE 4. *A bidimensional model of L2 proficiency*

Conclusion

This chapter has examined a number of sources of intra-learner variability in interlanguage use and has sought to relate these sources to the process of acquisition. In order to explain intra-learner variability it proved necessary to consider both social and psychological sources. Social sources account for the nature of the learner's knowledge; psychological sources account for the degree of control which the learner exercises over this knowledge. By distinguishing knowledge and control in this way it is possible to develop a coherent framework that can accommodate all the sources of variability I have examined.

Contrary to Bialystok & Sharwood-Smith, however, I have claimed that knowledge is sociolinguistic in nature. As Hymes long ago argued, we cannot understand rules of language without recourse to rules of language use. When the learner's language system changes over time, it is not just the linguistic representation of this knowledge that changes, but also the rules of use. Form and function are so closely intertwined in the process of interlanguage development that we cannot separate one from the other. Sampson (1982) captures the relationship like this:

> A person's personal history of the functions she or he has been engaged in will also be a history of the linguistic structures she or he has attended to. (Sampson, 1982:14)

The learner's hypotheses about the L2 are sociolinguistic in nature. Linguistic knowledge *grows* as the learner discovers the social value that can be placed upon it. The process of discovery itself affects the organisation of linguistic knowledge.

This might appear as a rejection of those theories of interlanguage that make claims regarding the independence of a purely linguistic competence. In part, it is intended to be just this. I do not believe that an adequate theory of interlanguage can be developed that seeks to separate language form from the communicative functions it serves. However, the position I have advanced in the preceding sections does not preclude explanations of acquisition based on purely linguistic arguments. Indeed, I consider it highly likely that some aspects of acquisition are linguistically determined. It is likely that the *sequence* of acquisition is a reflection of specifically linguistic or cognitive mechanisms that have little or nothing to do with communication. My point is not that we should stop investigating these mechanisms. They provide our best bet for accounting for how new forms get into interlanguage. It is of obvious importance that we establish what formal constraints there are on the acquisition of new linguistic forms. Investigating development-as-sequence, however, is only half the story; we also need to consider development-as-growth by finding out what happens to linguistic forms once they have entered interlanguage. This necessitates viewing competence sociolinguistically and studying variability in L2 use.

As has frequently been observed in the past, to focus research on formal features to the exclusion of social factors is not only unnecessarily restricting but ultimately misleading.

References

ANDERSEN, R., 1984, What's gender good for, anyway. In R. ANDERSEN (ed.), *Second Languages: A Cross-Linguistic Perspective*. Rowley, MA: Newbury House.

ATKINSON, J. and SHRIFFIN, R., 1968, Human memory: A proposed system and its control processes. In K. SPENCE & T. SPENCE (eds), *The Psychology of Learning and Motivation: Advances in Research and Theory*, Vol. 2. New York: Academic Press.

BAILEY, C.-J., 1973, *Variation and Linguistic Theory*. Washington DC: Center for Applied Linguistics.

BEEBE, L., 1981, Social and situational factors affecting the communicative strategy of dialect code-switching, *International Journal of the Sociology of Language*, 32, 139–49.

BEEBE, L. and ZUENGLER, J., 1983, Accommodation theory: An explanation for style-shifting in second language dialects. In N. WOLFSON & E. JUDD (eds), *Sociolinguistics and Language Acquisition*. Rowley, MA: Newbury House.

BELL, A., 1984, Language style as audience design, *Language in Society*, 13, 145–204.

BIALYSTOK, E., 1981, The role of linguistic knowledge in second language use, *Studies in Second Language Acquisition*, 4, 31–45.

——, 1982, On the relationship between knowing and using linguistic forms, *Applied Linguistics*, 3(2), 181–206.

BIALYSTOK, E. and SHARWOOD-SMITH, M., 1985, Interlanguage is not a state of mind: An evaluation of the construct for second language acquisition, *Applied Linguistics*, 6(3), 101–17.

BICKERTON, D., 1975, *Dynamics of a Creole System*. Cambridge: Cambridge University Press.

BLEY-VROMAN, R., 1983, The comparative fallacy in interlanguage studies: The case of systematicity, *Language Learning*, 33(1), 1–17.

BROWN, P. and LEVINSON, S., 1978, Universals in language usage: Politeness phenomena. In E. GOOD (ed.), *Questions and Politeness: Strategies in Social Interaction*. Cambridge: Cambridge University Press.

CAZDEN, C., CANCINO, H., ROSANSKY, E. and SCHUMANN, J., 1975, *Second Language Acquisition in Children, Adolescents and Adults*, Final Report, United States Department of Health, Education and Welfare,

CORNU, A. and DELAHAYE, M., 1987, Variability in interlanguage reconsidered: LSP vs. non-LSP IL talk, *English for Specific Purposes*, 6(2), 145–51.

DOWNES, W., 1984, *Language and Society*. London: Fontana.

EISENSTEIN, M., BAILEY, N. and MADDEN, C., 1982, It takes two: Contrasting tasks and contrasting structures, *TESOL Quarterly*, 16(3).

ELLIS, R., 1985a, *Understanding Second Language Acquisition*. Oxford: Oxford University Press.

——, 1985b, Sources of variability in interlanguage, *Applied Linguistics*, 6(2), 118–31.

——, 1987a, Interlanguage variability in narrative discourse: Style-shifting in the use of the past tense, *Studies in Second Language Acquisition*, 9(1), 1–20.

——, 1987b, 'Individual learning styles in classroom second language development.' Paper presented at the 8th AILA World Congress, Sydney.

——, 1988, The effects of linguistic environment on the second language acquisition of grammatical rules, *Applied Linguistics*, 9(3), 257–74.

ELLIS, R. and ROBERTS, C., 1987, Introduction. In R. ELLIS (ed.), *Second Language Acquisition in Context*. London: Prentice Hall International.

FAERCH, C., 1980, Describing interlanguage through interaction: Problems of systematicity and permeability, *Working Papers on Bilingualism*, 19, 59–78.

FASOLD, R., 1984, Variation theory and language learning. In P. TRUDGILL (ed.), *Applied Sociolinguistics*. London: Academic Press.

GATBONTON, E., 1978, Patterned phonetic variability in second language speech: A gradual diffusion model, *Canadian Modern Language Review*, 34(3), 335–47.

GILES, H. (ed.), 1977, *Language, Ethnicity and Intergroup Relations*. New York: Academic Press.

——, 1980, Accommodation theory: Some new directions. In S. DE SILVA (ed.), *Aspects of Linguistic Behaviour*. York: University of York.

GIVÓN, T., 1979, *On Understanding Grammar*. New York: Academic Press.

HALLIDAY, M., MCINTOSH, A. and STREVENS, P., 1964, *The Linguistic Sciences and Language Teaching*. London: Longman.

HUDSON, R., 1980, *Sociolinguistics*. Cambridge: Cambridge University Press.

HUEBNER, T., 1979, Order-of-acquisition vs. dynamic paradigm: A comparison of method in interlanguage research, *TESOL Quarterly*, 13(1), 21–8.

——, 1983, *A Longitudinal Analysis of the Acquisition of English*. Ann Arbor: Karoma.

HULSTIJN, J. and HULSTIJN, W., 1984, Grammatical errors as a function of processing constraints and explicit knowledge, *Language Learning*, 34, 23–44.

HYLTENSTAM, K., 1984, The use of typological markedness conditions as predictors in second language acquisition: The case of pronominal copies in relative clauses. In R. ANDERSEN (ed.), *Second Languages: A Cross-Linguistic Perspective*. Rowley, MA: Newbury House.

KRASHEN, S., 1981, *Second Language Acquisition and Second Language Learning*. Oxford: Pergamon.

LABOV, W., 1969, Contraction, deletion and inherent variability of the English copula, *Language*, 45(4), 715–52.

——, 1980, The social origins of sound change. In W. LABOV (ed.), *Locating Language in Time and Space*. New York: Academic Press.

MEISEL, J., 1983, Strategies of second language acquisition: More than one kind of simplification. In R. ANDERSEN (ed.), *Pidginization and Creolization as Language Acquisition*. Rowley, MA: Newbury House.

NICHOLAS, H., 1986, The acquisition of language as the acquisition of variation, *Australian Working Papers in Language Development*, 1(2), 1–30.

PARRISH, B. and TARONE, E., 1986, Article use in interlanguage: A study of task-related variability. Paper presented at the 20th Annual TESOL Convention, Anaheim, CA.

RAMPTON, B., 1987, Stylistic variability and not speaking 'normal' English: Some post-Labovian approaches and their implications for the study of inter-language. In R. ELLIS (ed.), *Second Language Acquisition in Context*. London: Prentice Hall International.

ROBERTS, C. and SIMONOT, M., 1987, 'This is my life': How interaction is interactionally accomplished. In R. ELLIS (ed.), *Second Language Acquisition in Context*. London: Prentice Hall International.

SAMPSON, G., 1982, Converging evidence for a dialectal model of function and form in second language learning, *Applied Linguistics*, 3(1), 1–28.

SATO, C., 1985, Task variation in interlanguage phonology. In S. GASS & C. MADDEN (eds), *Input in Second Language Acquisition*. Rowley, MA: Newbury House.

SCHACHTER, J., 1986, In search of systematicity in interlanguage production, *Studies in Second Language Acquisition*, 8(2), 119–34.

SELINKER, L., 1972, Interlanguage, *International Review of Applied Linguistics*, 10, 201–31.

SELINKER, L. and DOUGLAS, D., 1985, Wrestling with context in interlanguage theory, *Applied Linguistics*, 6(2), 190–204.

SKEHAN, P., 1987, Variability and language testing. In R. ELLIS (ed.), *Second Language Acquisition in Context*. London: Prentice Hall International.

SLOBIN, D., 1977, Language change in childhood and in history. In J. MACNAMARA (ed.), *Language Learning and Thought*. New York: Academic Press.

TARONE, E., 1979, Interlanguage as chameleon, *Language Learning*, 29(1), 181–92.

——, 1983, On the variability of interlanguage systems, *Applied Linguistics*, 4(2), 142–63.

——, 1985, Variability in interlanguage use: A study of style-shifting in morphology and syntax, *Language Learning*, 35(3), 373–404.

——, 1987, Methodologies for studying variability in second language acquisition. In R. ELLIS (ed.), *Second Language Acquisition in Context*. London: Prentice Hall International.

VALDMAN, A., 1987, 'Les aprennant americains avances devant la norme.' Paper presented at the 8th AILA World Congress, Sydney.

WAGNER-GOUGH, J., 1975, Comparative studies in second language learning, *CAL-ERIC/CLL Series on Language and Linguistics*, 26.

WIDDOWSON, H., 1978, *Teaching Language as Communication*. Oxford: Oxford University Press.

4 The theoretical status of variation in interlanguage development

ROGER W. ANDERSEN
University of California, Los Angeles

The purpose of this chapter is to place the study of variation in inter-language development within a theoretical framework. Important as the technical aspects of the study of variation are—and they are very important—without a sound theoretical framework to help the analyst to *explain* the variation found, such technical details simply display it. What is needed is a principled explanation of why variation occurs the way it does. Moreover, by explaining that variation, we are also much closer to explaining the nature of acquisition itself. That is, dealing with variation in SLA is not a marginal pursuit but an obligatory part of SLA research itself.

Variation can mean a number of different things: (1) variation across learners: i.e. learners go about learning a language in different ways, (2) variation across individual styles, registers or tasks, or (3) variation within the same sample of interlanguage of an individual speaker as well as over time. The focus in this chapter is on this last type of variation: the same person using different linguistic forms or constructions for what appears to be the same intended meaning. For example, why doesn't the speaker always use a past morpheme when the intended reference is past or a definite article when the referent is specific, or in second language Spanish why does the speaker place a first person clitic pronoun before the verb but a third person clitic after the verb, when in native Spanish all clitics are preverbal? The approach taken here will be to assume that *all such surface variation can be reduced to invariance and a set of principles that govern distribution of forms and change* (i.e. restructuring) *over time*. This is the assumption behind the *implicational model* for SLA developed in Andersen (1976, 1978) to deal with variation in second language data.

This does not mean, however, that all variation can indeed be reduced to invariance. The importance of *assuming* that it can be so reduced is that we can more easily tell whether it can or cannot in any particular case and thus will understand variation better. That is, we wish to test the null hypothesis that a particular occurrence of variation cannot be reduced to invariance plus a set of principles that govern the surface variation. If we cannot reject the null hypothesis, it may be that the given occurrence of variation is not systematic or that it is indeed systematic but we have not discovered the principle or principles which govern it. It is this second case that would constitute progress in our field, provided this result eventually led to discovery of the correct principles or a better theory. In fact, if systematic variation cannot be reduced to clear principles and their relationships to each other, then we simply can't do *anything* with variation.

On the following pages I will discuss aspects of a theory of SLA (the Cognitive–Interactionist Theory) which I believe is capable of explaining a large part of the variation found in second language developmental data. Before doing so, however, it seems appropriate to state a number of basic assumptions about the nature of linguistic variation in second language data which form part of the background to this chapter. These assumptions have a number of different sources: variation theory in sociolinguistics, within the tradition established by Labov (e.g. 1966, 1972), as well as the partly competing tradition represented by DeCamp (1971), Bailey (1973), Bickerton (1973, 1975) and Rickford (1979, 1987), but especially my own interpretation of empirical evidence for variation in second language studies. I will simply state these assumptions and not attempt to defend them here.

1. The ideal goal of the study of variation is to reduce variation to invariance plus principles that account for the variation.

2. Variation can be either systematic or nonsystematic. We must know the difference and be able to explain the first, i.e. systematic variation.

3. Variation is due to both cognitive–linguistic and social–interactionist factors. Of the two, cognitive–linguistic factors are the more basic and universal.

4. In a dynamic framework of acquisition over time, systematic variation reflects a transition from an (idealised) earlier *invariant* state S_1 to a second (idealised) later *invariant* state S_2.

5. Within a cognitive–interactionist theory of SLA the greatest part of the systematic variation found in the interlanguage system of a given learner over time (from S_1 to S_2), across a *population* of learners at one time, or

across different *styles* or *registers* of the same learner, is due to the interaction of the cognitive operating principles as they guide learners in their perception of structural relations and incorporation of these perceptions into their interlanguage.

6. Additional variation can come from other sources (formal learning, socio-economic status variables, degree of literacy, learning style, discourse type, task, etc.). Cognitive–interactionist theory does not attempt to account for these and they must be controlled for in research on variation within a cognitive–interactionist theory.

A cognitive–interactionist theory of second language acquisition

The theory of SLA that I offer as an adequate explanatory framework for dealing with variation in SLA I will call a 'cognitive–interactionist' theory of second language development, for want of a better term. It is the theory I believe many researchers take for granted in their discussion of how a learner acquires a second language naturally through social interaction and attempts to give and receive meaning through the second language. By developing the 'cognitive–interactionist' theory of SLA, I am trying to specify more explicitly and verify empirically a model of SLA and the principles which operate within that model.[1] The model is the *Nativisation Model* I have discussed elsewhere (e.g. Andersen, 1979b, 1980, 1983a, 1984a) and the principles are cognitive operating principles of the type Slobin has worked on in first language acquisition for the past fifteen years (e.g. Slobin, 1973, 1977, 1982, 1985).

The nativisation model

> *Nativization* refers to the composite of (presumably universal) processes by which an individual language learner creates an internal representation of the language he is acquiring and the subsequent assimilation ... of new input to the learner's gradually evolving internal representation of that second language. (Andersen, 1979b: 109)

Nativisation, unrestricted by accurate perceptions of structural relations in the input, would lead to a linguistic system very different from that of the input. This is what happens in situations where pidgin and creole languages evolve (see Andersen, 1983a). In other contexts, where access to the input is not restricted, the learner's linguistic system or interlanguage evolves towards that of the input, as I have tried to capture with the notion of 'denativisation' (not a totally satisfactory term).

> *Denativization* is the gradual restructuring of the learner's somewhat unique and idiosyncratic internal representation of the language he is acquiring in terms of the input he processes during language acquisition. (Andersen, 1979b:109)

Over the past several years I have attempted to arrive at a theoretically more satisfying interpretation of data on natural and non-instructed second language acquisition of English by speakers of various languages and of Spanish by English speakers, as well as instructed SLA by Spanish speakers learning English in classrooms and, through the published and unpublished literature and through contact with colleagues, of second language acquisition of a number of other languages, especially German, French, Dutch and Swedish. Through this effort I arrived at the current set of 12 operating principles that I will discuss briefly in this chapter. I will state each principle, with examples, and then elaborate further on how any one principle or group of principles might account for empirically verifiable variation.

The Nativisation Model and the related operating principles are in an ongoing state of development. It is anyone's guess what the final expression of each principle should look like and how many principles there might be. My approach so far has been to develop one principle at a time as motivated by consistent patterns in the data. I certainly owe an important debt to Dan Slobin, since I have drawn where possible on his in-depth research on cognitive operating principles (OPs) in first language acquisition. I have done this only where insights from his work have helped me understand a particular problem in SLA. I have not simply assumed that each of his 40 principles automatically applies to SLA. If I had, I would have more than 12 principles.

Cognitive operating principles

Before beginning with the principles, I should make clear a simple example that I will use throughout this presentation to try to make the operation of each principle as clear as possible. I have chosen second language acquisition of English negation to illustrate the application of the principles, primarily because this area of research is well documented, but also because it is easier to use for purposes of illustration than many other linguistic constructions. I will refer throughout this chapter to the 'simple example' given below. This example is meant to represent the basic development in negation from the earliest (the examples in (1)) to the latest (2 & 3) stages of development. Obviously many details are omitted.[2]

A simple example:

	(A)	(B)		(C)		(D)	
1.	**No!**	No	the dog. He	**no**	eat.	1'. I **dunno**.	
2.	**No!**	Not	the dog. He	**don**	eat.	2'. I **don**	know.
3.	**No!**	Not	the dog. He	**didn't**	eat it.	3'. I **didn't**	know.

Line 3 in this 'simple example' is meant to represent the end-point of second language acquisition of English negation, obviously oversimplified. 'No!' in column (A) represents anaphoric negation, '**Not** the dog' in column (B) negation of a constituent of a sentence, in this case a noun phrase,[3] and 'He **didn't** eat it' in column (C) sentence-level or propositional negation. (3) 'I **didn't** know' (column D) represents the rule-generated version of what begins as a memorised chunk or routine in SLA. In (1) the hypothetical learner treats all three cases the same, using an invariant **no** before the entity to be negated. In (1') the learner uses a memorised expression, 'I **dunno**' with the meaning of (3'). At time (2) the learner has differentiated anaphoric, constituent and propositional negation and, in (2'), has generated 'I **don** know' presumably in the same way as 'He **don** eat'. At this time, however, the learner gives no evidence of having a clear auxiliary node. That is, **don** is simply a variant form of **no**. Moreover the learner does not encode past time reference at this stage. I take this as a noncontroversial and well-established description of SLA of English negation (essentially that of Cazden *et al.*, 1975 and Schumann, 1978).

Basic psycholinguistic processes of perception and storage

I will now illustrate, again in oversimplified fashion, each of the 12 principles with this developmental sequence of negation and other linguistic domains where necessary. I have divided these principles into two groups, the first four as 'Basic psycholinguistic processes of perception and storage', taken verbatim from Slobin's (1985) version of Peters' (1985) principles for perceiving, storing and tagging segments of speech. There are more than four (Slobin uses eight), but these four seem especially basic. All the other principles, discussed later under the heading 'Additional Principles', have these as prerequisites and must be consistent with these basic processing principles.

1. Attention (sounds): *Store any perceptually salient stretches of speech.* (Slobin, 1985:1165)

Principle 1 is straightforward. For the negation example this means basic vocabulary, at least **no** as a lexical item, and the memorised expression 'I **dunno**'.

2. Attention (stress): *Pay attention to stressed syllables in extracted speech units. Store such syllables separately and also in relation to the units with which they occur.* (Slobin, 1985:1166)

Principle 2 contributes to perception of **no** as the all-purpose negative morpheme, since it is more often stressed than the other variants in the input, which are most typically unstressed.

3. Storage (frequency): *Keep track of the frequency of occurrence of every unit and pattern that you store.* (Slobin, 1985: 1166)

No is also initially favoured because of its high frequency in anaphoric negation. It appears that **not** (or often a variant without the final [t]—**na**) is also perceived early because of frequency as well as possibility of being stressed. And the early use of **don**, long before number (**doesn't**) and tense (**didn't**) are encoded in the negated auxiliary, is also favoured by the high frequency of **dont** in the input, relative to the much lower occurrence of **doesn't** and **didn't**.

4. Storage (units): *Determine whether a newly extracted stretch of speech seems to be the same as or different from anything you have already stored. If it is different, store it separately; if it is the same, take note of this sameness by increasing its frequency count by one.*

This principle contributes to the learner beginning to differentiate the forms **no, not** and **dont** (and eventually **didn't, doesn't** and others) as well as their functions and distribution. As learners encounter more and more tokens of each form, so does the internal representation of that form in their interlanguage strengthen, long before they spontaneously use them.

Additional principles

The remaining eight principles build on these four basic principles. Principle 5, the One-to-One principle, states that:

5. The One-to-One Principle: *An interlanguage system should be constructed in such a way that an intended underlying meaning is expressed with one clear invariant surface form (or construction).* (Andersen, 1984a:79)

This principle has been discussed considerably in the literature on first language acquisition, historical change, and pidgin and creole linguistics. I also devoted an article to it several years ago (Andersen, 1984a). Returning to our miniature negation continuum, this principle motivates the preference for one and only one negator (**no** in our example) and one simple rule for its position: directly before the entity negated. Research on SLA of German and Swedish gives similar results[4] (e.g. Meisel, 1983 and Clahsen, 1984 for German; Hyltenstam, 1977, 1982 and Jordens 1980, 1982 for Swedish). Although pidgin and creole languages maintain this simplest type of negation system, in normal SLA there is a counter-tendency to develop a more multifunctional system, which all natural languages have. A one-to-one principle is simply inefficient and close to disfunctional for natural language use, as can be seen in probably any language. This observable fact is captured in Principle 6, the Multifunctionality Principle.

6. The Multifunctionality Principle: *(a) Where there is clear evidence in the input that more than one form marks the meaning conveyed by only one form in the interlanguage, try to discover the distribution and additional meaning (if any) of the new form. (b) Where there is evidence in the input that an interlanguage form conveys only one of the meanings that the same form has in the input, try to discover the additional meanings of the form in the input.*

Depending on the particular circumstances of the learner, some learners barely follow this principle and are stuck for a long time (perhaps forever) in an IL system based entirely or partially on the One-to-One principle. Returning to our negation example, the Multifunctionality Principle motivates discovery of the multiple surface forms for negation: the learner comes to reserve **no** for anaphoric negation, **not** for constituent negation (and perhaps negated predicates with copulas), and **don**[5] for sentence negation. The evidence for doing this is in the input and it simply takes time for the learner to discover the different forms and their distribution. Stage 2 in our simple example is meant to capture this. Part (b) of this principle would presumably lead the learner at some later stage to use **no** not only for anaphoric negation but also for the negative quantifier as in 'Yes, we have **no** bananas'. This is clearly different from '**not** bananas, coconuts'.

Principle 7 contributes to the learner's discovery of multifunctionality in the input when his own interlanguage is still unifunctional.

7. Formal Determinism: *When the form:meaning relationship is clearly and uniformly encoded in the input, the learner will discover it earlier than other form:meaning relationships and will incorporate it more consistently within his interlanguage system.*

Following our negation example, **dont** clearly and uniformly encodes propositional negation, which helps the learner perceive it fairly early. Learners hardly ever confuse this form with anaphoric or constituent negation, precisely because it is clearly reserved for propositional negation. **Didn't** and **doesn't**, however, are much more opaque (and less frequent) and take longer for the learner to figure out, which is what is predicted by this principle.

The next principle, the Distributional Bias Principle, also guides the learner towards multifunctionality, but also has the potential of leading the learner into a dead-end. Again, using our negation example, since **dont** is so much more frequent for propositional negation than the forms **didn't** and **doesn't**, this constitutes a distributional bias within the input that causes the leaerner to mis-perceive **dont** as the only negator for propositions and to not perceive the obligatory tense and agreement marking. (See Andersen, 1986c, for extensive discussion of this principle, based on data on the acquisition of Spanish tense and aspect by English speakers.) This principle states that:

8. Distributional Bias: *If both X and Y can occur in the same environments A and B, but a bias in the distribution of X and Y makes it appear that X only occurs in environment A and Y only occurs in environment B, when you acquire X and Y, restrict X to environment A and Y to environment B.*

Bybee (1985) is the source of Principle 9, the Relevance Principle. This is Slobin's (1985) version of it.

9. Relevance: *OP (POSITION): RELEVANCE. If two or more functors apply to a content word, try to place them so that the more relevant the meaning of a functor is to the meaning of the content word, the closer it is placed to the content word. If you find that a Notion is marked in several places, at first mark it only in the position closest to the relevant content word.* (Slobin, 1985:1255)

The negation continuum example is only partially relevant here. The initial rule for negator placement causes the negator to be placed immediately in front of the constituent to be negated. This is close to how native English works and this makes English L2 data of limited use in studying this principle. In German and Swedish, however, syntactic rules require the negator to be separated from the negated constituent. Learners take a long time to learn that this is the case and initially follow the Relevance Principle and place the negator immediately in front of (or at least next to) the negated constituent (see Clahsen, 1984; Hyltenstam 1977, 1982; Jordens 1980, 1982; and Meisel, 1983).

More revealing of the operation of the Relevance Principle is the acquisition of verbal morphology in L2 Spanish. Spanish verbal morphology conveys, among other things, primarily aspect, tense and person—

number agreement. As Bybee's Relevance Principle explicitly predicts, aspect marking is acquired first, since aspect is more relevant to the intrinsic meaning of the verb. Tense marking develops afterwards, but before agreement, because tense-marking, while relevant to the entire proposition, which includes the verb to which it is attached, is still more relevant to the verb than is agreement marking. Her principle thus accounts for what is actually observed (see Andersen, 1986a,b, for further details).

We can return to our simple example on negation for Principle 10, which has two parts. First part (a):

10. Constituent Structure: *(a) When a new form is incorporated into your interlanguage system, place it within the existing constituent structure of that system.*

Until an auxiliary node develops in the interlanguage system—and this takes a long time—**dont** can only be categorised as a negator, specific to propositional negation, but not as an auxiliary plus phonologically reduced negator as in native English. When **dont** is initially acquired, it can only be acquired in this fashion and must fit into the existing constituent structure of the interlanguage.

(b) When you notice a mis-match between a given form's position within the interlanguage constituent structure and the position it has in the native input constituent structure, restructure your interlanguage in the direction of the input constituent structure, with regard to that particular form.

Part (b) of this principle motivates restructuring of **dont** into **do** in the auxiliary node and **not** as negator, phonologically reduced and cliticised to the aux. This can only take place after the auxiliary node has developed, however, which then provides grounds for the learner to perceive a mis-match between the constituent structure in which *his* **dont** fits and the constituent structure of the **dont**s in the input. Once this happens, he is also ready to perceive tense and person–number marking on the negative auxiliary. We might want to add a special clause in small print to this principle that reads, 'No constituent structure will develop before its time'.

So far we have acted as if the learner's native language didn't matter. But we know better. The next two principles are meant to capture what I believe is the way first language transfer operates. I would prefer to have only one principle. Having the second one, the Relexification Principle, puts me in the uncomfortable position of sounding like I'm saying, 'I can handle L1 transfer, but whenever I can't, I'll just call it something else—relexification. So I can never be wrong.' This is certainly not my intention, and I have been forced into this position by what I believe are the facts of interlanguage data. The first of these, Principle 11, the Transfer to Somewhere Principle, reads as follows:

> **11. Transfer to Somewhere:** *A grammatical form or structure will occur consistently and to a significant extent in the interlanguage as a result of transfer* if and only if *(1) natural acquisitional principles are consistent with the L1 structure or (2) there already exists within the L2 input the potential for (mis-)generalization from the input to produce the same form or structure. Furthermore, in such transfer preference is given in the resulting interlanguage to* free, invariant, *functionally* simple *morphemes which are congruent with the L1 and L2 (or there is congruence between the L1 and natural acquisitional processes) and* [to] *morphemes* [which] *occur frequently in the L1 and/or the L2.* (Andersen, 1983b:182)

This basically states that L1 transfer can operate consistently and persist only if it operates within the scope of the preceding ten operating principles. What does this mean for our minicontinuum for English negation? Spanish speakers more consistently use **no** as the general negator in English than Japanese speakers, for whom **no** is restricted to a very short early stage or to speakers stuck in the One-to-One Principle for the rest of their lives. Although Japanese speakers do use **no** as a negator for both constituent and propositional negation, they more commonly discover **not** and **dont** as negators, much faster than do Spanish speakers. The explanation within the Transfer to Somewhere (TTS) Principle is that Spanish negation matches what the One-to-One Principle produces independent of transfer and thus Spanish speakers have something to transfer to. And, once they take the bait, they are hooked for a long time.[6] Japanese negation, however, is post-verbal and the verb is sentence final, two characteristics which operate against any sort of transfer. For verb- and sentence-final negation there is no 'somewhere' to transfer to.

We can take up another case of transfer involving negation which fits the TTS principle. Wode (1976) showed over ten years ago that German post-verbal position of the negator **nicht** transfers to English only after the learner has developed a set of auxiliaries (in effect, the operation of the Constituent Structure Principle). Once the learner can say 'He **must** not go', which matches German negation for auxiliaries, he can transfer from German to produce incorrect 'He **goes** not', which matches German word order for main verbs. In this case the 'somewhere' to which the learner transfers must be developed in the learner's interlanguage before the transfer can take place.[7]

Some interpretations of first language transfer treat it simply as a case of plugging target language words into a native language structure when the learner doesn't know the target language structure. This is how I read Krashen's (1983) version of L1 transfer. While this can and does take place, I believe this is the least interesting type of L1 influence and not the type that the TTS Principle is meant to explain. This view of transfer is better called 'Relexification' as it is called in pidgin and creole studies. My interpretation of SLA data and the pidgin and creole literature is that relexification only applies when learners cannot get adequate access to target language input on which to base their interlanguage development. This is stated as Principle 12, the Relexification Principle.

12. Relexification: *When you cannot perceive the structural pattern used by the language you are trying to acquire, use your native language structure with lexical items from the second language.*

It is very revealing that Japanese speakers of Hawaiian Pidgin English, who clearly rely heavily on relexification in many areas, do not relexify their post-verbal and sentence-final Japanese negation in their Pidgin English. Instead they use one-to-one principle negation. But they do frequently relexify the basic subject—object—verb word order of Japanese. Bickerton reports that this object—verb order reaches as high as 60% in Japanese speakers of Hawaiian Pidgin English (Bickerton & Odo, 1976). Example (1) illustrates the effect of this principle for the extreme case of SLA called pidginisation.

(1)   Japanese Pidgin English in Hawaii:

as kerosin, plaenteishan, wan mans, fo gaelan **giv**
The plantation **gave** us four gallons of kerosene a month.
(Bickerton, 1977:53)

This word order can only be attributed to the severely restricted access to native English input in Hawaii when Hawaiian Pidgin English first developed in Hawaii. In naturalistic acquisition of English by Japanese speakers in the continental US, where they have much better access to native English than the pidgin speakers did in Hawaii, such relexification is not common. It does exist, however, as in example (2). The speaker in example (2) began to learn English in Japan, however, where her access to native English input would have been much more limited than after she arrived in the United States. Most of her English is clearly verb + object order. In this example verbs are italic and objects are enclosed in square brackets. Parentheses enclose uncertain transcriptions.

(2)   Japanese-English in natural SLA:

> (In response to the question: 'Why didn't you *like* [English]?')
> 1. Because ... I never *talk* [to American people],
> 2.   I'm never learn.
> 3. Then, I'm (gonna) marry,
> 4.   *must be* [English] I *am study*.
> 5. Then, I'*m* not *marry* ... [(the) American people],
> 6.   I not [English], *take* [the class]. (laughs)
> 7. I *have* [a Junior high school],
> 8.   never [English] *take* [the class].
> (Kuwahata, 1984)

[= 1. Because since I never talked to Americans,
  2.   I never learned English.
  3.   But when I was going to marry an American,
  4.   I had to study English.
  5.   If I weren't going to marry an American,
  6.   I wouldn't have taken English classes. (laughs)
  7.   In junior high school,
  8.   I never took English class.]

I interpret this passage as the speaker's preference for Japanese processing, which causes her to plan her sentence with sentence-final placement of the verb, which she then repairs by inserting a second object after the verb, which semantically fits the meaning. Thus, in clauses 6 and 8, she appears to have planned to say 'I not English class take' and 'Junior High, I never English class take'. She was able to catch herself soon enough to put *class* after the verb. Thus, if my interpretation is correct, relexification is highly restricted and her low frequency of such constructions is due to the Transfer to Somewhere Principle. Since she does have contact with native English, such potential relexification does not survive because there is no 'where' for it to transfer to in native English.

What then does all of this do for us in trying to understand and explain variation in interlanguage development?

The role of variation within a cognitive–interactionist theory of SLA

In this section I will discuss how the Nativisation Model and the twelve cognitive operating principles apply to three variable linguistic phenomena

in interlanguage development, beginning with the area of negation which I
used as illustration of each of the principles.

Negation

The One-to-One Principle and the Multifunctionality Principle com-
pete, one drawing the learner towards the simplest system shown in stage 1
in our simple example, the other motivating the learner to discover formal
and distributional differences between **no, not**, and **dont**, and later to
include **doesn't** and **didn't** as well. The Principle of Formal Determinism
operates in support of the Multifunctionality Principle. If the learner is in a
situation where he can easily perceive the clearest form and distribution
distinctions in English negation in the input, then he will move away from
the One-to-One Principle. If, however, he either has limited access to such
input or other factors keep him from paying attention to available input,
the One-to-One Principle will prevail for some time. This in itself introduces
principled variation in the negation system. Added to this variation is the
variation introduced by means of the Transfer to Somewhere Principle. For
example, Spanish learners of English may persist with the use of **no** as a
general negator placed before the constituent to be negated for a long time,
whereas a Japanese speaker would discover **not** as a general negator much
more rapidly. In addition, if the learner is delayed in developing an auxiliary
node, this will fix his development at a stage prior to restructuring of **dont**
into an auxiliary and a negator, which potentially introduces further
variation into the system, following the Constituent Structure Principle.
This prediction can be verified by an analysis of auxiliaries in the learner's
interlanguage.

The three English S's

The next example involves the three English 's's: plural 's', possessive
's', and third person singular 's'. In both first and second language
acquisition these morphemes appear to be acquired in this order. If there is
quantitative variation in their use—and there is at many stages of development—the plural is more developed than the possessive and both are more
developed than third person singular 's'. The Relevance Principle, the
One-to-One Principle, and the Frequency Principle all can account for this
order. The plural 's' is most relevant to the noun to which it is attached and
should develop before the possessive and the verb morpheme. The plural
morpheme is also more frequent in the input than both the possessive and
the verb inflection (and the possessive 's' is more frequent than the verb

inflection, although they are close). And the One-to-One Principle promotes development of the plural inflection and lack of development of the
other two: the plural 's' clearly and uniformly encodes the notion 'more
than one', while for possession the order of possessor + possessed already
encodes the meaning adequately and the 's' is superfluous.[8] For the verb
inflection, in most cases the information provided by the 's' is already
present in the subject. Additional variation can be introduced into this
order, however, by L1 transfer, which follows the TTS Principle. Spanish
speakers accelerate development of plural 's' and delay development of
possessive 's', while Japanese speakers accelerate development of the
possessive 's' and delay development of plural 's', both because of L1
transfer.[9]

Spanish clitics and agreement markers

The next example of how variation can be explained within the
cognitive–interactionist theory has to do with variation in the development
of Spanish clitic pronouns and person-number agreement markers on the
verb in L2 Spanish. The relevant examples and paradigms are given as
examples (3), (4) and (5). The basic facts to be accounted for are, first of all,
that initially in L2 Spanish, learners place object pronouns postverbally, the
same as full NP objects, as in example (3).[10]

(3) **learners:**   la policía quiere **él**   'the police want him'
     native Spanish: la policía **lo** quiere

The One-to-One Principle promotes maintenance of verb–object word
order, since clitics violate this order. And the Stress Principle favours the
use of stressed pronouns like **él**. Clitic pronouns are unstressed and, being
preverbal, harder to perceive by the learner.

When the learner does begin to place pronouns in preverbal position as
clitics, s/he first does so with first person pronouns and continues either to
omit third person pronouns or to place them postverbally and use stressed
forms. The interpretation of this variation in form and placement of
stressed and unstressed clitic pronouns within this theory is that there is
competition between the One-to-One Principle which initially keeps object
pronouns stressed and postverbal, and the Multifunctional Principle which
motivates a special position and lack of stress for object pronouns. The
Formal Determinism Principle begins to resolve this competition because
the first person clitics are clear and consistent across the paradigm and they
are the first to be perceived in the correct form and position in the input.

This is seen in example (4). The third person pronouns come in too many shapes and sizes to be perceived clearly for a while. Thus, what on the surface appears to be accidental variation is really principled variation when dealt with within the cognitive–interactionist theory I have outlined.

(4) CLITICS:

	D.O.	I.O.	REFLEXIVE
1sg.	**me**	**me**	**me**
1pl.	**nos**	**nos**	**nos**
3sg. masc.	lo	le	se
3sg. fem.	la	le	se
3pl. masc.	los	les	se
3pl. fem.	las	les	se

This explanation finds further support when we consider the development of verbal inflections in Spanish for person–number agreement, shown in example (5). In this case the plural inflections develop faster and reach a greater percentage of accuracy than the singular forms for the same reason: the plural forms are clearer and more consistent in the paradigm, which also increases their relative frequency in the input. Before any agreement markers are used, the One-to-One Principle requires person and number marking to be expressed only once, on the subject. But when the Multifunctionality Principle begins to promote acquisition of the agreement markers, the Principle of Formal Determinism causes plural markers to be perceived and internalised before the singular markers. This variation thus has a principled explanation.

(5) Agreement markers on verb:

	Present ind. subj.		Imperfect ind. subj.		Preterit (1)	(2 & 3)	Future	Conditional	Perf./Prog. auxiliaries
1sg.	– o	–	–	–	– é	– í	– (r) é	– (ría) –	he /estoy
3sg.	–	–	–	–	– ó	– ió	– (r) á	– (ría) –	ha /está
1pl.	– mos	– mos	– mos	– mos	– mos	– mos	– (re) mos	– (ría) mos	hemos /estamos
3pl.	– n	– n	– n	– n	– ron	– ron	– (rá) n	– (ría) n	han /están

Conclusion

The type of variation accounted for in this brief treatment is variation within the same style of speech by the same learner. As stated in the assumptions, however, I believe these explanations apply as well to variation over time and to variation between different styles or registers or different tasks. Showing that this is indeed the case will take more research, however.

The purpose of this chapter has been to outline aspects of a theoretical framework for SLA which is meant to account for the linguistic variation inherent in developmental data. Careful validation of this theory requires quantitative studies on a broad and varied data base. It would take another, quite different paper to deal with the analytical tools needed in such studies. What has been offered here certainly does not begin to fulfil the need to provide careful empirical evidence for each of the 12 operating principles discussed here and the ways in which these principles interact, sometimes operating in conjunction with each other and at other times counteracting each other. There is a considerable amount of quantitative research needed to elaborate further on this theoretical framework.

Some researchers might find this framework lacking in certain respects. Earlier SLA research had considered and rejected Slobin's operating principles (OPs) as an explanatory framework for SLA. Dulay & Burt (1974) and Larsen-Freeman (1975), for example, objected that Slobin's (1973) operating principles were difficult to test and were not mutually exclusive. As Bowerman's (1985) critical evaluation of the revised operating principles reveals, these limitations are still there. Such criticism would also apply to the principles discussed here for SLA. My position on this criticism is that rather than rejecting the OPs (with nothing comparable to replace them), we should work with them as they are and improve on them with further research. More important, however, it is quite possible—I would say probable—that the difficulties faced in testing some of the operating principles as well as the interrelatedness of certain of the principles with each other are the result of the complexity of language and human cognition, not necessarily a weakness in the operating principles themselves or the theoretical framework.

Notes to Chapter 4

1. In this chapter I will elaborate on the 'cognitive' half of the theory and will not discuss the 'interactionist' half.

2. I have relied primarily on Cazden *et al.*, 1975; Rickford, 1983; Schumann, 1978, 1979; Stauble, 1978, 1981, 1984; and Schumann & Stauble, 1983 for the descriptive facts on acquisition of English negation.

3. Other constituents can be negated also as in:
   Not now. **Not** green, blue. **Not** many. **Not** in the morning.

4. Similar with regard to placement of the negator, although not with regard to choice of only *one* negator for all uses. Other details specific to German and Swedish produce results different from what is found in English. These differences can be explained, however, in terms of the principles discussed in this chapter.

5. I use spellings like **don** and **dont** to represent that fact that the learner may perceive the form and its structure differently from how a native speaker does.

6. See Zobl, 1980.

7. This case is from Zobl (1980:49).

8. See Andersen, 1977, 1979a.

9. See Cancino, 1976, and the summary of this work in Andersen, 1983b.

10. These examples are from Andersen, 1983b, 1984b, 1986a, 1986b. Native Spanish requires preverbal placement of clitic object pronouns.

References

ANDERSEN, R. W., 1976, 'A search for a second language functor acquisition hierarchy in the acquisition of English as a second language in Puerto Rico.' Paper presented at the Tenth Annual TESOL Convention, New York City.

——, 1977, The impoverished state of cross-sectional morpheme acquisition/accuracy methodology (or: The leftovers are more nourishing than the main course), *Working Papers in Bilingualism*, 14, 47–82.

——, 1978, An implicational model for second language research, *Language Learning*, 26, 221–82.

——, 1979a, The relationship between first language transfer and second language overgeneralization: Data from the English of Spanish speakers. In R. W. ANDERSEN (ed.) *The Acquisition and Use of Spanish and English as First and Second Languages*. Washington, DC: TESOL.

——, 1979b, Expanding Schumann's pidginization hypothesis, *Language Learning*, 29, 105–19.

——, 1980, Creolization as the acquisition of a second language as a first language. In A. VALDMAN & A. HIGHFIELD (eds), *Theoretical Orientations in Creole Studies*. New York: Academic Press.

——, (ed.), 1983a, *Pidginization and Creolization as Language Acquisition*. Rowley, MA: Newbury House.

——, 1983b, Transfer to somewhere. In S. GASS & L. SELINKER (eds), *Language Transfer in Language Learning*. Rowley, MA: Newbury House.

——, 1984a, The One to One Principle of interlanguage construction, *Language Learning*, 34, 77–95.

——, 1984b, What's gender good for, anyway? In R. W. ANDERSEN (ed.), *Second Languages: A Cross-Linguistic Perspective*. Rowley, MA: Newbury House.

——, 1986a, El desarrollo de la morfología verbal en el español como segundo idioma. In J. M. MEISEL (ed.), *Adquisición de lenguaje/Aquisição da linguagem*. Frankfurt:Vervuert.

——, 1986b, 'Interpreting data: Second language acquisition of verbal aspect.' Unpublished manuscript.

——, 1986c, 'The need for native language comparison data in interpreting second language data.' Forum Lecture, TESOL Summer Institute, University of Hawaii.

BAILEY, C.-J., 1973, *Variation and Linguistic Theory*. Washington, DC: Center for Applied Linguistics.

BICKERTON, D., 1973, On the nature of a creole continuum, *Language*, 49, 640–69.

——, 1975, *Dynamics of a Creole System*. Cambridge: Cambridge University Press.

——, 1977, *Change and Variation in Hawaiian English: Creole Syntax*, Vol. 2 of Final Report on NSF Grant No. GS-39748.

BICKERTON, D. and ODO, C., 1976, *Change and Variation in Hawaiian English: General Phonology and Pidgin Syntax*. Vol. 1 of Final Report on NSF Grant No. GS-39748.

BOWERMAN, M., 1985, What shapes children's grammar? In D. I. SLOBIN (ed.), *The Crosslinguistic Study of Language Acquisition*. Hillsdale. NJ: Lawrence Erlbaum Associates.

BYBEE, J., 1985, *Morphology*. Amsterdam & Philadelphia: John Benjamins.

CANCINO, H., 1976, Grammatical morphemes in second language acquisition— Marta. Unpublished qualifying paper, Harvard University.

CAZDEN, C. B., CANCINO, H., ROSANSKY, E. J. and SCHUMANN, J. H., 1975, *Second Language Acquisition Sequences in Children, Adolescents, and Adults*. Final Report, Project no. 730744, National Institute of Education.

CLAHSEN, H., 1984, The acquisition of German word order: A test case for cognitive approaches to L2 development. In R. W. ANDERSEN (ed.), *Second Languages: A Cross-linguistic Perspective*. Cambridge, MA: Newbury House.

DECAMP, D., 1971, Toward a generative analysis of a post-creole continuum. In D. HYMES (ed.), *Pidginization and Creolization of Languages*. London & New York: Cambridge University Press.

DULAY, H. and BURT, M. K., 1974, A new perspective on the creative construction processes in child second language acquisition, *Language Learning*, 24, 253–78.

HYLTENSTAM, K., 1977, Implicational patterns in interlanguage syntax variation, *Language Learning*, 27, 383–411.

——, 1982, Descriptive adequacy and psychological plausibility, *Language Learning*, 32, 167–73.

JORDENS, P., 1980, Interlanguage research: interpretation or explanation, *Language Learning*, 30, 195–207.

——, 1982, How to make your facts fit: A response from Jordens, *Language Learning*, 32, 175–81.

KRASHEN, S., 1983, Newmark's 'ignorance hypothesis' and current second language acquisition theory. In S. GASS & L. SELINKER (eds), *Language Transfer in Language Learning*. Rowley, MA: Newbury House.

LABOV, W., 1966, *The Social Stratification of English in New York City*. Arlington, VA: Center for Applied Linguistics.

——, 1972, *Sociolinguistic Patterns*. Philadelphia: University of Pennsylvania Press.

LARSEN-FREEMAN, D., 1975, The acquisition of grammatical morphemes by adult ESL students, *TESOL Quarterly*, 9, 409–19.

MEISEL, J., 1983, Strategies of second language acquisition: More than one kind of simplification. In R. W. ANDERSEN (ed.), *Pidginization and Creolization as Language Acquisition*. Rowley, MA: Newbury House.

PETERS, A. M., 1985, Language segmentation: Operating principles for the perception and analysis of language. In D. I. SLOBIN (ed.), *The Crosslinguistic Study of Language Acquisition*, Vol. 2. Hillsdale, NJ: Lawrence Erlbaum.

RICKFORD, J., 1979, 'Variation in a creole continuum: Quantitative and implicational approaches.' Ph.D. dissertation, University of Pennsylvania.

——, 1983, What happens in decreolization. In R. W. ANDERSEN (ed.), *Pidginization and Creolization as Language Acquisition*. Rowley, MA: Newbury House.

——, 1987, *Dimensions of a Creole Continuum. History, Texts, & Linguistic Analysis of Guyanese Creole*. Stanford: Stanford University Press.

SCHUMANN, J. H., 1978, *The Pidginization Process: A Model for Second Language Acquisition*. Rowley, MA: Newbury House.

——, 1979, The acquisition of English negation by speakers of Spanish. In R. W. ANDERSEN (ed.), *The Acquisition and Use of Spanish and English as First and Second Languages*. Washington, DC: TESOL.

SCHUMANN, J. H. and STAUBLE, A., 1983, A discussion of second language acquisition and decreolization. In R. W. ANDERSEN (ed.), *Pidginization and Creolization as Language Acquisition*. Rowley, MA: Newbury House.

SLOBIN, D. I., 1973, Cognitive prerequisites for the development of grammar. In C.A. FERGUSON & D. I. SLOBIN (eds), *Studies of Child Language Development*. New York: Holt, Rinehart & Winston.

——, 1977, Language change in childhood and history. In J. MACNAMARA (ed.), *Language Learning and Thought*. New York: Academic Press.

——, 1982, Universal and particular in the acquisition of language. In E. WANNER & L. R. GLEITMAN (eds), *Language Acquisition: The State of the Art*. Cambridge: Cambridge University Press.

——, 1985, Crosslinguistic evidence for the language-making capacity. In D. I. SLOBIN (ed.), *The Crosslinguistic Study of Language Acquisition, Vol. 2, Theoretical Issues*. Hillsdale, NJ: Lawrence Erlbaum.

STAUBLE, A., 1978, The process of decreolization: A model for second language development, *Language Learning*, 28, 29–54.

——, 1981, 'A comparative study of a Spanish–English and Japanese–English second language continuum.' Ph.D. dissertation, UCLA.

——, 1984, A comparison of a Spanish–English and a Japanese–English second language continuum: Negation and verb morphology. In R. W. ANDERSEN (ed.), *Second Languages: A Crosslinguistic Perspective*. Rowley, MA: Newbury House.

WODE, H., 1976, Developmental sequences in naturalistic L2 acquisition, *Working Papers in Bilingualism*, 11, 1–31.

ZOBL, H., 1980, The formal and developmental selectivity of L1 influence on L2 acquisition, *Language Learning*, 30(1), 43–57.

5 Ends and means: Methods for the study of interlanguage variation

RICHARD YOUNG
University of Pennsylvania

Introduction

Variation is an accepted fact of interlanguage and one of the most pressing problems for second language acquisition theory is how to describe and explain the highly variable speech of learners of second languages. The facts of variation have been described in interlanguage pragmatics (Selinker & Douglas, 1985), syntax (Fairbanks, 1982), morphology (Larsen-Freeman, 1975; Adamson & Kovac, 1981; Tarone, 1985; Young, 1986), and phonology (Dickerson & Dickerson, 1977; Schmidt, 1977; Gatbonton, 1978; Beebe, 1980; Beebe & Zuengler, 1983; Sato, 1985) by researchers who have carried out empirical investigations in these areas, while theoreticians have constructed models which attempt to identify the causes of variation and to relate them to established sociolinguistic and psycholinguistic theories of second language acquisition (Littlewood, 1981; Tarone, 1983; Ellis, 1985a,b, this volume). Yet there remain a number of unresolved questions regarding the nature of interlanguage variation and the ways in which investigators go about studying the phenomenon. First of all, the term 'variation' is used as a label for many differences in interlanguage among different learners or within the interlanguage of one learner on different occasions. However, in order to more precisely define the term variation, it is preferable to consider it as referring only to 'different ways of saying the same thing' (Labov, 1969:72) in different contexts. That is, the set of alternants of a given variable form—the so-called 'envelope of variation'—must be well-defined and there should be no suspicion that different variants have different semantic functions in order for differences in interlanguage forms within the speech of one learner or across learners to be considered variation. In the second place, we do not yet have a coherent research methodology for studying interlanguage variation and this makes it difficult to compare studies of different variable forms or even studies of the same form carried out using different methods of data collection and analysis. And last, although most previous studies of interlanguage variation have acknowledged the effect of the physical, social, and cultural context of speech (which I will call 'situational context') on the variation found in interlanguage, we still have only a rudimentary, almost intuitive, way of describing and analysing that context.

In this chapter I will address these three issues in the context of an empirical study of variation in interlanguage morphophonology.[1] I hope to show that the analysis of a variable with a one-to-one relation between form and function and with a well-defined envelope of variation provides concrete, though partial, evidence to support the claim that interlanguage is systematic (Selinker, 1969, 1972). I will further show that the design of studies of variation must take into account the multiple factors which influence it, including situational context, stage of acquisition, linguistic environment, and communicative redundancy. And I will suggest that previous analyses of situational context in terms of formality, degree of attention to speech, and task, are inadequate and suggest an alternative set of categories for the componential analysis of context, based on those proposed by Hymes (1967).

Designs of empirical studies of interlanguage variation: a critique

The design of almost all the previously cited studies of variation in interlanguage has followed a familiar mode of psycholinguistic experimentation: a relevant population of speakers of a second language is identified, certain independent variables in the situational context are manipulated, and the production of certain dependent variables in the informants' interlanguage is measured. Now, a research design which relates variable linguistic forms to the contexts in which they occur is attempting to answer two questions. The first question is how changes in *one* particular contextual feature such as style, interlocutor, or phonological environment, influence variation in the form. The second question is how to evaluate the relative impact on variation of *different* contextual features. With the exception of the studies by Dickerson & Dickerson (1977) and by Adamson & Kovac (1981), all previous studies of interlanguage variation have addressed the first question but have remained silent on the second.

INDEPENDENT VARIABLES
(Contextual features)

		One	Many
DEPENDENT VARIABLE (Variable	Dichotomous	**A**	**B**
linguistic form)	Multinomial	**C**	**D**

FIGURE 1. *Relationships between independent and dependent variables in research designs for the study of interlanguage variation*

The possible relationships between dependent and independent variables in models of research design for the study of variation may be represented as the two-by-two matrix in Figure 1.[2] Cell A in the matrix represents a research design in which the relationship between a dichotomous dependent variable and one independent variable is investigated. A dichotomous variable is measured on a nominal scale which has only two categories. The measurement level of the independent variable depends on the nature of that variable, but type A designs measure the effect of only one independent variable. Cell B represents a research design in which the effects of many independent variables are measured on one dichotomous linguistic variable. Cell C represents a research design which is similar to a type A design in that the effect of only one independent variable is investigated, but differs from a type A design in its treatment of the dependent variable. The difference lies in the fact that type C designs measure the dependent variable on a nominal scale with more than two categories (which I have called a multinomial scale). Cell D represents a design which measures the effects of many different independent variables on a multinomial linguistic variable. The implications of these different approaches to research design in the investigation of interlanguage variation are important in reviewing and disentangling the claims made by previous studies in this area.

The designs of the vast majority of previous studies of variation fall into cell A in the matrix. Tarone (1985) is representative of these studies. She carries out four separate investigations of the effect of one independent variable (speech style, measured on an ordinal scale) on different morphemes. In the methodological tradition of suppliance in obligatory context (SOC) used in much early morpheme research, she considers each linguistic variable (i.e. each morpheme) as a dichotomous variable. The two values of the variable are zero—omission in a context in which it is obligatory in the target, and one—suppliance in such a context. Tarone's failure to find a consistent relationship between independent and dependent variables in her study may well be due to the fact that she takes only one contextual feature into consideration. If other independent variables which were not taken into account in her design are in fact exerting an influence on the dependent variable, this would explain the lack of regularity in the relationships between the variables she observes.

In addition to the problems inherent in type A designs in identifying a consistent relationship between dependent and independent variables, a further problem arises when two separate studies investigate the same dependent variable but study the effects of different independent variables. In this case, the results of one study may appear to contradict the results of a previous study of the same linguistic variable. An example of this is the differing interpretations put forward by Wolfson (1982) and Wolfram (1985) on the phenomenon of variable tense marking in conversational narratives. Both authors take as their dependent linguistic variable the alternation between present and past tense forms of verbs referring to events which occurred in the past. Wolfson convincingly relates the alternation between present and past tense verb forms in conversational narratives to the episode boundaries within the narratives, and she finds that a switch between one tense and another is a way in which the speaker makes explicit the organisation of a conversational narrative. On the other hand, Wolfram contends that the tense marking may be better explained by lower-level features of linguistic environment. When Wolfram examines a narrative from one of his informants he does find some relationship between tense shifts and episode boundaries, although:

> it is difficult to see them merely as a function of episodic or continuity shifts [...]. It thus appears that, in this instance, the distribution of tense marking in the discourse is more constrained by the surface considerations than by factors of discourse. (Wolfram, 1985:250–1)

That two scholars should come to such different conclusions concerning the cause of tense alternation in narrative is surprising. However, when one considers that the two studies both used a type A design which relates the observed variation to different independent variables, the contradiction appears less surprising. If, as appears likely, variation is a consequence of the effects of many different contextual factors, including discourse organisation *as well as* phonological environment and membership in lexical form classes, then what is needed is a way of evaluating the relative importance of the different independent variables in a research design which takes all relevant contextual features into consideration. Such a design would fit into cell B in Figure 1 and would include within the design some way of evaluating the relative impacts of the different contextual variables.

One further limitation of type A designs in the investigation of interlanguage variation is that they allow only two values of the dependent variable. In almost all previous studies of interlanguage variation these two values have been identified as the suppliance or omission of the variable form in a context in which it is obligatory in prescriptive grammars of the target. Although there may be certain research questions which are best approached through the study of dichotomous variables which are best measured in this way, there are two reasons why such an approach to data may give a distorted picture of variation. First, as Pica (1983) has pointed out, when more values of the variable than the two allowed by SOC analysis are taken into consideration, the analysis of morpheme production may produce very different results. Pica proposes a target-like use analysis (TLU) in which, in addition to the omission or suppliance in obligatory context of SOC analysis, instances of overgeneralisation of a form to contexts in which it is not required in the target are taken into consideration. In the case of TLU analysis, the dependent variable is measured on a three-category nominal scale, and the research design falls into cells C or D of Figure 1.

Second, it may well be the case that the alternation among variants is not simply a matter of presence or absence of the form. There may be more than two variants, such as in the case of third person singular copula, which has a morphologically free form *is*, a bound form *'s* and the absence of either form, represented by zero, *0*. Beebe (1980) has taken the possibility of the dependent variable having more than two values into account in her study of phonological variation in the production of (r) in the English interlanguage of native speakers of Thai. She recognises at least ten phonetic variants of word-initial and final (r), which she subdivides into three categories: (a) the correct L2 variant, (b) L1 variants, and (c) new variants not present in either the L2 or L1. However, when she comes to describe the relationship between her independent variable (speech style, with two values—conversation and listing) and the dependent linguistic variable (r), Beebe collapses (r) to a dichotomous variable with the familiar values of target-like or non-target-like. Thus, although it resembles a type C design, Beebe's study in fact fits more closely into a type A research design.

It should be clear from the foregoing discussion that type A studies suffer from a number of serious defects. In the first place, we have convincing evidence from different studies of separate contextual variables that many contextual factors such as phonological environment (Gatbonton, 1978; Beebe, 1980; Dickerson, 1975), speech style (Dickerson, 1975; Tarone, 1985; Beebe, 1980), task (Larsen-Freeman, 1975), and interlocutor (Young, 1986; Berkowitz, 1987) exert an influence on variation. The effects of these factors are well-motivated by psycholinguistic and sociolinguistic theories of language acquisition and use. Since so many different factors have been identified, future studies which examine the effect of any one variable and do not control for the effects of others are likely to produce unreliable and inconclusive results. In the second place, even if other relevant factors could be controlled in a type A design, the investigation of the effect of one factor gives us no information about the relative importance of that contextual factor in comparison with others. And finally, as we have seen, some dependent linguistic variables may be best measured on a nominal scale with more than two values, rather than as a dichotomous variable.

Future studies must attempt to overcome some of the defects inherent in type A designs by adopting a type B design in which a much larger number of theoretically-motivated independent variables are taken into account, and their effects are measured. Since their effects may be measured with a common metric, it should also be possible to rank the relative impact of each factor on the variable under consideration.

The situational context of interlanguage variation: a componential analysis

One of the functions of variation in native-speaking speech communities is as a resource to communicate such social meanings as marking other participants in the speech events as members of an in-group or an out-group, indicating the relative social importance or triviality of the topic of speech, asserting the speaker's own status *vis-à-vis* other participants in the speech event, marking the speech event as belonging to a certain socially recognised genre, and so on. These resources may exist independently of any of the linguistic levels of phonology, syntax, discourse, or even choice of code; alternatively, they may involve complex interactions between different levels. Such sociolinguistic resources Gumperz (1964) has called speakers' *verbal repertoire*, which he defines as 'the totality of linguistic forms employed in the course of socially significant interaction' (Gumperz, 1964:152).

The learner's hypothesised competence to command a verbal repertoire in a second language is the source of what Corder (1977) called *horizontal variability*. It should be noted that the learner's repertoire, such as it is, is not necessarily equivalent to the repertoire of a full member of the speech community. This was convincingly shown by Beebe (1980), who found that while Thai speakers of English as a second language were able to mark conversation and reading word lists as different genres by means of phonological variation, at least one of the variables involved (trilled (r) in word lists and flapped (r) in conversation) owed more to transfer from their L1 verbal repertoire than to any known sociolinguistic rules of English.

Other work by Beebe & Zuengler (1983) and by Young (1986) has shown that the identity of an interlocutor as a member of the learner's in-group also has an effect on the speech of second language learners at all levels of overall proficiency in the second language. However, much work which has examined horizontal variability has not focused on it as a sociolinguistic phenomenon. Instead, some writers have attempted to reduce the observed variation across different situational contexts to an underlying psychological or psycholinguistic motive. The reductionist position was stated most clearly by Labov (1972:208):

> There are a great many styles and stylistic dimensions that can be isolated by an analyst. But we find that *styles can be ranged along a single dimension, measured by the amount of attention paid to speech*. The most important way in which this attention is exerted is in audio-monitoring one's own speech, though other forms of monitoring also take place.

Following this reductionist point of view, Tarone (Tarone *et al.*, 1976; Tarone, 1979, 1982, 1983, 1985) carried out a number of studies and reviews of the literature which analysed horizontal variation as being a product of psycholinguistic processing constraints such as degree of monitoring or attention to speech. However, the shaky foundations on which this approach to variation is built were roundly criticised by Wolfson (1976: 203):

> The monitoring of speech is a psychological reaction about which a great deal is assumed but very little is really known. The relationship between audio-monitoring and speech style has yet to be proved. Before we can use it as an index of style, it would seem to be a good idea to measure attention to speech independently in order to find out just what it involves. At present we have no idea *what* people monitor when they pay attention to their speech.

In general, it has to be admitted that situational context is a notion which has been treated rather superficially in studies of interlanguage variation. If one takes the categories proposed by Hymes (1967) for the analysis of speech events—*setting, participants, ends, art characteristics, communicative key, instrumentality, norms* and *genre*—then it is rare to find a study in the second language acquisition literature in which speech has been observed in situations involving the manipulation of elements within one of these categories while maintaining the others constant. In Tarone's own work this is especially evident. Her 1985 study reports the production of groups of learners on (1) a written grammaticality judgement task, (2) an oral narrative to a non-native speaking listener, and (3) an oral interview with a native speaker of English; three tasks which she arranges on a continuum of hypothetical degree of attention to speech. That the results she reports are unclear is not surprising given the multiple ways in which her tasks contrast. If 'attention to speech' is indeed a matter of degree (i.e. a variable which can be measured on an ordinal scale), and if three such different tasks can indeed be ranged on such a continuum in the way that Tarone suggests, then one would expect a better fit for the data than Tarone in fact obtains.[3] The results of this and other studies which take situational context as an independent variable may be more comprehensible if it is assumed that no ordinal variables are involved here, and that the situational contexts or tasks differ in terms of three pairs of contrasts, specifically: instrumentality (spoken versus written), participants (native speaker versus non-native speaker), and genre (interactive versus non-interactive).

Another putative continuum which has been invoked in the analysis of variation in interlanguage according to situational context by Tarone (1985), Labov (1966) and Beebe (1980) is that of *formality/informality*. Irvine (1979), however, supplies evidence that terms such as 'formality' and 'informality' cover the four conceptually distinct features of (1) the degree of structuring of the code, (2) the consistency of code choices made, (3) the positional identities invoked by participants, and (4) the emergence of a central situational focus. She concludes that it is impossible to identify features of formality or informality which are valid in all cultures, a point which is especially relevant when we are dealing with stylistic variation in the second language speech of people from different cultures for whom norms of formality and informality may pattern very differently from the way they pattern in the target language community. Irvine suggests that we need to seek different and more universally valid constructs than formality and informality when describing ways of speaking crossculturally. In her own words:

> it is appropriate in few instances to speak of 'formality' generally without specifying precisely what one has in mind. Otherwise, there is

too great a risk of mistaking one kind of formality for another or assuming that kinds of formality are really the same. (Irvine, 1979: 226)

The situational contexts which have been used in previous studies of interlanguage variation have also varied along a dimension of what the authors of those studies call *task*. Task is an unanalysed construct which comprises such different speech events as conversation (also known as free or spontaneous speech), reading aloud (of minimal pairs, word lists, paragraphs or dialogues), interviews, elicited narratives, imitation, written tests and translation. It has been assumed in each study that one particular task chosen by the authors requires more attention to speech, or is more formal than some other. In contrast, the approach to situational context taken here is to eschew seemingly useful but in fact misleading constructs such as formality, degree of attention to speech and task, in favour of a componential description of situational context in the terms outlined by Hymes (1967).

Variation in (s) plural marking

The critique of previous studies of interlanguage variation which has been made in the preceding pages has centred on two weaknesses of these studies: (1) an unjustified assumption that variation is caused by only one independent variable, and (2) an inadequate analysis of the role of situational context in causing variation in interlanguage. The second half of this chapter will demonstrate how a multivariate model of variation and a Hymesian componential analysis of the context of situation may be used to overcome the defects of these approaches.

The study I report on here (Young, 1988, 1989) was designed to evaluate the degree of systematicity in one area of morphophonology in the English interlanguage of native speakers of Chinese. The variable form under investigation is (s) marking on semantically plural count nouns. The phenomenon of marking semantically plural count nouns with an (s) plural suffix is a highly variable one in the speech of the twelve informants who participated in this study. Out of a total of 1,564 semantically plural count nouns only 1,021 or 65% are marked with an (s). At first sight, this variation appears to be difficult to account for since it is observed on the same lexical item within the speech of one speaker. For example, informant Mary has the following tokens within five lines of each other in the transcript.

Mary:　　　The store is . a . just sells all the *books* for Christian.

all the *book* is have to ship from Taiwan

And informant Jennifer switches between -*s* and zero marking on the same semantically plural lexical item in a similar way.

Jennifer:　... I think because my brother . a . hate *girls* when he was a
Yun-yun:　Really?
Jennifer:　Mm . was terrib- . he she . he's very strange I mean he . you know even he was in the high school he wouldn't talk to *girl* you know ...

In general, although highly proficient speakers of English as a second language exhibit a higher rate of (s) plural marking than less proficient learners, the acquisition of a categorical target rule is by no means complete in even the most proficient informant in the study, Sally,[4] for example,

> it's such a nice place for *tourist*
> some fur *coat* just gorgeous

Part of the reason for the low rate of (s) plural marking may be found in the effect of transfer from Chinese. Chinese marks plural only on personal pronouns and [+ human] vocatives.[5] Plural is not marked on third person nouns in Chinese; if plural is marked at all, it is marked lexically by other elements of the NP, for example,

yīge xuésheng
INDEF-CLASSIFIER STUDENT
'a student'

liǎngge xuésheng
TWO-CLASSIFIER STUDENT
'two students'

hěn duō xuésheng
VERY MANY STUDENT

'a lot of students'

yīxiē xuésheng
INDEF-QUANTIFIER
STUDENT
'some students'

If plural is not marked lexically then semantic plurality must be inferred from the discourse or situational context, for example,

nǐde xuésheng láile
YOU-POSSESSIVE STUDENT COME-COMPLETIVE
'your student has arrived', or 'your students have arrived'

It is therefore to be expected that the overall rate of morphological plural marking for Chinese speakers of English will be low. However, since third person noun plurals are *never* marked morphologically in Chinese, considerations of transfer alone do not give us any indication of where to expect (s) plural marking in the interlanguage of Chinese speakers and where to expect that (s) plurals will not be produced.

If we limit the role of transfer to a determinant of the gross level of (s) plural marking, we still need to explain variation at the micro level: which stems are pluralised in the interlanguage of which speakers and why? Before describing how the results of the study provide an answer to that question, I would like first to describe in detail the design of the present study and contrast it with designs of previous studies of variation in interlanguage.

Since a major objective of this study was to identify some possible effects of situational context on linguistic variation in interlanguage, the research design called for data collection in two different and contrasting situational contexts. Data were gathered by means of interviews with each of the twelve informants in either their own home or the home of a friend. Each informant was interviewed twice in English on separate occasions, once by a native speaker of English and once by a non-native speaker who was a fellow native speaker of Chinese. Interviews lasted for approximately one hour and were recorded by the investigator who was also present in the room while the interview was taking place. Forty-five minutes of each of the 24 interviews were transcribed and analysed.

The informants were seven females and five males who had been born and had grown up in Mainland China or Taiwan. Ages ranged between 26 and 65 and the informants came from a variety of social and educational backgrounds. All informants spoke either *Pǔtōnghuà* (the Mainland standard dialect of Chinese) or *Guóyǔ* (the Taiwanese standard) as their home language. TOEFL tests were administered to all informants and results showed that the twelve could be divided into two distinct groups on the basis of their proficiency in English as a second language. Six informants scored below 410 on TOEFL and are referred to as the low proficiency group while the remaining six scored above 470 and are referred to as the high proficiency group.

In order to contrast the two interviews on only one dimension of Hymes' components for the analysis of speech events, an attempt was made to control all components of the situational context except for that one. The two speech events are best described as 'spontaneous interviews' (Wolfson, 1976), and the dimension on which the two situational contexts differed was that of the participants involved. As described below, all other components of situational context—settings, ends, art characteristics, communicative key, instrumentality, norms, and genre—were, as far as possible, the same for the two interviews.

Setting

Both interviews took place in a private, homely setting which was almost always a room in the informant's house or apartment. A small number of interviews were conducted in the home of a friend of the informant when informants felt that conducting the interview in their own homes was not convenient. While no previous studies of interlanguage variation have identified an effect for setting or scene, most of the data in previous studies were collected in more public settings such as offices or classrooms. The choice of a private setting for interviews in the present study was made so that informants would feel as relaxed as possible and it would be possible to gather a large amount of speech data, and also to mimic as closely as possible an authentic (i.e. non-experimental) situational context for speech.

Ends

For the two participants, the purpose of the two interviews—what Hymes (1967) called the 'ends in view'—was simply to talk about any topic which they found of interest. The interviews generally began with the interlocutor asking a few general questions about the informant's background, but initiation of new topics and questioning was by no means a sole prerogative of the interlocutor. Perhaps because informants felt at ease in their home surroundings, or because they felt that it was incumbent on them, as the hosts, to keep their visitors entertained, they would often initiate new topics of their own and tell long narratives concerning their own personal history and those of their family members. There was no special outcome of the interviews. When, after an hour's recording, the investigator switched off the tape recorder, the participants would usually break off the conversation, get up and move around the room, but they would often sit down again and continue the conversation where they had left off or else try to involve the investigator and other family members in the conversation.

Art characteristics

As regards the component of speech events which Hymes labels 'art characteristics', both informant and interlocutor were aware that to a certain extent they were performers. The interviews had been arranged in advance by the investigator, the interlocutors had been prepared for their role, and the informants had agreed to spend a couple of hours talking to an interlocutor. In addition, each informant signed a consent form, and some informants were paid a small sum of money for their participation. The 'performance' aspect of the interview was underlined by the presence of the investigator and his small tape recorder and the lavaliere microphone which was attached to the informant's clothing. The obtrusive nature of the data collection procedure no doubt had some effect on the spoken interaction between informant and interlocutor. However, the characteristics of the speech event which made for a performance rather than an unselfconscious event—the appointment, the tape recorder, the length of time spent in the interview—were identical for both interviews. In this way it was hoped that whatever effect there was on interlanguage would be similar in both situational contexts.

Communicative key

Despite the obtrusive data collection procedure, the communicative key of the interviews was mostly light, friendly and humorous. Informant and interlocutor usually sat side by side on a soft couch, turning their bodies half way round to face each other comfortably as they talked. They often touched as they talked and all the interviews contained some laughter, this being especially noticeable on the occasions when the interlocutor was a fellow Chinese.

Instrumentality

The channel used in the interviews was, of course, primarily speech. No interviews contained any reading aloud or references to writing present in the setting, but a lot of information was conveyed non-verbally. Participants maintained eye contact for most of the interview and used gesture to help with the description of physical scenes and also to indicate when they felt at a loss for a word in English. The code throughout the interviews was predominantly English. Both participants knew that they were expected to speak English during the interview, and the presence of the investigator and the fact that they were being recorded served as reminders of that expectation. None the less, when the interlocutor was a fellow Chinese, and especially when both participants came from the same part of China, the informant would sometimes switch into Chinese to describe a familiar place, activity or way of doing things. Nor surprisingly, this code-switching into Chinese happened most frequently when informants had difficulty expressing themselves in English, which was noticeable with the very low proficiency informants. However, the amount of Chinese spoken even by these informants made up a very small proportion of the sixty-minute interview.

Norms

The norms of the interaction were those of the spontaneous interview and similar to (although significantly different from) the norms of conversation among acquaintances or friends. Turn-taking was very smooth, with one participant interrupting the other only on very rare occasions. The informants generally held the floor in the sense that they did most of the talking and the interlocutors' role was that of indicating that they were paying attention to what the informants were saying by means of eye contact, body position and conversational fillers such as 'Uhuh', 'Oh really', or 'Mm'. One norm which was particularly apparent was that the interview was limited to only two participants—the informant and the interlocutor. This was made clear when the norm was violated on occasions when the informant tried to involve the investigator in the conversation, or other family members present in the room tried to join in. In the former case the investigator always sat out of line of sight of the two participants with his back turned and refused to acknowledge remarks which the participants addressed to him. In the latter case the interlocutor managed to skilfully acknowledge the contribution from outside by means of a gesture or a smile but made no attempt to respond. Violations of the dyadic norm for the interviews occurred briefly in only three out of the twenty-four interviews.

Genre

The genre of the events was, from the standpoint of the investigator and analyst, a spontaneous interview. The interlocutors also normally referred to the events as interviews, and the investigator used the word 'interview' to describe the event to informants. It differed from conversation in terms of the components of the event mentioned above. It took place during a protracted but circumscribed time period, an appointment was required, the event was limited to two participants, and both participants were fully aware that they were being recorded. When described in terms of the components of situational context as has been done here, the spontaneous interview genre may well be similar to what others have labelled 'conversation' (Beebe, 1980; Sato, 1985), 'free speech' (Dickerson & Dickerson, 1977), or 'spontaneous speech' (Gatbonton, 1978). However, the distinction between a spontaneous interview and conversation is an important one to make although it limits the generality of the findings of this study.

In terms of setting, ends (both purposes and outcomes), art characteristics, communicative key, instrumentality (channel and code), norms, and genre, the two interviews with each informant were identical and were also comparable across informants. The sole difference between each pair of interviews was the participants. In the first interview the interlocutor was an ethnic Chinese and a fellow native speaker of Chinese, while in the second interview the interlocutor was a non-Chinese and a native speaker of English. While this difference of ethnicity and first language is the most striking difference between the two interviews, there appeared more subtle differences when the backgrounds of both informant and interlocutor were compared in terms of sex, age, educational attainment, occupation and place of origin, in addition to the ethnic and linguistic differences. These additional differences are described in greater detail in the following section.

Hypotheses and results

Four major hypotheses were tested in this study. It was predicted that the degree of (s) plural marking would be a complex function of factors deriving from four major influences: (1) the situational context of the interview, (2) the informants' overall proficiency in English, (3) certain linguistic features of the noun stem and its phonological environment, and (4) a tendency to eliminate redundant marking of plural number in the same clause.

The data were analysed by means of the VARBRUL multivariate procedure, first used by Cedergren & Sankoff (1974), in its latest formulation by Rousseau & Sankoff (1978) implemented for the IBM personal computer by Pintzuk (1987). This procedure has been shown to be applicable to type B and type D designs involving multidimensional variation such as that investigated here, for which conventional multivariate techniques such as ANOVA are inadequate due to the large number of cells containing zero or very few tokens because they represent linguistically impossible or improbable combinations of factors. The VARBRUL procedure has been used in much quantitative work in the sociolinguistic analysis of variation (e.g. Guy, 1980; Weiner & Labov, 1983), and the conceptual basis underlying it has been reviewed in a debate between Kay & McDaniel (1979) and Sankoff & Labov (1979), and in Kroch's (1985) review of Romaine (1982).

The effect of each factor on the dependent variable is expressed as a probability ranging between zero and one. A probability (p_i) of 1.00 for a given factor indicates that if that factor is present, then it is certain that plural will be marked with (s), while a value of 0.00 indicates with certainty that a plural will not be marked with (s). A value of 0.50 indicates that the factor has no effect on (s) plural marking, a value between 0.01 and 0.49 indicates that the factor inhibits (s) plural marking, and a value between 0.51 and 0.99 indicates that the factor promotes it. The results of this

TABLE 1. *Comparison of factor probabilities for low and high proficiency speakers with those for the combined data*

Factor group	Factors	Low p_i	High p_i	Combined p_i
1. Social	High convergence with a NS	ns*	ns	0.62
convergence	High convergence with a NNS	ns	0.59	0.57
with an	Low convergence with a NNS	ns	na	0.43
interlocutor	Low convergence with a NS	ns	0.26	0.38
2. ESL profici-	High	na†	na	0.59
ency level	Low	na	na	0.41
3. Definiteness	Indefinite	ns	ns	ns
	Definite	ns	ns	ns
4. Animacy	Animate	0.41	0.57	ns
	Inanimate	0.59	0.43	ns
5. Position of	Prenominal modifier	0.72	0.75	0.71
noun within	Head	0.28	0.25	0.29
the NP				
6. Syntactic	Adverbial	0.70	0.58	0.62
function of	Complement	0.51	0.60	0.57
NP	Subject	0.40	0.40	0.41
	Object	0.38	0.42	0.40
7. Preceding	Non-sibilant fricative	na	ns	0.67
segment	Vowel	0.69	ns	0.54
(final	Stop	0.73	ns	0.54
segment	Nasal	0.63	ns	0.48
of stem)	Sibilant	0.47	ns	0.42
	Lateral	0.10	ns	0.34
8. Following	Vowel or Glide	ns	ns	0.54
segment	Pause	ns	ns	0.49
	Consonant or liquid	ns	ns	0.46
9. Redundant	Numeral	0.70	0.61	0.66
plural	Plural demonstrative	0.50	0.67	0.65
marking	Quantifier	0.45	0.49	0.46
within the NP	Partitive	0.45	0.38	0.38
	No redundant plural marking	0.39	0.35	0.35
10. Noun–verb	Subject of – s inflected verb	ns	ns	ns
concord	Subject of uninflected verb	ns	ns	ns
	Complement of *there is/was*	ns	ns	ns
	Complement of *there are/were*	ns	ns	ns

* ns = not statistically significant.   † na = factor does not apply

analysis are shown in Table 1. The three columns of figures in this table represent three different analyses of the data: the first column (low p_i) is the result of an analysis of semantically plural nouns occurring only in the transcripts of interviews involving the six low proficiency speakers, the second column (high p_i) is an analysis of the data from the six high proficiency speakers and the third column (combined p_i) is the analysis of the combined data from all twelve speakers.

It was found that seven out of the ten factor groups had a statistically significant effect on (s) plural marking in the combined speech data from all speakers in the corpus ($p < 0.05$). The three which had no significant effect were definiteness (factor group 3), animacy (factor group 4),[6] and noun–verb concord (factor group 10).[7] The significant factor groups were, as predicted, a combination of contextual, developmental, linguistic, and information processing features. These results will be discussed in detail below.

Social convergence with an interlocutor

Many studies of interlanguage variation (e.g. Ellis, this volume) have drawn on Bell's theory of audience design (Bell, 1984) as a fruitful source of hypotheses regarding interlanguage variation. Basing his theory on earlier work by Brown & Gilman (1960) and by Giles (Thakerar *et al.*, 1982), Bell formulates a theory of style-shifting as design of speech with reference to the speech patterns of an audience. According to this theory, the effect of hearers on the speech patterns of a speaker depends on whether the hearers are addressed, ratified and known. If these conditions all hold, as is the case in the dyadic interviews which compose the data in this study, audience design theory predicts that the perceived speech patterns of the hearer will have a significant effect on the speech of a speaker. If a second language learner's interlocutor is a native speaker of the target language, then audience design theory predicts that the learner's speech will shift in the direction of the target speech forms of his or her interlocutor. Conversely, if the learner's interlocutor is a fellow non-native speaker whose speech patterns deviate significantly from those of the target, then audience design theory predicts that the learner's speech will shift away from the target.

One hypothesis of the present study was that audience design would be a significant factor in the variation found in the speech of second language learners, but that the effect of this variable would be mediated by the degree to which speaker and interlocutor shared certain sociocultural attributes. It was predicted that informants who shared with interlocutors a number of relevant sociocultural attributes would tend to vary in their speech patterns toward the speech of their interlocutors. Each of the 24 interviews was graded according to whether informant and interlocutor shared or differed on the six attributes of (1) ethnicity, (2) age, (3) sex, (4) educational attainment, (5) occupation, and (6) place of origin. Each interview could thus be graded on a scale of between zero and six attributes shared by the two participants. The number of shared attributes is referred to as the *convergence index* for that interview. For the purposes of this study the convergence index was categorised as either *high* (with a value between four and six) or *low* (with a value between zero and three). It was predicted that if the convergence index was high and the interlocutor was a native speaker of English, then informants would accommodate their speech forms toward those of their interlocutors and consequently produce a higher rate of (s) plural marking. Furthermore, it was predicted that if the convergence index was high and the interlocutor was a non-native speaker of English then speakers would accommodate to the non-target-like forms found in their interlocutor's speech.

Table 1 shows that the first of these hypotheses was confirmed, since high convergence with a NS favours (s) plural marking ($p_i = 0.62$), but the second hypothesis was not confirmed since high convergence with a non-native speaker also favours (s) plural marking ($p_i = 0.57$).

Proficiency in English

The second group of factors under investigation is the degree of proficiency in English as a second language of informants, as measured by their scores on a TOEFL test. Two effects of proficiency were investigated in this study. First, it was predicted that the probability for the high proficiency group to mark plurals with (s) would be greater than the probability for the low proficiency group. However, previous work in creole linguistics (e.g. Mühlhäusler, 1981) and in second language acquisition (Huebner, 1983) has led us to expect in the development of a pidgin and also in the acquisition of a second language that the pattern of variation will change as acquisition proceeds. As a result, it was also predicted that the pattern of factors influencing variation in (s) plural marking among the low proficiency group would be significantly different from the pattern of factors influencing variation in the high proficiency group.

Both of these hypotheses were confirmed by the results. Table 1 shows that a high level of proficiency as measured by TOEFL scores promotes (s) plural ($p_i = 0.59$), whereas a low level of proficiency inhibits it ($p_i = 0.41$).

TABLE 2. *Developmental differences in the effects of factor groups on variation in (s) plural marking*

Low proficiency	High proficiency
Preceding segment	Social convergence
Animacy (inhibits)	Animacy (promotes)
Redundant plural in NP	Redundant plural in NP
Syntactic function of NP	Syntactic function of NP
Position of noun in NP	Position of noun in NP

Furthermore, Table 2 shows that the pattern of factors exerting a significant effect on (s) plural marking differs between high and low proficiency learners. Thus, while three factors—redundant plural marking in the same NP, the syntactic function of the NP, and the position of the noun as head or prenominal modifier—affect (s) plural marking irrespective of learners' proficiency level, it was found that phonological environment affects variation *only* for low proficiency learners and that social convergence with a NS interlocutor appears to promote (s) plural marking *only* for high proficiency learners. In addition, animacy exerts an effect on (s) plural marking in opposite directions for low and high proficiency learners.

Linguistic factors

Factor groups 3 to 8 examined the effects of semantic, syntactic and phonological factors on (s) plural marking. On the basis of findings in pidgin and creole studies (Mühlhäusler, 1981; Sabino, 1983; Dijkhoff, 1983), it was predicted that the two semantic factors of definiteness and animacy would both favour marking of (s) plurals. As we have seen, neither of these factor groups had a significant effect of variation in the combined data.

Syntactic features of nouns and NPs were also hypothesised to have an effect on (s) plural marking. Each noun was coded as either an NP head or alternatively a prenominal modifier. The relation of prenominal noun modifier to head in English is very similar to that of the genitive relation of possessor to possessed which is marked by an -s suffix attached to mostly animate nouns. In this case, regular nouns have the genitive plural inflection identical to the plural. In addition, Chinese has a bound form *de* to mark both the genitive and the prenominal modifier in a complex NP. This combination of factors leads us to predict that prenominal position for a plural noun will strongly favour marking with (s). However, it will not be possible to say whether the (s) in this position represents a plural or a genitive. Table 1 shows that this factor did indeed exert the strongest effect on (s) with a factor probability of 0.71.

The syntactic function of the NP within the matrix clause was also considered to influence (s) plural marking. Those NPs which occurred in matrix clauses were coded as subjects, objects, complements of *be*, or adverbials. It was predicted that subject position would favour plural marking because of the greater number of animate agents occurring in this position, but this prediction was not borne out by the results. It appears that the strongest syntactic factors promoting (s) are adverbials ($p_i = 0.62$) and complements ($p_i = 0.57$), and that subjects in fact inhibit (s) plural ($p_i = 0.41$).

All quantitative studies of variation in the Labovian tradition have found that preceding and following phonological environments of a form exert an influence on the deletion or retention of that form. It was predicted that a combination of preceding and following vowels would favour (s) plural marking since insertion of a consonant between two vowels will preserve the predominantly CVCV syllable structure of the informants' first language. In addition, it was predicted that stem-final sibilants will inhibit (s) plural marking since, as has been found for children learning English as their first language (Innes, 1974), in this case plural marking already appears to be present, and moreover the insertion of an epenthetic vowel to form the so-called 'long plural' /Iz/ appears to be a fine-tuning of the (s) pluralisation rule which appears only in the later stages of acquisition. A final hypothesis regarding phonological environment predicted that the effect of the preceding phonological segment would differ between members of the low and high proficiency groups.

All four hypotheses concerning the effects of phonological environment were confirmed but it was found that phonological environment had a significant effect on (s) plural only for low proficiency learners. It appears that for high proficiency learners phonological environment (specifically the final segment of the noun stem) does not affect the decision as to *whether* to mark plurals with (s) but rather, as in the target, it affects the decision as to *how* to mark plural, that is, the shape of the plural allomorph.

The functional hypothesis

Finally, two factor groups examined what Kiparsky (1972), Poplack (1980) and Guy (1981) have called the 'functional hypothesis', that is, if information concerning the semantic number of the noun can be retrieved from any other part of surface structure, then there will be a tendency not to mark such information redundantly by means of an (s) inflection on the noun. Such information may be given in two ways in English: by redundantly marking number within the NP or by concord between the verb and its arguments. Redundant marking of number within the NP is accomplished by means of numerals, partitive constructions, quantifiers or plural demonstratives; while concord may indicate the number of a noun in one of two ways, either by marking a subject as singular by means of a third person singular -s in the present tense, or by concord between existential expressions (*there is/was/are/were*) and complements. It was predicted that numerals, partitives, quantifiers and plural demonstratives would inhibit (s) plural marking on the noun, whereas a lack of redundant plural marking within the NP would favour it. Similarly, it was predicted that an -s inflection on a third person present tense verb would be a salient marker of singular and hence a factor inhibiting (s) plural marking on the subject of the verb. And last, it was predicted that plural marking on existentials would inhibit redundant (s) plurals on noun complements.

Of the two factor groups which investigated the functional hypothesis, only one yielded enough tokens for a significant result. Concord between noun and verb (factor group 10) had no significant effect due to the fact that only 142 tokens could be coded in this factor group. Redundant plural marking within the NP (factor group 9) did reveal a highly significant effect, however, but in precisely the opposite direction to that predicted. That is, the most salient markers of plural number—numerals and *these/those*—appear to strongly favour redundant marking of plural on the head noun, whereas if number is not marked anywhere else in the NP, there is a very good chance that it will not be marked on the head noun either.

Summary and conclusions

In summary, the model of multidimensional variation proposed accounts well for the variation in (s) marking on semantically plural count nouns in the spoken English interlanguage of native speakers of Chinese. Significant effects on variation have been found for three major groups of factors: the situational context, the informant's overall proficiency in English, and linguistic features of the noun stem and its phonological environment. Of the four major hypotheses motivating this study, only the functional hypothesis is not confirmed by these results; in fact it appears that there is a tendency to maintain rather than eliminate redundant marking of plural within the same clause.

What is particularly interesting in the results of the present study is the confirmation of the hypothesis suggested by Mühlhäusler's (1981) and Huebner's (1983) findings that different factors exert different influences on variation as learners acquire greater competence in the target language. In the present study, the phonological environment of (s)—most significantly the final segment of the noun stem but also the immediately following segment—is a major factor in accounting for variation in the speech of learners with TOEFL scores below 410. However, phonological environment is *not* a significant factor in accounting for variation in the speech of informants with TOEFL scores above 477. Social convergence with a native English speaking interlocutor becomes a significant factor in accounting for variation in the speech of these high proficiency informants. The picture which emerges is one of variation of forms in early interlanguage being conditioned by widespread phonotactic processes which have been observed in early first language acquisition (Innes, 1974), early creolisation (Mühlhäusler, 1981), and other studies of second language acquisition (Eckman, 1981). In more developed interlanguage, however, these processes lose their influence, to be supplanted by the sociolinguistic effects of audience design and social convergence with an interlocutor. Variation in later interlanguage has become more sociolinguistic in nature, forming part of learners' burgeoning verbal repertoire which allows them to communicate social as well as propositional meanings. Such resources appear not to be available in early interlanguage.

I have argued in this chapter that the goal of a descriptively adequate analysis of interlanguage variation is inextricably linked to the methodological approaches which researchers use to elicit, record and analyse interlanguage data. By defining variation in a narrow sense as alternation among a closed set of 'ways of saying the same thing', it is possible to construct a robust model of variation in interlanguage. Such a model not only avoids the vagueness of statement inherent in approaches in which the envelope of variation is not well defined, but also avoids the confounding influence of plurifunctional forms. Furthermore, all the empirical work which has been carried out to date on interlanguage variation has shown it to be subject to the influence of many different independent factors, including situational context, stage of interlanguage development, linguistic environment, and also possibly the learner's first language. Further analysis of interlanguage variation must therefore apply a multivariate procedure such as the VARBRUL procedure described in this chapter in order to separate the independent variables and evaluate their effects relative to one another. Finally, if interlanguage variation, at least in the later stages of interlanguage development, is a sociolinguistic phenomenon, then second language acquisition researchers need a more subtle and profound way of describing situational context than is provided by the familiar descriptive categories of formality, task and degree of attention to speech.

Notes to Chapter 5

1. The study cited here is reported in greater detail in Young (1988, 1989).

2. The following discussion of models of research design and levels of measurement of the variables involved is based on the treatment given in Blalock (1979).

3. Tarone's intuitive ordering of the three tasks from that requiring the greatest attention to speech to that requiring the least attention is (1) grammaticality judgement, (2) narrative, (3) interview.

4. Sally had a TOEFL score of 573. TOEFL scores for the other relevent informants ranged between 270 and 523, with two subranges of 270–407 (low proficiency speakers) and 477–573 (high proficiency speakers).

5. Chinese pronouns mark plural by means of the suffix -men: wǒ ('I') ~ wǒ-men (exclusive 'we'). Vocatives used on infrequent and formal occasions also show plural marking with -men. Thus tóngzhì ('Comrade') contrasts with tóngzhì-men ('Comrades!').

6. The two semantic factor groups of animacy and concord did not show significant effects on (s) plural marking in the combined data from high and low proficiency speakers. However, in the case of animacy a significant effect was found for low proficiency speakers ($p < 0.02$) and for high proficiency speakers ($p < 0.01$) when data from these two groups were modelled separately. Tables 1 and 2 show that the effects were in different directions for the two groups, with animacy inhibiting (s) plural marking for low proficiency speakers but promoting it for high proficiency speakers. When data from the two groups were combined these effects naturally cancelled each other out.

7. With only 142 tokens, less than 10% of the total, there were too few instances of noun–verb concord in the data to allow any significant findings with respect to this variable.

References

ADAMSON, H. D. and KOVAC, C., 1981, Variation theory and second language acquisition: An analysis of Schumann's data. In D. SANKOFF & H. J. CEDERGREN (eds), *Variation Omnibus*. Edmonton, Alberta: Linguistic Research.

BEEBE, L. M., 1980, Sociolinguistic variation and style shifting in second language acquisition, *Language Learning*, 30, 433–48.

BEEBE, L. M. and ZUENGLER, J., 1983, Accommodation theory: An explanation for style shifting in second language dialects. In N. WOLFSON & E. JUDD (eds), *Sociolinguistics and Language Acquisition*. Rowley, MA: Newbury House.

BELL, A., 1984, Language style as audience design, *Language in Society*, 13, 145–204.

BERKOWITZ, D., 1987, 'Cultural empathy and second language phonological production.' Paper presented at the 21st Annual TESOL Convention, Miami Beach.

BLALOCK, H. M., 1979, *Social Statistics*, 2nd edn. New York: McGraw-Hill.

BROWN, R. and GILMAN, A., 1960, The pronouns of power and solidarity. In T. A. SEBEOK (ed.), *Style in Language*. Cambridge, MA: MIT Press.

CEDERGREN, H. and SANKOFF, D., 1974, Variable rules: Performance as a statistical reflection of competence, *Language*, 50, 333–55.

CORDER, S. P., 1977, Language continua and the interlanguage hypothesis. In S. P. CORDER & E. ROULET (eds), *The Notions of Simplification, Interlanguages and Pidgins and their Relation to Second Language Learning*. Geneva: Droz.

DICKERSON, L. J., 1975, The learner's interlanguage as a system of variable rules, *TESOL Quarterly*, 9, 401–7.

DICKERSON, L. J. and DICKERSON, W. B., 1977, Interlanguage phonology: Current research and future directions. In S. P. CORDER & E. ROULET (eds), *The Notions of Simplification, Interlanguages and Pidgins and their Relation to Second Language Learning*. Geneva: Droz.

DIJKHOFF, M. B., 1983, The process of pluralization in Papiamentu. In L. D. CARRINGTON (ed.), *Studies in Caribbean Language*. St. Augustine, Trinidad: Society for Caribbean Linguistics.

ECKMAN, F. R., 1981, On the naturalness of interlanguage phonological rules, *Language Learning*, 31, 195–216.

ELLIS, R. J., 1985a, Sources of variability in interlanguage, *Applied Linguistics*, 6, 118–31.

——, 1985b, A variable model of second language acquisition, *International Review of Applied Linguistics*, 13, 47–65.

FAIRBANKS, K., 1982, 'Variability in interlanguage.' Unpublished manuscript, University of Minnesota.

GATBONTON, E., 1978, Patterned phonetic variability in second language speech: A gradual diffusion model, *Canadian Modern Language Review*, 34, 335–47.

GUMPERZ, J. J., 1964, Linguistic and social interaction in two communities, *American Anthropologist*, 66 (6, part 2), 137–153. Reprinted in A. S. DIL (ed.), *Language in Social Groups: Essays by John J. Gumperz*. Stanford, CA: Stanford University Press, pp. 151–76.

GUY, G. R., 1980, Variation in the group and the individual: The case of final stop deletion. In W. LABOV (ed.), *Locating Language in Time and Space*. New York: Academic Press.

——, 1981, 'Linguistic variation in Brazilian Portuguese: Aspects of the phonology, syntax, and language history.' Ph.D. dissertation, University of Pennsylvania. *Dissertation Abstracts International*, 42, 1127-A. (University Microfilms International order no. DEN81-17786.)

HUEBNER, T., 1983, *A Longitudinal Analysis of the Acquisition of English*. Ann Arbor: Karoma.

HYMES, D., 1967, Models of the interaction of language and social setting, *Journal of Social Issues*, 23(2), 8–28.

INNES, S., 1974, 'Developmental aspects of the plural formation in English.' M.Sc. thesis, University of Alberta.

IRVINE, J. T., 1979, Formality and informality in communicative events, *American Anthropologist*, 81, 773–90.

KAY, P. and McDANIEL, C. K., 1979, On the logic of variable rules, *Language in Society*, 8, 151–87.

KIPARSKY, P., 1972, Explanation in phonology. In S. PETERS (ed.), *Goals of Linguistic Theory*. Englewood Cliffs, NJ: Prentice-Hall.

KROCH, A. S., 1985, Review of Romaine (1982): Socio-historical linguistics: Its status and methodology, *Language*, 61, 698–704.

LABOV, W., 1966, *The Social Stratification of English in New York City*. Washington, DC: Center for Applied Linguistics.

——, 1969, Contraction, deletion, and inherent variability of the English copula, *Language*, 45, 715–62.

——, 1972, *Sociolinguistic Patterns*. Philadelphia, PA: University of Pennsylvania Press.

LARSEN-FREEMAN, D., 1975, The acquisition of grammatical morphemes by adult ESL students, *TESOL Quarterly*, 9, 409–19.

LITTLEWOOD, W. T., 1981, Language variation and language acquisition theory, *Applied Linguistics*, 2, 150–8.

MÜHLHÄUSLER, P., 1981, The development of the category of number in Tok Pisin. In P. MUYSKEN (ed.), *Generative Studies in Creole Languages*. Dordrecht: Foris.

PICA, T., 1983, Methods of morpheme quantification: Their effect on the interpretation of second language data, *Studies in Second Language Acquisition*, 6, 69–78.

PINTZUK, S., 1987, *VARBRUL Programs for the IBM Personal Computer and the VAX*. University of Pennsylvania, Department of Linguistics.

POPLACK, S., 1980, The notion of the plural in Puerto Rican Spanish: Competing constraints on (s) deletion. In W. LABOV (ed.), *Locating Language in Time and Space*. New York: Academic Press.

ROMAINE, S., 1982, *Socio-historical Linguistics: Its Status and Methodology*. Cambridge: Cambridge University Press.

ROUSSEAU, P. and SANKOFF, D., 1978, Advances in variable rule methodology. In D. SANKOFF (ed.), *Linguistic Variation: Models and Methods*. New York: Academic Press.

SABINO, R., 1983, Plural marking in the Virgin Islands English Creole in the St. Thomas–St. John community, *Penn Review of Linguistics*, 7, 3–11.

SANKOFF, D. and LABOV, W., 1979, On the uses of variable rules, *Language in Society*, 8, 189–222.

SATO, C. J., 1985, Task variation in interlanguage phonology. In S. M. GASS & C. G. MADDEN (eds), *Input in Second Language Acquisition*. Rowley, MA: Newbury House.

SCHMIDT, R. W., 1977, Sociolinguistic variation and language transfer in phonology, *Working Papers in Bilingualism*, 12, 79–95.

SELINKER, L., 1969, Language transfer, *General Linguistics*, 9, 67–92.

——, 1972, Interlanguage, *International Review of Applied Linguistics*, 10, 219–31.

SELINKER, L. and DOUGLAS, D., 1985, Wrestling with 'context' in interlanguage theory, *Applied Linguistics*, 6, 190–204.

TARONE, E. E., 1979, Interlanguage as chameleon, *Language Learning*, 29, 181–91.

——, 1982, Systematicity and attention in interlanguage, *Language Learning*, 32, 69–84.

——, 1983, On the variability of interlanguage systems, *Applied Linguistics*, 4, 142–63.

——, 1985, Variability in interlanguage use: A study of style-shifting in morphology and syntax, *Language Learning*, 35, 373–404.

TARONE, E. E., FRAUENFELDER, U. and SELINKER, L., 1976, Systematicity/variability and stability/instability in interlanguage systems. In H. D. BROWN (ed.), *Papers in Second Language Acquisition*. (Special issue) *Language Learning* 4, 93–104.

THAKERAR, J. N., GILES, H. and CHESHIRE, J., 1982, Psychological and linguistic parameters of speech accommodation theory. In C. FRASER & K. R. SCHERER (eds), *Advances in the Social Psychology of Language*. New York: Cambridge University Press.

WEINER, E. J. and LABOV, W., 1983, Constraints on the agentless passive, *Journal of Linguistics*, 19, 29–58.

WOLFRAM, W., 1985, Variability in tense marking: A case for the obvious, *Language Learning*, 35, 229–54.

WOLFSON, N., 1976, Speech events and natural speech: Some implications for sociolinguistic methodology, *Language in Society*, 5, 189–209.

——, 1982, On tense alternation and the need for analysis of native speaker usage in second language acquisition, *Language Learning*, 32, 53–68.

YOUNG, R., 1986, The acquisition of a verbal repertoire in a second language, *Penn Working Papers in Educational Linguistics*, 2(1), 85–119.

——, 1988, Variation and the interlanguage hypothesis, *Studies in Second Language Acquisition*, 10 (3), 281–302.

——, 1989, 'Approaches to variation in interlanguage morphology: Plural marking in the speech of Chinese learners of English.' Ph.D. dissertation, University of Pennsylvania.

Section Three:
Topic and Task

6 Psycholinguistic perspectives on interlanguage variation: A Vygotskyan analysis

JAMES P. LANTOLF
MOHAMMED K. AHMED
University of Delaware

Introduction

Over the past few years, there has been an increased effort on the part of scholars working within Vygotskyan psycholinguistic theory to extend the theory developed by Vygotsky, Luria, Leontiev and their colleagues and students to the area of second language learning (see, for example, Appel, 1986; Di Pietro, 1987; Frawley & Lantolf, 1984, 1985; Groff, 1985; John-Steiner, 1985; Lantolf & Frawley, 1984, 1985; and Lantolf *et al.*, 1987). When one surveys the field of second language research, one is struck by the similarity between the present state of affairs in our discipline and the chaotic state of psychology to which Vygotsky so profoundly reacted more than sixty years ago as he began to develop his theory of human cognitive processes.[1] Long (1985:389), for instance, estimates that approximately fifteen to twenty theories, models, metaphors and perspectives appear in the current second language literature. Felix (1986:6) presents an even more pessimistic view when he warns that unless the findings of second language research can be unified within a theoretical framework, the field is doomed to fossilise at the stage of data collection.

According to Vygotsky, it was only through the creation of a unified psychology operating from the perspective of a consistent methodology that progress could be made in understanding the nature of human cognitive processes. Vocate (1987:154–58) argues that Vygotsky's theory, especially as elaborated by Luria, meets the metatheoretical criteria by which theories are usually assessed; that is, it is logically self-consistent, exhaustive in dealing with data, parsimonious, and it has a powerful heuristic value for stimulating research. In fact, Velichkovskii (1987:29–30) goes so far as to say that Vygotskyan theory is the only truly unified theory of cognitive processes.[2]

While we do not intend to enter into the general debate on the current status of cognitive psychology, we do concur with the implication of Long's and Felix's observations that one of its subfields, second language acquisition research, lacks a unified theoretical perspective. This is not to say that there are no interesting models nor a dearth of interesting data; but the problem, from our perspective, is that there is no unified theory to link the models and the data in any coherent and consistent way. In fact, what often counts as data for one model or hypothesis is frequently overlooked by another. For Vygotskyan theory, a theory that focuses on humans as eminently thinking beings, actively involved in the creation of their world, all data are both relevant and revelatory (Frawley & Lantolf, 1985:19). In what follows we undertake a brief analysis of one individual L2 speaker of English and offer an explanation of the variation observed in his performance in terms of Vygotskyan psycholinguistic theory.

Overview of Vygotskyan theory

Vygotskyan theory represents an essentially hermeneutic rather than nomological approach to science. As such, it is not directly concerned about predicting human behaviour as much as it is with seeking to understand behaviour as it actually unfolds. Thus, the theory does not seek out *causes* of human mental phenomena as is the case for theories of natural phenomena. For Vygotsky there is no necessary equation of *scientific* with natural scientific (Davydov & Radzikhovskii, 1985:43). Those, like Vygotsky, who approach science from a hermeneutic perspective, are

> profoundly concerned with the peculiar subject–subject relation in assessment of linguistically mediated meaning as opposed to the subject–object relation in natural scientific search for causal laws, with the embeddedness of such meaning in contexts of human communication, and with inherently social and collective features of language. These are precisely the issues that were consistently evaded and/or deliberately put into brackets in mainstream American psycholinguistics more than twenty years ago. (Rommetveit, 1987)

For Vygotsky then, an inseparable link is forged between semiotically mediated human social interaction and individual cognitive activity—a link that has been ignored in Western paradigms and has consequently led to the creation of isolated disciplines which could not be integrated even if researchers were interested in doing so (Wertsch, 1985:230–1). Specific features of Vygotskyan theory will be brought out during the discussion of the findings.

Subject

The data for the present study are taken from a series of interactions conducted with a single Arabic speaker of English as a second language. The subject, M, was a male graduate student enrolled in the civil engineering programme at the University of Delaware. At the time of the initial interview, M had been in the United States for ten months and was also taking an advanced level English language class in the university's ELI. He had previously studied English for five years in his homeland.

It should be pointed out that the original intent of the study was to investigate the variable interlanguage performance of five ESL speakers. As it turned out, however, quite by chance, the interviews conducted with M took on an aspect which changed the entire focus of our study. In an earlier paper, Lantolf & Khanji (1983) reported on some of the findings from the project and attempted an explanation of M's variable performance in terms of interactional factors, including those proposed by social psychologists such as Giles & Powesland (1975). The problem with the Lantolf & Khanji study is that its explanatory principles are largely *ad hoc*, since like much of the research in our field, they were formulated specifically to deal with the data we had uncovered. Among other things, the present chapter seeks to remedy this situation.

Tasks

The five subjects who participated in the initial round of data collection were asked to perform two tasks:

1. An oral narrative, based on the *Bilingual Syntax Measure* (BSM), which required the subjects to relate on-line the story depicted by the sequence of pictures from the BSM. The story was told to the principal investigator (L), a native speaker of English.

2. An oral interview in which the subjects were asked questions on their experiences with the American way of life. The interviews were conducted by L.

Prior to beginning the activities, the subjects were told that they would be taking part in a project to study the performance of ESL speakers. The activities were carried out in the office of the principal investigator, L.

Data

As mentioned earlier, the data to be discussed in the present chapter are taken from one of the five participants only. At the outset, we had hypothesised, as is often the case in interlanguage variation studies, that the BSM would be a task which required the participants to pay more attention to form than did the interview. Thus, we anticipated that the speech of the subjects would reflect a higher degree of accuracy on the more structured BSM than on the less constrained interview activity. As reported in Lantolf & Khanji (1983) this indeed proved to be the case. As we proceeded with the initial study, however, M, the focus of the present discussion, showed considerable interest in engaging L in a conversation about the similarities and differences between Islam and Christianity. This, of course, was not a planned part of the study. In fact, M did not express his interest in religion until completion of the interview task when he and L were initiating the leave-taking ritual that usually follows such sessions. At this point, M and L began what amounted to an extended discussion on the topic of religion. M then returned at a later time in order to continue the conversation. A total of four hours of conversation between M and L on the topic of religion were recorded on sound tape. Although some data from the three activities are presented here, the focus of our analysis is on the interview and the conversation.

Table 1 summarises the data on the formation of NP Plural -s and article use in M's performance across the three tasks (i.e. BSM, interview, conversation) as reported in Lantolf & Khanji (1983).

It is clear from Table 1 that there is a marked decline in the accuracy of both morphemes across activities. The decline in accuracy from the BSM to

TABLE 1. *Correct use of NP Plural -s and article*

	BSM %	Interview %	Conversation %
NP Pl -s	96	53	36
Article	65	55	35

TABLE 2. *Copula deletion and past tense markers*

	Interview	Conversation
Copula deletion	3/39 = 8%	13/41 = 32%
Correct formation of past irregular	8/12 = 66%	7/23 = 30%
Correct formation of past regular	4/4 = 100%	7/18 = 39%
* Present for past	3/16 = 19%	23/64 = 36%

* Some specific examples of use of the present tense in place of the past are presented in Table 3.

TABLE 3. *Use of present tense for past tense*

Interview
- **L:** Have you travelled around at all while you've been here?
- **M:** I *am going* to Washington, to France and/ ... to New York five times/ ... to Niagara falls, that's it.
- **L:** Why did you go, Why did you go there?
- **M:** There *is* a round trip to ... in the State College.

Conversation
This, the second book about how the Christ *live*.
The following examples occurred when M spoke of his childhood:
I *say* to myself there is no God.
When I was fifteen, I *think* I *can't* agree with him.
I *begin* to talk about it.

the interview is not surprising, since the former task is, relatively speaking, more structured than the latter activity, which was expected to elicit less controlled speech.

Table 2 provides additional evidence on the morphological changes observed in M's performance across the tasks. We do not include data from the BSM, because other than in the two cases presented in Table 1, M's morphology on the BSM task was virtually 100% accurate with respect to the specific elements under consideration.

The data in Tables 1 to 3 show that M's morphological accuracy declined consistently from the interview to the conversation. According to Givón (1979, 1984), a change in morphological patterns such as observed in the preceding tables is characteristic of a shift from a more syntactic to a more pragmatic mode of speech. The syntactic and pragmatic modes of speaking are the extremes of a continuum 'with varying degrees of the two styles in between' (Stauble & Schumann, 1983:76). An additional and salient feature of the pragmatic mode of speech is its high frequency of topic–comment configurations, while the syntactic mode is typified by subject–predicate constructions (Givón, 1979:98). Every known language exhibits both syntactic and pragmatic modes of speech (Givón, 1979:97). The occurrence of either mode, as will be discussed later, depends on the psycholinguistic circumstances surrounding an individual's act of speaking and reflects the degree of planning (i.e. attention to linguistic form) engaged in by the speaker.

Evidence of a shift from subject–predicate toward topic–comment configurations in M's performance is provided by the data presented in Tables 4 and 5. In addition to the morphological simplification noted above, the appearance of such a shift is a further indication of M's movement away from syntactic and towards pragmatic or unplanned speech across activities.

Before presenting the data, however, one caveat is in order. Schumann (1982:352) observes that it is sometimes quite difficult to determine whether

TABLE 4. *Examples of pragmatic utterances*

Interview
> **L:** How about reading and writing?
> **M:** Reading it is good but writing bad.
> **L:** What about the food?
> **M:** The same food we have.

Conversation
> **L:** I don't remember what we were talking about?
> **M:** Talking about the way you, the way you, ah, the way you ... fast .. the way you fast your religion. I talk about my, the way we fast.*
>
> **L:** You only have to fast on the first day.
> **M:** The first day, the first day and during Mondays.
>
> **M:** What I know something about fasting.
> **M:** The rules, its exist.

* According to Givón, difficulty in introducing a topic is a feature of pragmatic speech.

TABLE 5. *Frequency of pragmatic speech by task*

	Interview	Conversation
Total utterances	96	268
Pragmatic utterances	6	83
Percentage	6%	31%

an utterance is subject–predicate (syntactic) or topic–comment (pragmatic) in nature. In analysing M's performance along these lines, we adopted a conservative approach. That is, we only included those sentences which were clear examples of topic–comment and subject–predicate speech. All other cases were excluded from analysis. Although one-word utterances qualify as pragmatic rather than syntactic speech, we excluded these from our analysis as well. This is because M frequently used single-word utterances as a strategy to indicate that he had not understood a particular lexical item uttered by L. For example, when M first encountered the word *Protestants* in the conversation, he made several attempts to repeat the word with interrogative intonation in order to elicit a definition from L. No such strategy occurred during the interview.

Summary of data

We would characterise M's performance as variable across the three activities. His performance on the interview was more grammatical and syntactic in terms of morphological accuracy and frequency of subject–predicate utterances. His performance during the conversation was markedly different to the extent that his morphological accuracy decreased and he manifested an increase in topic–comment structures. Thus, we see a style shift from more syntactic to less syntactic speech from one activity to the other. To explain this variation simply as degree of attention to form is, in our opinion, to miss what really is going on as two individuals engage each other through the mediating tool of speech. It is here, we believe, that Vygotskyan theory can make an important contribution to variation research.

Discussion

Schumann (1982) and Stauble & Schumann (1983) argue, on the basis of evidence from adult learners of English, that interlanguage development proceeds along the lines predicted by Givón (1979, 1984) from a pragmatic to a syntactic mode. Despite the significance of Schumann's acculturation model of second language acquisition, it must be recognised that the model is not designed to account for variation within a learner's idiolect. As Beebe & Zuengler (1983) observe, while the acculturation model does take social and psychological factors as causal variables in determining the ultimate development of a learner's interlanguage,

> it does not help us in explaining the dynamics of an individual's second language speech within each interactional situation. It accounts for differential levels of success (i.e. variation across learners) in second language acquisition but does not explain any type of variation within each learner's speech. (Beebe & Zuengler, 1983:200)

In essence, the acculturation model views interlanguage development as a linear process in which the learner passes through a series of more or less well-defined stages on the way to target language competence. Givón, however, considers the relationship between pragmatic and syntactic speech to be dynamic rather than linear, as indicated by the following remarks:

> It is thus only to be expected that when communication is under severe stress, speakers of varying linguistic background revert to this more common communicative mode. It has persisted subterraneanly in some registers of linguistic-communicative behavior, those which hark back to early childhood and pre-syntactic communication (Givón, 1984:129).

A similar view of linguistic development is proposed by Ochs (1979) in her discussion of planned and unplanned discourse in which she argues against a replacement model of development and in favour of a retentive model. According to Ochs (1979:52), as people mature linguistically, they develop potentialities that are retained throughout life and which can be accessed 'under certain communicative conditions'. Ochs further claims that adults are likely to rely upon language with child-like features whenever communication is spontaneous and unpredictable (Ochs, 1979:53). Thus, it is not necessarily the case that people use pragmatic (unplanned) speech patterns only under conditions of stress. They may also utilise similar patterns 'under relaxed conditions without time pressure, where planning is simply NOT NECESSARY' (Givón, 1979:103).

The view of linguistic development outlined by Givón and Ochs is precisely in line with the theory of the development of all higher cognitive functions, including language development, proposed by Vygotsky. That is, unlike a Piagetian model of human development in which new forms of functioning are presumed to replace earlier forms (much in the same way as the acculturation model predicts linguistic development), a Vygotskyan model argues that

> different genetic forms coexist in thinking, just as different rock formations coexist in the earth's crust. Such a structure is not an exception, but rather a rule of behavior ... developmentally late forms coexist in behavior with younger formations (Vygotsky, 1986:140).

Ontogenetically prior forms of cognitive behaviour are especially evident in the everyday activities of adults (Vygotsky, 1986:140).

M's variable performance on the two tasks reflects this principle of Vygotskyan theory. In other words, his pragmatic mode of speaking represents a developmentally earlier mode of speech, while his syntactic mode is an ontogenetically later stage. This would appear to confirm Schumann and Stauble's findings, until we realise that both modes occur in the same speaker contemporaneously. More importantly, however, is that each mode takes on a specific function relative to the *individual* speaker who chooses to access a specific mode in order to carry out each of the two tasks. In what follows, we consider this critical point in more detail.

At first glance, both the interview and the conversation appear to be dialogic speech events in which the two participants are attempting to negotiate meaning, to use the current terminology. To be sure, not only are there significant differences in the speech performance of M, but data on L's performance also reveals considerable variation, as we will see.

The relevant feature of Vygotskyan theory to be considered here is what Wertsch (1984:8) refers to as *definition of situation*. According to Wertsch,

> a situation definition is the way in which a setting or context is represented—that is, defined—by those who are operating in that setting. I use the term *definition* because I want to emphasize that humans actively create a representation of a situation; they are not the passive recipients of this representation. (Wertsch, 1984:8)

Vygotsky cautioned that researchers often forget their experiments involve human beings who are always thinking about themselves and that 'this process is never without some influence on [their] behavior; a sudden shift in thought during an experiment always has some impact on the subject's overall behavior' (Vygotsky, 1979:7). The very act of informing an individual of the nature and intent of a given experiment (e.g. 'This is an experiment to determine how learners of English use their second language.') can lead that individual to act contrary to our predictions (Rommetveit, 1987). This means that regardless of how a researcher may characterise a task or activity, the ultimate responsibility in determining how a task is perceived and carried out rests with the individuals who take part in the activity. When this happens, researchers are often hard pressed to explain apparent aberrations in their data and often seek explanations in factors that in a real sense reside outside the individual.

Tarone (1985), for example, in a study of morphemic variability in L2 speakers, argues that style shifting may not only be governed by attention to form but also by text type. Specifically, she hypothesises that in narrating a story, one of the tasks in her study,

> the speaker must make sure that references to the various protagonists and objects which are crucial to the story line are clear; articles and pronouns are very important in maintaining this sort of clear reference. (Tarone, 1985:392)

In interviews, on the other hand, turn taking 'may be interrupted at unpredictable intervals by the interviewer and thus may be less cohesive' (Tarone, 1985:392). From this she concludes that style shifting may not only be governed by attention to form but also by discourse type.[3]

While we appreciate the significance of Tarone's findings and her claims on style-shifting, we nevertheless believe that in order to develop full understanding of variability, it is necessary to realise that explanations of all linguistic phenomena must ultimately relate to people and how they orient themselves to what they are doing with their language. As Yngve (1986:38) cogently remarks,

> it would be possible to develop explanations of linguistic phenomena of the sort we have been striving for, in terms of people, directly on the basis of the evidence from people, not indirectly through language. Such a linguistics would be a human linguistics rather than a linguistics of language ... Without language blocking the way, we are free to move directly from the data obtained from people to theories and proposed explanations in terms of people.

In order to fully understand the implication of the above discussion with regard to situation definition and the subject-based approach to behaviour, we introduce the concept of *intersubjectivity*—a concept initially introduced by Rommetveit (see Wertsch, 1985:159). Traditional approaches to human dialogic interaction assume that 'when interlocutors come together in a speech situation, they share a fund of "background knowledge" that provides an agreed-upon foundation for communication' (Wertsch, 1985:160). Rommetveit argues that this approach forces researchers to focus on how each utterance in a dialogue merely adds to already established information and overlooks the crucial fact that communication 'creates and transforms a situation' (Wertsch, 1985:160).

For Rommetveit, the problem of intersubjectivity is really an issue of how well humans are able to transcend their private worlds through linguistic means. What is negotiated, according to Rommetveit, is not meaning, in the usual sense of the term, but a dynamic social world which emerges from the coming together of two private worlds. Thus, at the outset of a dialogic exchange the interlocutors may and usually do have vastly different perspectives, or, at best, a 'vague interpretation of what is taken for granted and what the utterances are intended to convey' (Wertsch, 1985:161). It is out of this that attempts are made to negotiate a temporarily shared social world.

Rommetveit (1985:187) claims that a state of intersubjectivity is achieved between two communicating individuals if, and only if, some state of affairs is brought into focus by one of the participants and is jointly attended to by both of them. In other words, 'intersubjectivity exists between two interlocutors in a task setting when they share the same situation definition and know that they share the same situation definition' (Wertsch, 1984:12).

Whether or not a state of intersubjectivity is actually attained rests upon the mutual endorsement of dyadic patterns of control in the dialogue (Rommetveit, 1985:190). The question of control is crucial because it will determine whose private world will or will not be endorsed. The control relationship between interlocutors can either be symmetrical or asymmetrical. The former case allows for unlimited interchangeability of dialogue roles, i.e. recognition of two private worlds; and the latter promotes the world view of one of the participants at the expense of the other. In Vygotsky's terms, under conditions of symmetrical dialogue control both participants are said to be fully *self-regulated*, because they are free to introduce their respective world views into the creation of a shared social world, while under asymmetrical conditions, one of the participants is said to be *other-regulated*, because his/her world view is subverted to that of the partner. In this case, there is no true negotiation of intersubjectivity, and the situation definition is more or less imposed by one of the interlocutors, who, for whatever reason, has special status, and as such is allowed to control the focus of attention (see Habermas, 1970).

The point of all of this is that the degree of intersubjectivity and situation definition existing between two interlocutors is reflected in their linguistic performance (Wertsch, 1985:177). Specifically, we would like to argue that the speech produced by M during the interview and the conversation activities is a direct reflection of the degree of intersubjectivity *negotiated* between the interlocutors in the two tasks.

The interview was designed to do nothing more than elicit a representative sample of M's interlanguage. As such, the interview setting immediately established the interviewer L as the individual in control of the interaction; that is, as the person responsible for the direction of the dialogue, including such concerns as topic selection. Essentially, what transpired under the guise of a linguistic interaction was a linguistic reaction on the part of M to the questions posed by L in order to uncover M's English language capabilities. That this was indeed the case is graphically indicated by M's comments at the beginning and conclusion of the interview. These comments established a type of macrostructure for the entire exchange. At the outset, M made a series of revealing responses to L's remarks:

M: Because I don't like to .. to learn English.
L: Don't like to speak it or you don't like to .. you don't like studying?
M: I don't like languages in general.
L: You don't like languages?
M: I don't like Arabic.
L: It seems you don't like to talk.
M: No, I like to talk ... but when I have to.

Near the conclusion of the interview, M made the following comment to the research assistant, who entered, by design, to indicate that L was needed by someone outside his office:

M: Do you think it's enough to make me speak (laughs). It's your turn.

On the basis of the preceding commentary, it would seem that M had a clear understanding of the situation definition imposed by L: he was to provide a representative sample of his speech in English and he apparently believed he had adequately complied with the situation definition as *imposed* by L.

During the interview it is readily apparent that L alone was free to be fully self-regulated, while M was simply expected to comply with the situation definition and was thus other-regulated by L. There was little if any negotiation of intersubjectivity, because there was in fact no need for such negotiation. Evidence of the asymmetrical nature of the interview is provided in Lantolf & Khanji (1983). They report, for example, that during the interview M did not ask a single question, whereas L asked a total of 43 questions, as clear indication of topic control. In fact, of the 26 topic shifts occurring in the interview, all were initiated by L. In the conversation, on the other hand, M asked 67 questions, while L only asked 16 during this activity. Of the 8 general topic shifts which occurred during the conversation, 6 were initiated by M.

A further analysis of the interactional features of the two activities also reveals the lack of intersubjectivity during the interview. The mean length of utterance (MLU) for M in the interview was 3.91 and his mean length of turn (MLT) was computed to be 7.5 with a range of from 1 to 32 words per turn (Lantolf & Khanji, 1983:464). During the conversation, a significant increase in both measures was calculated. M's MLU increased to 6.83 and his MLT increased to 16.09, with a range of from 1 to 129 words per turn. Of equal importance is the fact that L's MLU and MLT also changed across the two activities. In the interview his MLU was 7.3 and his MLT was 11.8, while during the conversation L's MLU increased slightly to 8.6, but his MLT declined to 9.7 with a range of from 1 to 24.

Finally, if we look at M's remarks at the beginning and conclusion of the conversation, we notice a sharp contrast in terms of the nature of the macrostructure which they frame for this activity:

(beginning)

M: I don't have anythings to discuss but ... I don't mind. I don't mind.

(conclusion)

M: I have English class now. We can talk more after?

At the outset, it appears that M was once again willing to comply with the general goal of eliciting data. As the conversation progressed, his interest in the topic obviously grew to the point that he was no longer concerned with providing data but with learning something through the comparison of the two religions. Just as obviously, L too became interested in this topic.

The claim we are making is that the speaking styles displayed by M in the two activities mean something in terms of the person who produced them. For Vygotsky, it is inappropriate and often misleading for the researcher to separate the syntactic organisation of an utterance from its psychological organisation. To say that an utterance is grammatically incorrect relative to some external norm tells us little in terms of the intentionality of the individual subject who produced the utterance. This is because grammatical constructs such as subject and predicate, gender, case, tense, etc. 'have their psychological doubles' (Vygotsky, 1986:221). Frawley & Lantolf (1985) showed this to be the case in ESL speakers' use of the atemporal, past, and progressive constructions in narrative discourse.

The point is, that M's production of syntactically well-formed utterances in the interview indicates that he in fact had ceded control of the activity to L and that his speech was other-regulated. In essence, M did what he was supposed to do: produce well-formed English utterances. There was no attempt to negotiate intersubjectivity. The lack of intersubjectivity is much more likely to stimulate a speaker to produce explicit (nonelliptical) utterances (Wertsch, 1985:177). M's shift to a more pragmatic mode of interactions during the conversation is a clear indication that control was shared by both interlocutors. This is another way of saying that M's speech was self-regulated. The only way he could find out what he wanted was to move to this mode of speaking. Moreover, as intersubjectivity is negotiated and a common situation definition is freely agreed upon there is a decreased need for the participants in a dialogue to rely on fully syntactic speech, because of the movement toward a temporarily shared social world.

Conclusion

The relationship between pragmatic and syntactic speech is not simply a developmental issue in which an individual moves from pragmatic to syntactic mode over time. Rather, both forms of speaking have clear psychological significance for the individual who produces them. In the case of M, we argue that only the conversation represented a true dialogue—a dialogue which allowed, indeed required, M to access his self-regulated mode of speaking. The task does not determine what the individual will or will not do; rather, it is the individual that ultimately determines the task and how it will be carried out.

Notes to Chapter 6

1. In his address to the Second All-Union Congress of Psychoneurologists held in Leningrad in 1924, Vygotsky pointed out that in psychology there existed as many separate theories as there were problems to be solved (Vygotsky, 1979). Each particular psychological problem gave rise to a theoretical perspective specifically designed to solve each problem—clearly, no way for science to progress.

2. In this regard, Velichkovskii cites numerous American and European researchers such as Johnson-Laird, Fodor, Neisser, Tulving and Newell, among others, who present a rather pessimistic view of developments within cognitive psychology. Velichkovskii (1987:34) quotes Neisser as an example in this regard: 'briefly put, the results of a hundred years of investigation of memory are somewhat discouraging. We have established some valid empirical generalizations, but most of them are so self-evident that even a ten-year-old child knows them.'

3. Frawley & Lantolf (1985) found that use of pronouns and articles among native speakers as well as L2 speakers of English on a storytelling task was not at all consistent and accurate, at least from the perspective of some interlocutor. To be sure, these two features of discursive cohesion did make sense from the viewpoint of the speaker, if one assumed that the speaker was, in fact, speaking to no one other than the self.

References

APPEL, G., 1986, 'L1 and L2 narrative and expository discourse production: A Vygotskyan analysis.' Ph.D. dissertation, University of Delaware.

BEEBE, L. M. and ZUENGLER, J., 1983, Accommodation theory: An explanation for style shifting in second language dialects. In N. WOLFSON & E. JUDD (eds), *Sociolinguistics and Language Acquisition*. Rowley, MA: Newbury House.

DAVYDOV, V. V. and RADZIKHOVSKII, L. A., 1985, Vygotsky's theory and the activity-oriented approach in psychology. In J. V. WERTSCH (ed.), *Culture, Communication, and Cognition: Vygotskian Perspectives*. Cambridge: Cambridge University Press.

DI PIETRO, R. J., 1987, *Strategic Interaction: Learning Language Through Scenarios*. Cambridge: Cambridge University Press.

FELIX, S., 1986, *Cognition and Language Growth*. Dordrecht: Foris.

FRAWLEY, W., and LANTOLF, J. P., 1984, Speaking and self-order: A critique of orthodox L2 research, *Studies in Second Language Acquisition*, 6(2), 143–59.

——, 1985, Second language discourse: A Vygotskyan perspective, *Applied Linguistics*, 6(1), 19–44.

GILES, H. and POWESLAND, P. F., 1975, *Speech Style and Social Evaluation*. London: Academic Press.

GIVÓN, T., 1979, From discourse to syntax: Grammar as a processing strategy. In T. GIVÓN (ed.), *Syntax and Semantics, Vol. 12: Discourse and Syntax*. New York: Academic Press.

——, 1984, Universals of discourse structure and second language acquisition. In W. E. RUTHERFORD (ed.), *Language Universals and Second Language Acquisition*. Amsterdam: John Benjamins.

GROFF, K. A., 1985, 'Perception and context: Language acquisition grounded on activity theories of Lev Vygotsky.' Ph.D. dissertation, Ohio State University.

HABERMAS, J., 1970, Towards a theory of communicative competence, *Inquiry*, 13(4), 360–75.

JOHN-STEINER, V., 1985, The road to competence in an alien land: A Vygotskian perspective on bilingualism. In J. V. WERTSCH (ed.), *Culture, Communication, and Cognition: Vygotskian Perspectives*. Cambridge: Cambridge University Press.

LANTOLF, J. P. and FRAWLEY, W., 1984, Second language performance and Vygotskyan psycholinguistics: Implications for L2 instruction. In A. MANNING, P. MARTIN & K. MCCALLA (eds), *Tenth LACUS Forum, 1983*. Columbia, SC: Hornbeam.

——, 1985, On communication strategies: A functional perspective, *Rassegna italiana di linguistica applicata*, 17(2–3), 143–57.

LANTOLF, J. P. and KHANJI, R., 1983, Non-linguistic parameters of interlanguage performance: Expanding the research paradigm. In J. MORREALL (ed.), *The Ninth LACUS Forum, 1982*. Columbia, SC: Hornbeam.

LANTOLF, J. P., MATHEWS, T., HOWARD, D. and KELSEY, G., 1987, 'Language play in adult L2 learning: An activity-based perspective.' Paper presented at the Second International Congress on Applied Psycholinguistics, Kassel, Federal Republic of Germany.

LONG, M. H., 1985, Input and second language acquisition theory. In S. M. GASS & C. G. MADDEN (eds), *Input in Second Language Acquisition*. Rowley, MA: Newbury House.

OCHS, E., 1979, Planned and unplanned discourse. In T. GIVÓN (ed.), *Syntax and Semantics, Vol. 12: Discourse and Syntax*. New York: Academic Press.

ROMMETVEIT, R., 1985, Language acquisition as increasing linguistic structuring of experience and symbolic behavior control. In J. V. WERTSCH (ed.), *Culture, Communication, and Cognition: Vygotskian Perspectives*. Cambridge: Cambridge University Press.

——, 1987, 'Psycholinguistics, hermeneutics, and cognitive science.' Paper presented at the Second International Symposium on Applied Psycholinguistics, Kassel, Federal Republic of Germany.

SCHUMANN, J. H., 1982, Simplification, transfer, and relexification as aspects of pidginization and early second language acquisition, *Language Learning*, 32(4), 337–66.

STAUBLE, A.-M. and SCHUMANN J. H., 1983, Toward a description of the Spanish–English basilang. In K. M. BAILEY, M. H. LONG & S. PECK (eds), *Second Language Acquisition Studies*. Rowley, MA: Newbury House.

TARONE, E., 1985, Variability in interlanguage use: A study of style-shifting in morphology and syntax, *Language Learning*, 35(4), 373–95.

VELICHKOVSKII, B. M., 1987, Methodological problems in cognitive psychology, *Soviet Psychology*, 25(1–2), 29–77.

VOCATE, D. R., 1987, *The Theory of A. R. Luria: Functions of Spoken Language in the Development of Higher Mental Processes*. Hillsdale, NJ: Lawrence Erlbaum.

VYGOTSKY, L. S., 1979, Consciousness as a problem of psychology of behavior, *Soviet Psychology*, 17(1), 5–35.

——, 1986, *Thought and Language*. Cambridge, MA: MIT Press.

WERTSCH, J. V., 1984, The zone of proximal development: Some conceptual issues. In B. ROGOFF & J. V. WERTSCH (eds), *Children's Learning in the 'Zone of Proximal Development'*. San Francisco: Jossey-Bass.

——, 1985, *Vygotsky and the Social Formation of Mind*. Cambridge, MA: Harvard University Press.

YNGVE, V. H., 1986, *Linguistics as a Science*. Bloomington: Indiana University Press.

7 Theoretical implications of the acquisition of the English simple past and past progressive: Putting together the pieces of the puzzle

NATHALIE BAILEY
Lehman College, CUNY

An area of second language acquisition theory which has a long history of polar opposition is the relationship of form and function as explanations of language development. Researchers continually call for a consideration of both (Hatch & Wagner-Gough, 1976; Hakuta, 1985; Ellis, 1986; Rutherford, 1987). But, as Hakuta has acknowledged, it is still unclear how the development of grammar, meaning and communication are related to each other. He concludes that they are distinct levels of language. Ellis (this volume, chapter 3) claims that form and function are inseparable. Work currently being done on universal grammar focuses on the importance of form in explaining SLA; sociolinguistic research focuses on function. Rutherford (1987) in a masterful analysis of the state of the art suggests that far from attaining a paradigm, SLA may have achieved an unprecedented level of 'cognitive tolerance'. He sees each of the diverse areas of SLA research interacting to create a whole. With this chapter I would like to add to the literature on the interdependence of form and function learning along the lines of Huebner (1985). Using the variable development of the progressive in English in the present and in the past, I will show how very similar forms are learned very differently depending on their function. My hypothesis is that an unmarked (simpler and more natural) meaning or discourse function will be learned before a marked one.

Many explanations have been proposed for early progressive acquisition in English. Most have concluded that either form or frequency is responsible for the ease of progressive acquisition with no consideration of the role of meaning or function. For that reason I think that these explanations have been insufficient. Hatch & Wagner-Gough (1976) suggested, among other things, that the simplicity of the progressive form was what made it easy. They cited the perceptual salience of the progressive -*ing* and its phonological stability (one form). Wagner-Gough (1975), looking at children, went on to study the acquisition of the function of the progressive, but due to its lack of semantic contrast with the simple present, she decided that form is learned before function in second language learning. Olshtain (1979), also looking at a child second language learner, came to the same conclusion.

Larsen-Freeman (1976), studying adults, proposed that the answer to early progressive acquisition was frequency. She confirmed its high frequency in teacher talk to university students. Long & Sato (1983), however, failed to confirm the high frequency of the progressive in teacher input in their study of ESL learners.

Lightbown (1983), looking at adolescents, claimed that excessive and unnatural classroom input was the reason why the progressive was learned early although she failed to confirm high frequency of use of the progressive either in teacher talk or in textbook use.

Failing form and frequency, what can explain progressive -*ing* learning?

Bailey & Madden (1980) show that meaning rather than form or frequency was what was responsible for the success of the progressive -*ing*. We had noticed that the past progressive was frequently lumped with the present progressive in researchers' minds. As one researcher (Frith, 1977) put it, 'One should not expect the past and present progressive to be learned any differently because both function as background to the moment of speaking'. We did not agree that the present progressive had a background function. If anything, we felt that the simple present had a background function, and we were supported in this analysis by the work of Woiset-schlaeger (1980) who analysed the progressive as having the meaning *observable* as opposed to *known*. He used illustrations such as

(1)   The car is burning oil

of an observable event as contrasted with

(2)   The car burns oil

which is a structural or known characteristic. Thus it could be argued that the simple present actually has a background function since the information that it conveys is not just temporary and true 'now' but unchanging and true 'always'. The present progressive could be said to occur on the main time axis and the simple present before, around or off it since it functions to express habits, universal truths and characteristics that do not advance the action of a story line but actually represent discourse digressions. In a recent study of English tense and aspect acquisition by Hatori *et al.* (1987) the simple present was found to be learned later than practically all other tenses and aspects in English. The reason they gave was its lack of temporal reference.

I turn now to an analysis of the past. The background function of the past progressive is widely attested. Labov (1972) found a distinct pattern of past progressive distribution in narrative whereby the past progressive occurred principally at the beginning of narratives to set the scene. Hopper (1979) and Hopper & Thompson (1980) strongly argue for the background function of the progressive though they never distinguish the function of the present progressive from the function of the past progressive. Nor did Woisetschlaeger. This is a curious omission. It betrays an assumption on the part of some linguists that the progressive is a unitary phenomenon with a single discourse function. I disagree with this premise of consistency. The discourse function of the progressive varies from the present to the past because the unmarked/core meaning of the present is temporariness and changing and the unmarked/core meaning of the past is non-changing. In fact if one were to imagine a main time axis, it might be visualised as a straight line for the simple past turning into a broken line representing the changeable present progressive, with the past progressive revolving around the main time in the past and the simple present revolving around it in the present (see Figure 1).

The experiment which I will now explain was designed to show that the progressive, despite its form simplicity, is not learned early in the past. Rather the simple past, despite its form irregularity, is learned before the past progressive.

The design of my experiment was, very simply, five tasks given to four levels (of five to eight learners each) of tutored adult ESL learners (26 in all), repeated twice. Four of the tasks were varieties of production tasks,

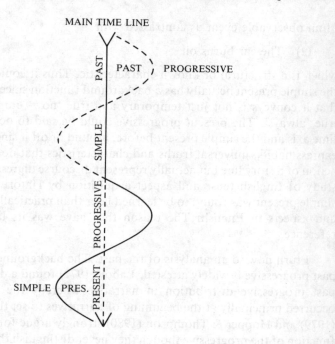

FIGURE 1.

written and oral, and one was imitation. Both questions and statements were tested. The types of production tasks are given in Table 1.

At the initial testing (Time 1) subjects were first asked to write a personal story about a dangerous or embarrassing incident that had happened to them (following Labov, who originated danger-of-death narratives). A day or two later they were asked to retell the same story orally. At that time they were also given two cued picture tasks, one in which they told about and one in which they asked about a series of single frame cartoons. After that they were given an imitation task based on four-frame wordless Louie cartoons.

TABLE 1. *Production tasks*

Types	Time 1		Time 2
Writing	Personal story	=	Re-tell story
Oral story	Personal story	=	Cartoon story
Picture Task I	Tell about	=	Tell about
Picture Task II	Ask about	=	Ask about

At Time 2 the oral story task was changed from a personal story to a re-telling of the Louie cartoon stories which they knew from the imitation task. (Level 5 was given this task at Time 1 as well as Time 2 as a pilot.) The written production task also changed from a personal story at Time 1 to a retold story at Time 2. This time a modelled composition was read aloud to them and they were asked to recreate it in writing. This was a balanced task in which eight simple past verbs and eight past progressive verbs were used in the modelled story. Both cued picture tasks were repeated at Time 2.

The imitation task requires more explanation. On this task I controlled for the relationship of the simple past and past progressive. All 24 sentences for imitation consisted of two clauses. I varied the order in which the simple past and past progressive were presented in those sentences but held constant main clause before subordinate clause. In a small number of items (four of each), two progressives or two simple pasts were presented together in one sentence. Examples of each of these kinds of sentences are the following:

Contrasting clause sentences

1 *Louie's wife was carrying some food when she saw a mouse.*
2 *She forgot the mouse when she was talking on the phone.*

Non-contrasting clause sentences

3 *Louie was reading the newspaper while he was eating breakfast.*
4 *She changed her clothes when she read about the dress sale.*

On the imitation task only accuracy was scored since frequency was supplied. On the production tasks both accuracy and frequency were scored by obligatory occasion.

All four production tasks were compared to get a global impression of whether the simple past or the past progressive was acquired earlier. Variation in task performance was carefully considered and turned out to be quite interesting.

Overall the results of the production tasks showed the simple past to be both more accurate and more frequent than the past progressive, strongly supporting its earlier acquisition. This can be seen in Figures 2 to 11. Figures 2 and 3 show frequency results and all the rest show accuracy results.

As can be seen in Figures 2 and 3 the only exceptions to the rule of greater simple past than past progressive frequency was on the *ask about* task. I will return to that below. Another interesting variation of frequency

Figures 2 and 3 are based on mean number of occurrences. PP stands for past progressive; SP for simple past.

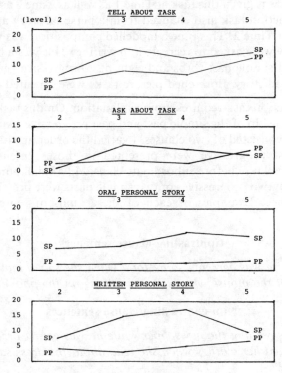

FIGURE 2. *Production frequency, Time 1*

was that three of the four production tasks show a U-shaped curve for past progressive learning at Time 1. That is, on the highest proficiency level, 5, and on the lowest, 2, the past progressive was close in frequency to the simple past. That is seen in the way the lines connecting the levels come together at level 2 and at level 5. By contrast, the simple past and past progressive are widely separate on level 2 at Time 2 (seen in Figure 3). Just five weeks after the first testing the simple past was strongly favoured over the past progressive by these low proficiency learners. This suggested to me that the impression that some researchers have that the past progressive is learned easily may be based on an early stage of acquisition where *intra*language transfer is going on because of the ease of learning of the present progressive. Learners may try to use it as the unmarked past before discovering the simple past.

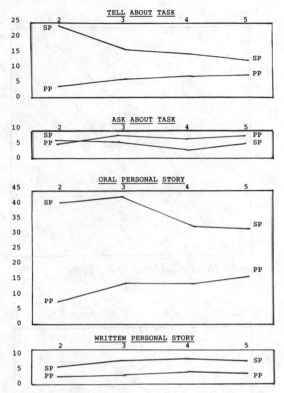

FIGURE 3. *Production frequency, Time 2*

The accuracy results can be found in Figures 4–11. They show that the simple past was almost always produced more accurately than the past progressive. It wasn't until level 5 that past progressive accuracy nearly equalled or exceeded simple past accuracy with any regularity. This occurred on the two story telling tasks shown in Figures 9 and 11. On the writing task, Figure 11, past progressive accuracy was higher than simple past accuracy from level 3 on. Significantly, at level 5 on this task, simple past accuracy actually decreased 16% from Time 1 accuracy. I interpret this as an interaction in the learning of the simple past and past progressive. Apparently the sorting out of these two past tense aspects is not accomplished until a very advanced level of learning.

The results of other tasks helped to clarify what it is that is difficult

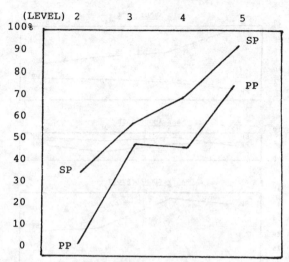

FIGURE 4. *Accuracy on the Tell About task, Time 1*

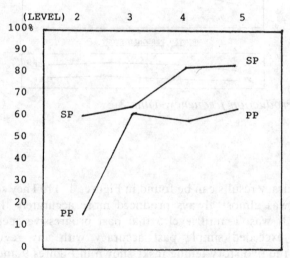

FIGURE 5. *Accuracy on the Tell About task, Time 2*

about the past progressive, that causes it to be learned so late. The strongest evidence of what causes the past progressive to be learned late came from the imitation task. Examples of the most accurately imitated sentences are given in Table 2.

The past progressive was significantly more accurate than the simple

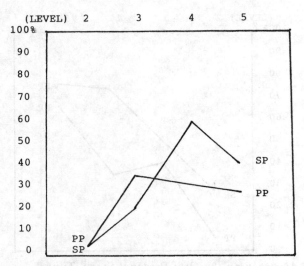

FIGURE 6. *Accuracy on the Ask About task, Time 1*

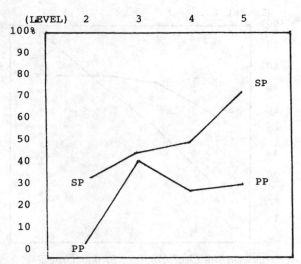

FIGURE 7. *Accuracy on the Ask About task, Time 2*

past when it occurred in the first clause position in a sentence as in the first example of contrasting clause sentences in Table 2.

1   *Louie's wife was carrying some food when she saw a mouse.*

In that order the scene-setting past progressive was mentioned before the simple past so that events were roughly chronological. In the opposite

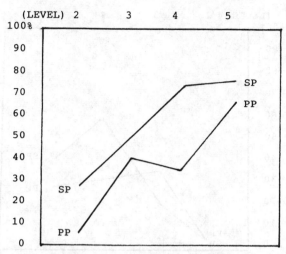

FIGURE 8. *Accuracy on the Oral Personal Story, Time 1*

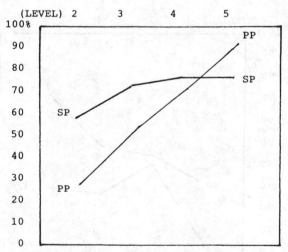

FIGURE 9. *Accuracy on the Oral Cartoon Story, Time 2*

order, with the simple past in the first clause and the past progressive in the second, what occurred first was mentioned second; i.e.:

2   *She forgot about the mouse when she was talking on the phone.*

Another discourse conditioned result was found in the non-contrasting clause condition where both clauses were simple past or both were past

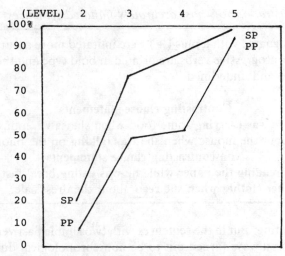

FIGURE 10. *Accuracy on the Written Personal Story, Time 1*

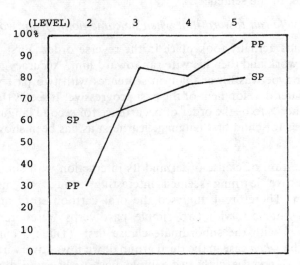

FIGURE 11. *Accuracy on the Written Nasreddin Story, Time 2*

progressive. Two past progressive clauses in one sentence were imitated with greater accuracy than two simple past clauses, an example of which is:

3 *Louie was reading when he was eating breakfast.*

The reason for this is that there is no need to order two past progressive verbs chronologically since they represent overlapping events such as

TABLE 2. *Illustrations of most accurately imitated sentences*

Sentences designated with a plus (+) were imitated more accurately in each pair. The past progressive verbs are printed in bold type and the simple past verbs are bold and underlined.

Contrasting clause statements
+ Louie's wife **was carrying** some food when she **saw** a mouse.
She **forgot** about the mouse when she **was talking** on the phone.
Non-contrasting clause statements
+ Louie **was reading** the paper while he **was eating** breakfast.
She **changed her clothes when she read** about the dress sale.

---

reading and eating. But in the sentences with two simple past verbs the order of presentation always turned out to be non-chronological due to the fact that the main clause always preceded the subordinate clause on this task. For example, in the sentence

4 *Louie's wife ran toward him when he came home from work*,

the two events actually took place in the reverse order. First Louie came home from work and then his wife ran toward him. Accuracy on sentences of the latter type was lower than on sentences with two past progressives despite the later development of the past progressive. It seems that the order of mention needs to be the order of occurrence for second language learners just as it does for child first language learners, as has been shown by Clark (1970).

The question of clause order and its interaction with simple past and past progressive learning seemed interesting enough to merit further investigation. Therefore I analysed the oral cartoon story at Time 2 to discover if sentences with two simple past verbs were ordered chronologically, i.e. with the subordinate clause first. (Table 3 contains these results.) In the *when* case in the third group down it was overwhelmingly the case that in sentences with two simple past verbs subordinate clauses appeared before main clauses. Two such sentences produced by subjects were

1 *When Louie came back from his work, his wife went out rapidly*

and

2 *When Louie came home, his wife seemed to run to him.*

The past progressive appeared much less commonly in two-clause

TABLE 3. *Patterns of clause production*

Clause 1, 2		Level 2	Level 3	Level 4	Level 5 Time 1	Time 2
1	When PP,SP	3	7	9	3	3
	While PP,SP	0	0	11	2	3
2	When PP,SP	2	2	1	0	1
	While PP,SP	0	0	2	1	1
3	When SP,SP	20	13	25	14	14
	While SP,SP	0	0	7	0	0
4	When SP,PP	0	5	3	0	0
	While SP,PP	0	0	2	0	0
5	SP *when* PP	1	0	0	0	0
	SP *while* PP	0	0	6	0	0
6	PP *when* SP	1	0	8	5	13
	PP *while* SP	0	0	0	0	0
7	PP *when* PP	0	0	1	0	2
	PP *while* PP	0	0	1	1	1
8	SP *when* SP	1	0	2	4	2
	SP *while* SP	1	0	0	1	0

sentences. And discourse function appeared to be what was conditioning this; subjects in this experiment used the past progressive mainly in single clause sentences that occurred predominantly in the very first sentence of a narrative. In the oral cartoon stories, the average number of past progressives used per subject in the first sentence position increased from 2 on level 2, to 3 on level 3, to 4½ on level 4, to 5 on level 5. The second and the last sentence also had notable amounts of past progressive but far less than the first sentence. This finding concurs with Labov (1972) in which he reported a similarly high incidence of past progressive use in the first sentence of narratives of inner city native speakers. He also found that the last sentence or coda frequently brought the listener back to the beginning of the story with a past progressive.

Second language learners are obviously sensitive to the discourse function of the past progressive. Still another variation in the results of this experiment underscores this conclusion. On the *ask about* task the past progressive was more frequent than the simple past. This was the only task with greater past progressive frequency. Here subjects asked questions about pictures of which examiners gave them answers. In such limited two-utterance exchanges, past progressive use is apparently easier for learners. With so little pressure to maintain the 'thread of discourse' as it is called by Grimes (1975) they are much freer to use this aspect. Certainly the nature of the task, asking about pictures, lent itself to past progressive use, but what is interesting is that the same pictures, used to cue statements, elicited more simple past use.

What has been learned by putting together the pieces of the puzzle? First of all I would say that task variation has been invaluable in determining not only the order of acquisition of the simple past and past progressive but also the explanation for it; i.e. simple meaning and discourse function. The role of form cannot be denied, however, especially order: clause order and sentence order. An especially interesting form finding was that verbs that have irregular past tense forms were favoured in the simple past and in exactly inverse proportion were disfavoured in the past progressive. That is, two-thirds of all the verbs used in the simple past were irregular types and two-thirds of those used in the past progressive were regular types. Apparently it was hard for learners to change from *ran* to *was running*; some came up with *ranning*. Another interesting form result is shown in Figure 12. Accuracy of usage of irregular type verbs alternated between the simple past and past progressive across levels.

In general we have seen that form, meaning and discourse function (or, more simply, form and function) are interdependent modules in second

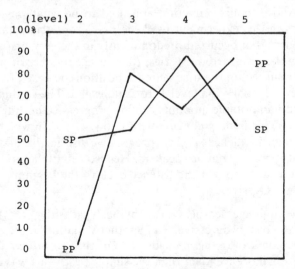

FIGURE 12. *Accuracy of irregular verbs, Time 2: past progressive (PP) and simple past (SP)*

language acquisition. In this experiment I have shown that variation in the learning of the progressive depends upon the tense and is conditioned by discourse function. The learner's need to order events clearly in time has constrained progressive learning in the past.

It has been necessary to utilise a macro-linguistic approach to understand the acquisition of the progressive in English, one which takes a broad look at form/function relationships and includes the role of the hearer. The sensitivity of second language learners to the need for chronological ordering in narratives reflects their own needs as listeners in discourse.

This interedependent relationship of form and function in second language learning could be compared with Einstein's general theory of the relativity of time and space. Einstein succeeded in separating the share of the observer and the share of external reality in the things we see happen. He pointed out that the motion of the observer changes perception. The gravitational field of the sun, as observer, for example, bends the light of stars.

I have tried to show in this chapter the relativity of form and function learning. Discourse, especially the role of the hearer/observer, can 'bend' the relationship of form and function. We have seen that progressive learnability varies from the present to the past tense because the progressive in the past has a marked discourse function, that of supplying background information, in relation to the simple past which sequences the more important foreground events. One of the implications of this research is that meaning and function differences probably underlie much additional *intra*lingual learning variation. Another implication is that markedness theory can be useful in explaining this variation through its contrast of core (more natural and useful) vs. peripheral grammar.

Acknowledgement

I would like to thank Carlos Yorio, Miriam Eisenstein, Georgette Ioup, Carolyn Madden and Sue Gass for their helpful suggestions and comments.

References

BAILEY, N. and MADDEN, C. 1980, 'Beyond grammatical morphemes: The effect of function on form.' Paper presented at the 14th Annual TESOL Convention, San Francisco.

CLARKE, E., 1970, How children describe events in time. In F. D'ARCAIS & W. LEVELT (eds), *Advances in Psycholinguistics*. New York: American Elsevier.

ELLIS, R., 1986, *Understanding Second Language Acquisition*. Oxford: Oxford University Press.

FRITH, M. B., 1977, *A Study of Form and Function at Two Stages of Developing Interlanguages*. Bloomington, Indiana: Indiana University Linguistics Club.

GRIMES, J., 1975, *The Thread of Discourse*. New York: Mouton.

HAKUTA, K. 1985, *Mirror of Language: The Debate on Bilingualism*. New York: Basic Books.

HATCH, E. and WAGNER-GOUGH, J. 1976, Explaining sequence and variation in second language acquisition. In H. D. BROWN (ed.) *Papers in Second Language Acquisition* (Special issue *Language Learning*), 4, 39–57.

HATORI, H., TOSHIKAZU, T., ITOH, K., KANTANI, K., NODA, T., MURAI, M. and YAMAUCHI, Y., 1987, Acquisition of English tense and aspect: In the case of Japanese learners of English. Interlanguage Development Research Project, Report No. 1. Tokyo: Tokyo Gakugei University.

HOPPER, P., 1979, Aspect and foregrounding in discourse. In T. GIVÓN (ed.), *Syntax and Semantics, Vol. 12: Discourse and Syntax*. New York: Academic Press.

HOPPER, P. and THOMPSON, S. 1980, Transitivity in grammar and discourse, *Language*, 56, 251–99.

HUEBNER, T., 1985, *A Longitudinal Analysis of the Acquisition of English*. Ann Arbor: Karoma.

LABOV, W., 1972, *Language in the Inner City: Studies in the Black English Vernacular*. Philadelphia: University of Pennsylvania Press.

LARSEN-FREEMAN, D., 1976, ESL teacher speech input to the ESL Learners. *Workpapers in TESL*, UCLA.

LIGHTBOWN, P., 1983, Exploring relationships between developmental and instructional sequences in L2 acquisition. In H. SELIGER & M. LONG (eds), *Classroom Oriented Research in Second Language Acquisition*. Rowley, MA: Newbury House.

LONG, M. and SATO, C. 1983, Classroom foreigner talk discourse: Forms and functions of teachers' questions. In H. SELIGER & M. LONG (eds), *Classroom Oriented Research in Second Language Acquisition*. Rowley, MA: Newbury House.

OLSHTAIN, E., 1979, The acquisition of the English progressive: A case study of a seven-year old Hebrew speaker, *Working Papers in Bilingualism*, 18, 81–102.

RUTHERFORD, W., 1987, *Second Language Grammar: Learning and Teaching*. New York: Longman.

WAGNER-GOUGH, J., 1975, Comparative studies in second language learning. M.A. Thesis, UCLA.

WOISETSCHLAEGER, E., 1980, *A Semantic Theory of the English Auxiliary System*. Bloomington, Indiana: Indiana University Linguistics Club.

8 The effect of emotional investment on L2 production

MIRIAM R. EISENSTEIN
ROBIN J. STARBUCK
New York University

As research in second language variation has progressed, it has become increasingly apparent that a number of factors can contribute to variability. The purpose of this chapter is to explore the possible influence of emotional investment on learners' interlanguage production.

Many researchers have noted that consciousness of linguistic form during second language production is an important factor in explaining variability. Both Tarone (1979) and Krashen (1982) claim that the more conscious a second language learner is of linguistic form, the more variability is to be found in her production. On the other hand, when the learner is more relaxed and less consciously concerned about performance, less variability is expected.

Tarone, in her landmark 1979 paper 'Interlanguage as chameleon', claimed that a formal style of speaking in a second language involved greater attention to form than the vernacular and extended Labov's earlier claim about L1 (Labov, 1970) to predict greater instability in formal as compared to informal L2 speech. More recently, theorists, including Tarone herself, have realised that variation cannot be accounted for by conscious attention to form alone. Sato (1985) has noted that variation in interlanguage cannot be determined simply on the basis of style or formality. Tarone (1982) reported that sometimes someone will do better on one grammatical item and worse on another in one task and then the reverse will occur in a different task, so that task and some aspect of syntax—perhaps complexity—must be considered when variation is observed. Task-based variation was also found by Dickerson (1975) in a study of the phonology of Japanese learners.

Huebner (1983) conducted a one-year longitudinal study of the inter-language production of an adult Hmong speaker acquiring English in a natural setting without formal instruction. In his analysis of the article system, he observed form–function relationships and concluded that there were two strategies being used: (1) the gradual elimination of a given form from one environment after another until the use of that form had ceased almost completely and (2) a form which had been used in a limited environment suddenly being used in a more general environment. Huebner (1985) argued that grammatical development is not only nonlinear but is also revealing of underlying cognitive processes. Godfrey (1980) studied the use of tense markers by Spanish and Japanese English learners and found variation based on first language background, difficulty of linguistic context, discourse context, learners' proficiency level and specific tokens used.

Wolfram (1985) reported on the tense marking of sixteen Vietnamese speakers learning English as a second language. He demonstrated that the analysis of tense marking in terms of higher-level language organisation must take into account surface constraints if it hopes to provide a valid, empirically based account of tense marking alternation in interlanguage. Variation in past tense use in narrative discourse was also studied by Ellis (1987). He found that past tense variability based on planning existed for regular past and copula, but little shifting took place in irregular past.

Douglas & Selinker (1987) in a study of discourse markers used by an American and a non-native teaching assistant suggest that discourse domain and activity type be added to the list of factors which appear to contribute to variation. Schachter (1986), in her discussion of syntactic variation in a learner's interlanguage, states, 'If differences in situational requirements produce variability in learner performance, then that variability is also a result of the interaction of the learner's processing system with situational demands.' Schachter also notes that different syntactic strategies condi-tioned by the discourse function of an utterance can result in variation. Young (1987) found that the following factors influence syntactic vari-ability: context of situation, stage of acquisition, linguistic environment and communicative redundancy.

Lantolf & Khanji (1983) studied second language learners whose degree of emotional investment in topic correlated with variation in accuracy. In this study, one learner spoke especially freely when he became emotionally involved in the topic (religion) and produced data that contained more errors than language elicited when talking on less invested topics. These findings are provocative but are based on limited data.

This study considers whether investment in topic does in fact impair accuracy of L2 production and examines aspects of discourse produced under this condition as revealed by the use of verbs and tenses in a learner's output.

Procedure

We consider the grammatical accuracy of verbs in second language learners' oral production in light of their investment in the topic under discussion. We have chosen to study the verb system because it is developmentally central to the language acquisition process and can potentially reveal variability at different stages of acquisition.

Correctness in formulation as well as usage was taken into account. Data came from open-ended discussions with participants described below. When questions arose, the intended meanings that the participants tried to convey through the verbs and tenses they chose were confirmed in *post hoc* interviews with them.

The subjects were ten advanced learners, chosen from an ESL class in a New York City university. The college's advanced placement of these students was confirmed by their performance on a cloze procedure, previously used by Eisenstein & Hopper (1983). Background information showed a range of socioeconomic status from working to upper class. Nine countries and six languages were represented by the learners along with a range of experience in foreign language acquisition.

The identification of invested and uninvested topics was accomplished as follows: participants listed (in writing) five areas that they cared a lot about and were interested in discussing, five areas that people talk about which they personally don't find very interesting, and five topics about which they had neutral feelings. On a different day prior to the study, subjects were asked to rate each of their 15 topics on a series of scales to further elucidate their feelings and reactions, and the topic that was most representative of each category was selected. For each subject, one high and one low investment topic were chosen based on his or her relative ranking of the topics elicited earlier. Thus, different topics were used with each individual. (Two subjects were dropped from the study because it later turned out that the topics they had listed as uninteresting were in fact topics they felt strongly about, but in a negative way.) The neutral topic was used to produce a writing sample. These written data will not be discussed in this chapter but will be explored at a later time.

Tape recordings were made of two ten-minute conversations with each one of the ten learners and the same native speaker; one conversation was on a high-investment topic and the other on a low-investment topic. The high-investment topic was presented first, since lower accuracy was expected under this condition. Thus, any drop in accuracy in invested conversation as compared with uninvested discourse would not be due to a speaker's greater fatigue. Order of topics was kept constant because of the small number of subjects in the study. The researcher opened the conversation with a simple request like, 'Tell me something about ...'. Interaction with the participant was limited as much as possible to minimise the extent of interlocutor influence on each subject. Occasionally the researcher brought the conversation back to the topic to maintain the 'high' or 'low' condition.

While some subjects spoke freely and needed little or no prompting, others required considerable prompting especially on the uninvested topic. This phenomenon varied considerably and seems to be idiosyncratic on the part of the participants. In general, all the participants had little difficulty conversing on the topics in which they had indicated a high interest. Some learners found it equally easy to talk on a topic that was not interesting to them, but others found this task quite challenging.

In view of Douglas & Selinker's (1987) findings, discourse domain needed to be accounted for. Therefore, subjects were asked *post hoc* how much they knew about each of the topics which they had discussed. (This check was done several weeks after the interviews were completed.) Based on the information given to us, we can say that all topics used in both conditions were familiar to the participants.

After the tasks were completed, a final meeting with each of the subjects was held to elicit comments regarding how they felt during each task. At this time any uncertainty about a subject's intended meaning in the oral interview data was clarified.

Data analysis

In analysing the taped interviews, a few minutes of tape were allowed to elapse before the transcription of a five-minute conversation sample. This was done to control for undue tension during the warm-up stage. Five minutes of conversation were then transcribed, and this procedure was repeated for each of the two topics used in the oral interviews.

Every verb in the transcripts was then listed on a chart with 'page and line' to show its location in the conversation. In addition to background data and cloze scores for each subject, the following information was coded for each verb:

1. *Tense used*—the tense attempted by the speaker was listed and coded for whether or not it was one of the tenses whose use would be appropriate for the context in which it appeared.

2. *Meaning of tense needed*—the grammatical meaning of the tense appropriate for the context was coded, based on the categories developed by Quirk *et al.* (1985).

3. *Lexical choice of verb*—the specific verb chosen by the speaker was coded for whether or not it made sense in the context in which it appeared.

4. *Meaning of verb needed*—the semantic category of verb needed for the context was coded, again based on Quirk *et al.* (1985). (The tense and verb categories described in 1, 2 and 4 are listed in the appendix.)

5. *Formation of verb*—each verb was coded for whether its grammatical form was produced accurately. (It was possible for a speaker to make a correct lexical choice and attempt a correct tense but to have a problem in this area.)

6. *Person of verb*—verbs were coded for first, second or third person, singular or plural.

7. *Clause type*—each verb was coded for the clause in which it appeared: affirmative, negative, interrogative, imperative, negative interrogative, negative imperative.

8. *Repetition*—each verb was coded for whether or not it was a repetition and if so, whether or not it corrected a previous error.

Quantitative results were computed using SPSS, version X. The total number of tokens coded was 1,906. The number of verbs produced under the two conditions was not dramatically different. In the uninvested (not emotionally invested) condition 979 verbs were produced by the ten learners compared to 927 in the invested topic. These figures include repetitions. There were 78 repetitions in the uninvested condition (7.9% of the verbs produced) and 70 repetitions in the invested condition (6.9%).

TABLE 1. *t-tests for uninvested and invested conditions**

	Invested %	sd	Uninvested %	sd	t value	d.f.	p
Total correct	69.9	8.8	92.7	3.1	− 7.49	9	0.000
Lexical	89.0	5.1	98.7	1.2	− 5.77	9	0.000
Tense attempted	77.6	2.5	95.9	2.9	− 7.19	9	0.000
Tense form	74.1	7.8	93.5	2.7	− 7.51	9	0.000
Repetitions	6.9	6.0	7.9	5.1	− 0.55	9	0.594

* These t-tests are based on aggregated data so that each subject is weighted equally.

T-tests were computed for the following variables under the two conditions: total verbs correct, lexical choice, tense attempted and tense form. For each of these variables, learners scored a higher percentage correct under the uninvested condition. Using a two-tailed probability score, these differences were highly significant at below the 0.001 level. While there were slightly more repetitions in the uninvested condition, these were not statistically significant (see Table 1).

Interestingly, the standard deviations show that there was greater variation in the invested condition. This was a surprise, since Labov and Tarone had both predicted increased variation in more monitored speech, and we had expected less monitoring when emotional investment was present. If the amount of repetition is an indication of monitoring, there is not a great difference under the two conditions. For purpose of control, accuracy rates were checked for all the data without the repetitions. The relationships reported remained virtually the same.

In terms of monitoring as measured by repetitions (which include self corrections), it would be illuminating to explain the lack of distinction under invested and uninvested conditions. One possible explanation is that because the invested topic was discussed first, monitoring was higher than normal while less monitoring in the uninvested discussion might have been caused by the fatigue of the speaker. This could have obscured a potential difference under the two conditions.

Another possible explanation is that the subjects in this study are 'monitor over-users' (Krashen, 1981). Since all interviews were conducted with the same professor from their university, the students could have been monitoring more than they would under other circumstances, regardless of investment in topic. An explanation that was suggested by Van Lier (personal communication) is that the repetitions in the two domains may have been serving different functions and thus are not necessarily comparable. For example, it is possible for a repetition to be a strategy for correction or emphasis; alternatively it could serve as a filler to provide the speaker with more time for planning.

Finally, it is possible that repetition is not a good measure of monitoring at all for these learners. Monitoring could be taking place at an earlier stage of processing so that the language produced under the two conditions would already reflect a difference in monitoring. If this were the case, greater monitoring under the uninvested condition could account for the significantly higher accuracy level observed.

The data on clause type used by speakers reveals that there were significant differences under the two conditions (chi square $= 17.9$, d.f. $= 5$, $p < 0.003$). There were more affirmatives in the invested condition (84.6%) as compared with the uninvested condition (78.3%). Interrogatives were used less in the invested conversation (13.7% vs. 18.2%) and negatives followed the same pattern (1% vs. 1.5%) as did imperatives (0.4% vs. 1.7%). The use of other clause types was very small (see Table 2). Since complexity as indicated by clause type was not greater in the invested condition, syntactic complexity does not appear to be a fruitful explanation for lower accuracy rates in invested conversation. Nevertheless, for purposes of control, the distribution of the other variables was recalculated for affirmative clauses only under the two conditions. The significance of other differences found when all clause types were included was not affected.

What accounted for the distribution of clause types under the two

TABLE 2. *Clause types in uninvested and invested conditions*

	Uninvested	Invested
Affirmative	767 (78.3%)	786 (84.8%)
Negative	15 (1.5%)	9 (1.0%)
Question	178 (18.2%)	127 (13.7%)
Imperative	17 (1.7%)	4 (0.4%)
Negative imperative	1 (0.1%)	1 (0.1%)
Negative question	1 (0.1%)	0

conditions? Perhaps they reflect different communicative goals on the part of the speaker. Greater reliance on affirmative statements and fewer negative ones might be an indication of more confidence on the part of the speaker in the invested condition. Fewer questions might reveal less focus on the opinions and ideas of the listener.

Person of verb was also significantly different in invested as compared with uninvested dialogue (chi square = 63.386, d.f = 5, $p < 0.0001$). There was more use of the first person singular in the uninvested condition (see Table 3). This was also true for the second person singular. Third

TABLE 3. *Person of verb*

	Uninvested	Invested
First singular	348 (35.5%)	273 (29.4%)
Second singular	142 (14.5%)	71 (7.7%)
Third singular	337 (34.4%)	320 (34.5%)
First plural	21 (2.1%)	42 (4.5%)
Second plural	1 (0.1%)	—
Third plural	130 (13.3%)	221 (23.8%)

TABLE 4. *Tenses used*

	Uninvested	Invested
Simple present	584 (59.9%)	500 (55.4%)
Present progressive	12 (1.2%)	24 (2.6%)
Present perfect	—	1 (0.1%)
Past	119 (12.2%)	110 (12.2%)
Past progressive	7 (0.7%)	11 (1.2%)
Past perfect	—	2 (0.2%)
Will/shall	14 (1.4%)	13 (1.4%)
Be going to	9 (0.9%)	5 (0.6%)
Will + progressive	1 (0.1%)	—
Modal present	65 (6.7%)	62 (6.9%)
Modal past	—	5 (0.6%)
Modal future	—	1 (0.1%)
Infinitive	70 (7.2%)	79 (8.8%)
Passive present	1 (0.1%)	5 (0.6%)
Passive past	2 (0.2%)	2 (0.2%)
Base form	76 (7.8%)	78 (8.6%)
Imperative	15 (1.5%)	4 (0.4%)

person plural use was highest for the invested condition. This seems to indicate a more personal or direct kind of interaction for the uninvested topic.

The general distribution of tenses used (or attempted) was significantly different under the two conditions (see Table 4). Present simple was used to a somewhat greater extent in the uninvested conversation as was the future with 'going to' and imperative. In the invested condition there was slightly more use of the present and past progressives, infinitives, and past modals. There was minimal use across the two conditions (less than five tokens) of present and past perfect, will + progressive, modal futures, and passive past.

A chi-square test showed the distribution of tenses under the two conditions significant at the < 0.03 level (chi square = 30.271, d.f. = 17). Speakers used a slightly wider range of tenses in the invested condition. This might be a sign of less monitoring and/or greater risk-taking. If a speaker who cares about a topic is thus encouraged to take greater linguistic risks, a lower accuracy rate could result. This would be consistent with Beebe's (1983) findings.

Tense needed based on context was found to be a very significant factor in the conversations under the two conditions (chi square = 65.441, d.f. = 16, $p < 0.000$). This seems to be an additional indication that for the ten speakers in this study, investment results in a difference in discourse style.

When we try to match the tenses needed with those actually used under the two conditions, we see that learners are more successful under the uninvested condition. While this is not surprising in view of total scores on correctness, it is interesting to note that choice of tense was part of the problem (see Table 5).

Meaning of tenses needed with and without emotional investment was significantly different (chi-square = 74.571, d.f. = 27, $p < 0.0001$). This showed more past definite state, past definite event and past definite temporary needed under the invested condition. The uninvested condition required more present state meaning for tenses.

Meanings of verbs were also significantly different under invested and uninvested conditions (chi square = 81.257, d.f. = 33, $p < 0.0001$). The five most common categories of verb meaning in the data and the extent of their distribution appear in Table 6.

Results of the cloze test ranged from 77% to 94% correct with a mean

TABLE 5. *A comparison of tense needed and tense used for five tenses*

Nature of Errors	Uninvested		Invested	
	needed	used	needed	used
Present simple	585 (59.8%)	584 (59.9%)	456 (49.2%)	500 (55.4%)
Present progressive	11 (1.1%)	12 (1.2%)	5 (0.5%)	24 (2.6%)
Past	117 (12.0%)	119 (12.2%)	166 (17.9%)	110 (12.2%)
Will/shall	19 (1.9%)	14 (1.4%)	21 (2.3%)	13 (1.4%)
Infinitive	70 (72%)	70 (7.2%)	75 (8.1%)	79 (8.8%)

TABLE 6. *Most common categories of verb meanings*

Meaning of verb	Uninvested	Invested
Stative	255 (26.0%)	272 (29.4%)
Activity	133 (13.6%)	133 (14.4%)
Intellectual state	132 (13.5%)	113 (12.2%)
Performative*	53 (5.4%)	55 (5.9%)
Emotive	53 (5.4%)	45 (4.9%)

* This category is referred to as 'speech act' in *A Comprehensive Grammar of the English Language* by Quirk *et al.* (1985) but since 'speech act' has a broader meaning in applied linguistics, 'performative' is a more descriptive term.

of 82.42 and sd of 5.57. The cloze scores did not significantly correlate with performance on the oral interviews. This could be an indication that oral accuracy is a different factor, or not one strong enough to emerge as significant with only ten subjects. It is also possible that since all speakers are advanced learners, scores on the cloze are all relatively high. The oral performance of learners with a greater range of ability might correlate more strongly with this cloze measure. At the very least, the cloze scores do provide independent verification of the subjects' advanced English level.

Conclusion

It is clear from the results of this study that investment in topic correlates with many kinds of differences in the discourse produced by second language speakers. Accuracy rate was significantly lower when subjects conversed on emotionally loaded topics. The extent to which cognitive load is increased by emotional investment and could potentially cause production errors can only be inferred from the data. An additional explanation for accuracy rates is indicated by the different discourse patterns observed, including clause types, verb tenses attempted by learners in the invested conditions and their meanings, and lexical choices. The broader range of tenses attempted by learners in the invested condition may be indicative of greater risk-taking and could contribute to an understanding of the lower accuracy rates.

There were some unexpected findings. Repetitions were not significantly correlated with investment in topic, so that the role of monitoring requires further investigation. In addition, the greater variation that appeared in the invested condition seems contrary to the expectations of Labov and Tarone discussed above. While a study limited to only ten subjects cannot be considered definitive, the notion of variation as it relates to formality, emotional investment, and conscious attention to speech must be evaluated more critically.

In this study, formality was controlled since all conversations took place in a university setting with a student (subject) speaking to a professor. Labov's suggestion that 'vernacular' speech can be elicited by an emotionally loaded question such as one that asks a speaker to relate a near-death experience appears to collapse what may be two independent dimensions—those of formality and emotion.

The data presented here do provide verification of Lantolf and Khanji's finding that emotional investment negatively affects accuracy and begin to elucidate the nature of discourse differences conditioned by such investment. Additional research with a larger number of subjects at different levels of proficiency and in a variety of social settings will provide more information on how investment interacts with other factors that emerge when variation is found.

Appendix: Categories of verbs and tenses

Tense used	Meaning of tense	* Meaning of verb
	A. PRESENT TIME	1—Accomplishment
		2—Activity
PRES (simple) = 01	01. State	3—Agentive
	02. Single event	4—Aspectual
	03. Habitual	5—Bodily sensation

Tense used	Meaning of tense	* Meaning of verb
PRES PROGressive = 02	04. Temporary	
	05. Temporary habit	6—Causative
	B. PAST TIME	7—Coercive
PRES PERFect = 03	06. State up to present time	8—Comparison
		11—Emotive
	07. Indefinite event(s)	13—Existential
	08. Habit up to present time	15—Goings-on
		17—Influencing
	09. With present results	18—Intellectual state
PRES PERF PROG = 04	10. Temporary state up to present time	19—Locative
	11. Temporary habit up to present time	20—Making
		21—Measure
	12. Temporary, with present result	22—Momentary Act
		23—Owning
PAST (simple) = 05	13. Definite state	27—Perception
	14. Definite event	28—Permission
	15. Definite habit	29—Placing
PAST PROGressive = 06	16. Definite temporary	30—Posture
PAST PERFect = 07	17. Past before past time (event)	31—Process
		33—Result
	18. State up to past time	35—Speech act
PAST PERF PROG = 08	19. Temporary state up to past time	36—Stance
		37—Stative
	C. FUTURE TIME	38—Suasive
WILL|SHALL = 09	20. Future time (neutral)	39—Transitional
BE GOING TO = 10	21. Future time (arising from present time)	40—Volitional
PRES PROG = 11	22. Future time (plan or arrangement)	**MODALS:**
		41—Advice
SIMPLE PRES FOR FUT = 12	23. Future time (as fact)	42—Necessity
WILL|SHALL + PROG = 13	24. Future time (as matter of course)	43—Future
		44—Ought
	25 Future time (temporary)	
WILL|SHALL + PERF = 14	26. Past in future time	45—Hypothetical
		46—Ability
	D. MISCELLANEOUS	
MODALS (PRES) = 15	27. Modals—present	**AUXILIARIES:**
MODALS (PAST) = 16	28. Modals—past	47—Have to
MODALS (FUTURE) = 18	29. Modals—future	48—Can
INFINITIVES = 19	30. Infinitives	49—May, Might
PASSIVE (PRES) = 20	31. Passive—present	
PASSIVE (PAST) = 21	32. Passive—past	
PASSIVE (FUTURE) = 22	33. Passive—future	50—Cond. passive

---

* Missing numbers indicate categories which did not appear in the data.

References

BEEBE, L. 1983, Risk-taking and the language learner. In H. SELIGER & M. LONG (eds), *Classroom Oriented Research in Second Language Acquisition*. Rowley, MA: Newbury House.

DICKERSON, L., 1975, Interlanguage as a system of variable rules, *TESOL Quarterly*, 9, 401–7.

DOUGLAS, D. and SELINKER, L., 1987, 'NS vs. NNS TA's: Markedness in discourse domains.' Paper presented at the 8th World AILA Congress, Sydney.

EISENSTEIN, M. and HOPPER, S., 1983, The intelligibility of English dialects for adult learners of English as a second language, *Indian Journal of Applied Linguistics*, 9, 43–52.

ELLIS, R., 1987, Interlanguage variability in narrative discourse: Style shifting in the use of the past tense, *Studies in Second Language Acquisition*, 9(1), 1–20.

GODFREY, D., 1980, A discourse analysis of tense in monologues. In D. LARSEN-FREEMAN (ed.), *Discourse Analysis in Second Language Research*. Rowley, MA: Newbury House.

HUEBNER, T., 1983, Linguistic systems and linguistic change in an interlanguage, *Studies in Second Language Acquisition*, 6(1), 33–53.

——, 1985, System and variability in interlanguage syntax, *Language Learning*, 35(2), 141–63.

KRASHEN, S., 1981, *Second Language Acquisition and Second Language Learning*. Oxford: Pergamon Press.

——, 1982, *Principles and Practice in Second Language Acquisition*. Oxford: Pergamon Press.

LABOV, W., 1970, The study of language in its social context, *Studium Generale*, 23, 30–87.

LANTOLF, J. P. and KHANJI, R., 1983, Non-linguistic parameters of interlanguage performance: Expanding the research paradigm. In J. MORREALL (ed.), *The Ninth LACUS Forum*. Columbia, SC: Hornbeam Press.

QUIRK, R., GREENBAUM, S., LEECH, G., and SVARTVIK, J., 1985, *A Comprehensive Grammar of the English Language*. New York: Longman.

SATO, C., 1985, Task variation in interlanguage phonology. In S. GASS & C. MADDEN (Eds), *Input in Second Language Acquisition: Series on Issues in Second Language Research*. Rowley, MA: Newbury House.

SCHACHTER, J., 1986. In search of systematicity in interlanguage production, *Studies in Second Language Acquisition*, 8(2), 119–33.

TARONE, E., 1979, Interlanguage as chameleon, *Language Learning*, 29(1), 181–91.

—— 1982, Systematicity and attention in interlanguage, *Language Learning*, 32(1), 69–84.

WOLFRAM, W., 1985, Variability in tense marking: A case for the obvious, *Language Learning*, 35(2), 229–53.

YOUNG, R., 1987, 'Variation and the interlanguage hypothesis.' Paper presented at the Second Language Acquisition Circle, New York University, NY., May, 1987.

Section Four:
Aptitude and Capacity

9   Exceptional second language learners

LORAINE K. OBLER
CUNY Graduate School

Among the sizeable monolingual population of the United States, the relatively few exceptionally *good* second language learners stand out; Selinker (1972) has estimated them to be perhaps 5% of the population. In bilingual classrooms and TEFL courses, exceptionally *poor* second language learners stand out as well. The question of how to account for these extremes in L2 learning has interested both teachers and theoreticians of L2 learning and acquisition, especially since virtually all humans seem to acquire their first language with relative ease and success.

Research to date addressing this question of who the exceptionally talented or untalented L2 learners are has generally been within the psychological framework, probing factors of attitude, cognitive style, and personality more generally. After reviewing briefly the approaches and findings of that literature, I will suggest a new framework for consideration of the question, that of the neurolinguist.

Most of the psychologically motivated research has depended on some sort of factor analytic paradigm. Learners along a broad continuum of talent are tested on a set of tests or evaluated on a set of characteristics, and then the component dimensions that predict which of the learners have been most or least successful are abstracted. For example, work by Snow & Hoefnagel-Hohle (1979) and Day (1979) focused on adult L2 acquisition; work by Vihman (1982), Peters (1981), Pienemann (1980) and Wong-Fillmore (1979) on child L2 learners suggests that both *language* factors, ranging on an *analytic* as compared to a *Gestalt* dimension, and *personality* factors contribute to determine who will be a successful learner or acquirer. Indeed similar studies suggest that the talented learner and the talented acquirer will not have the same psychological or psycholinguistic make up. As Gardner (1960) reported, two relatively independent factors predict second language success, the first characterised by those L2 skills taught specifically in the classroom, and the second characterised by L2 acquired through interacting with members of the target language community. For many individuals, of course, both learning and acquisition are in progress simultaneously. For example, the immigrant child learning English in the community as well as in the classroom is learning both formally and informally; the US college student of German who spends a year abroad has both formal and informal language experience. Indeed, like most individuals, those I will be concerned with in this chapter are neither purely L2 learners nor purely L2 acquirers. My claim is that within a group with similar opportunities to both learn and acquire an L2, some individuals will stand out as particularly good or particularly poor learners/acquirers.

Even within language abilities, factors have been abstracted that appear empirically and plausibly to associate with L2 learning abilities. Snow & Hoefnagel-Hohle (1979) demonstrated that there are learners for whom a factor loading on vocabulary and 'grammar' skills showed improvement, and others for whom phonological/oral skills developed independently.

The two language aptitude batteries—the Modern Language Aptitude Test and the Pimsleur Language Aptitude Battery—took a similar approach, giving learners a diversity of specifically language-related tests and discovering four dimensions that appear to contribute to successful L2 learning:

1. *phonetic coding ability*: the ability to associate sounds with unfamiliar symbols;

2. *grammatical sensitivity*: a skill or aptitude for the learning of linguistic rules;

3. *rote memory*: the ability to store and retrieve verbal information which may or may not be meaningful, and

4. *inductive language ability*: the ability to infer language rules for complex linguistic material.

It is important to point out that they determined that some components of language aptitude appear to be relatively unchangeable through formal training, thus indicating either a biological substrate for components of L2 learning and acquisition, or possibly a set of cognitive styles predisposing the learner towards effective or less effective processes to be employed in L2 acquisition. In particular, it would appear that phonetic coding and grammatical sensitivity may be more dependent upon individual aptitude in these areas than upon instruction. (Carroll, 1983, cites pertinent studies by Pike, 1959, and Politzer & Weiss, 1969.)

L2 research in cognitive style comes closest to treating neuro-psychological questions, indicating that the left and right hemispheres may be differentially involved in learning an L2, as has elsewhere been demonstrated when comparing lateral dominance for language between bilinguals and monolinguals (Albert & Obler, 1978). Hartnett (1976) studied the direction of lateral eye movement indirectly while two groups of college students were responding to questions, a technique believed to give a measure of contralateral hemisphere activation (Bakan, 1969). In Hartnett's study, those students who were more successful in learning L2 through the traditional teach-and-drill classroom approach were called 'deductive learners', while those who achieved more success while enrolled in a class emphasising L2 conversational skills were termed 'inductive learners', which led Hartnett to speculate that deductive L2 learners are more likely to utilise left hemisphere based processes in L2 learning than students who prefer an inductive style. *Successful* L2 learning *or* acquisition, I maintain, requires *both* sorts of abilities.

What reasons do we have to believe that the individual differences in L2 acquisition should be based on differences in the brain substrate for language? For one, despite a century of mapping out the similarities in human brain organisation for language that found it centred in the left hemisphere, it is also clear that even in monolinguals, there are individual differences in the anatomical structure of the brain. There are significant differences between people in the overall size of different areas of the brain (Geschwind & Levitsky, 1968), and in the configuration of the cerebral arteries that feed them (Whitaker & Selnes, 1979). There is enormous individual variation in the cellular cytoarchitectonic areas of the cortex, especially in the speech areas (Galaburda *et al.*, 1978). In some cases these variations in organisation have been shown to be associated with differences in function (Galaburda & Kemper, 1979), although specific linguistic functions still seem to be localised to the same general areas in different people (Ojemann, 1983). Thus, studies of individual differences in brain organisation suggest a possible neuropsychological basis for the wide variability of individual differences in cognitive skills, including the ability to learn or acquire a second language.

How then can we study the neuropsychology of talented L2 acquisition or learning?

The goal of neuropsychological theory is to understand the relationship between human behaviour and the brain substrate underlying it. The neuropsychologist wants to know what is going on in the brain of an adult performing an activity, and also how the brain developed to permit that individual to perform the cognitive activity. The major technique for studying these relations has been to observe and analyse the deficient behaviours of the brain-damaged patient, and then to draw conclusions about normal activity. For example, if the aphasic brain-damaged patient has difficulty with production of speech but not with comprehension, then we conclude that production and comprehension are dissociable components in the healthy performance of speech/language abilities. If the child but not the adult recovers language fully after a severe left hemisphere lesion, we conclude that in the normal non-brain-damaged child the right hemisphere is able to take over language processing, but then this ability is lost some time in young adulthood.

This paradigm has been applied to some case studies of individuals with exceptional talents who became brain-damaged, but not to exceptionally good or poor L2 learners. Schweiger (1988), for example, reports on the several visual artists who lost the ability to draw three-dimensional figures, or changed from a linear style to a more abstract style after a stroke. Judd (1988) reviews the case of a composer who lost the ability to synthesise musical elements into a unified piece, and was no longer able to experience music affectively after a right hemisphere stroke.

In most instances such studies have not yet questioned whether the components of the ability discovered through brain-damage would be those of any normal person who spent some time in composing or painting, say, or whether they are components of the ability in the famous and highly skilled artist, which have either developed due to biological proclivities or to years of exercising the ability.

A second newer approach to the study of talents that I have developed with Deborah Fein in our book *The Exceptional Brain: Neuropsychology of Talents and Special Abilities* (Obler & Fein, 1988) reverses the standard neuropsychological methodology. Instead of looking at the components of deficient abilities against the background of spared abilities, we analyse the exceptional ability against the background of merely normal abilities in the prodigy, or less than normal abilities in the case of the *idiot savant*.

Gardner exemplifies this methodology in his book *Frames of Mind: A Theory of Multiple Intelligences* (1983). Gardner's point in that book was to demonstrate that the seven types of 'intelligence' he has isolated do exist as independent categories. One of the arguments he used to support his thesis was the fact of prodigies and *idiots savants*. If we have the reports of an autistic boy who can build sophisticated electrical devices (p. 214), or recall music (p. 121), or a 5-year-old girl such as Nadia who draws like a talented adolescent (p. 188), and these individuals have few or no other exceptional or even normal abilities, that is a good argument for the fact that the talents are isolated capabilities. This should be true even for other individuals in whom the abilities do not stand out so starkly, but rather are seen in the context of other normal abilities.

Smith (1983) demonstrates that calculating abilities can occur in *idiots savants*, as well as in apparently normal individuals, and even in mathematical geniuses such as Gauss and von Neumann. Had we only studied the mathematical geniuses with the skill, we might have spent a long time looking for the connection between mathematical genius and calculating ability. Once we recognise that some mathematical geniuses and some autistic children have exceptional calculating ability and others do not, then we can appreciate that calculating is probably an independent skill.

In addition to demonstrating the independence of the skills and talents, however, it is useful to conduct more detailed neuropsychological testing of prodigies and *idiots savants* in order to discover both the components of their talent, and also the other neuropsychological skills which may be dissociated from it or associated with it. The study method appears simple: one selects especially talented individuals and administers to them a comprehensive set of neuropsychological and neurolinguistic tests chosen to address one's hypotheses. I will turn to an example of such a case after consideration of the third possible approach.

The third important approach to neuropsychological study of talent is the approach indicated by Normal Geschwind before his untimely death in 1984 (Geschwind & Galaburda, 1985a,b,c). Geschwind observed that certain phenomena—including talents and a set relating more obviously to brain lateralisation, such as handedness and dyslexia—cluster in certain families. He theorised that foetal hormonal environment accounts for the unusual development of cortical connections in individuals in these families. In particular, he suggested that testosterone levels interact with the 'normal' development of the two hemispheres (i.e. the right hemisphere in advance of the left hemisphere), resulting in a different developmental pattern of the hemispheres. Cells 'destined' for one area of the brain, by this analysis, either end up elsewhere, or die off in patterns different from those that usually follow birth (Galaburda, 1983). These cellular divisions then would account for the talents as well as the disabilities linked in the family constellation, and should explain certain combinations of talent and disability, such as the dyslexics—or even as Meg Humes-Bartlo has reported (in press), poor second language learners, who are particularly good at mathematical or visual–spatial abilities.

Geschwind takes great pains to emphasise that his theory is not simply a deterministic one. Stating that a talent or disability is biologically or genetically based does not mean that it will develop regardless of the conditions in which a child grows up. Certain environmental factors are crucial for the manifestation of talent, as they are for the manifestation of disability (Geschwind, 1983). For talent at second language learning, for example, one needs of course to be *exposed* to a second language, and to have some motivation for learning it.

In order to test Geschwind's theory at this time, the initial technique is to analyse questionnaires administered to individuals with the talent in question and determine how often they show the cluster of related phenomena as compared to a group of controls who do not show talent. Such research reinforces Geschwind's observations of the cluster, but does not speak directly to the theory by which he explained it. To do that, one might start with post-mortem examinations of the brains of talented individuals, along the lines of those carried out on dyslexics by Galaburda (1983), which clearly demonstrated unusual cortical and sub-cortical cellular development in several dyslexic individuals. Diamond & Scheibel (1985) have discovered extended dendritic growth in the cells of Einstein's brain, for example.

In sum, in order to discover the brain–behaviour relationships underlying talent, then, we must follow several paths. We must study talented individuals whose talent has been modified (or not) as a result of circumscribed brain-damage in order to determine components of the talent and gross brain areas underlying them. We must analyse neuropsychological test results of healthy individuals in whom talents stand out beside other merely normal or poorer than normal performance, in order to see which cognitive abilities dissociate from the talent and disability as they relate to cerebral lateralisation and potentially to foetal and post-birth environment, and thus suggest genetic and biological features related to talent. And we must undertake post-mortem neuropathological analyses of talented individuals who would show unusual cell patterning, in order to see the neuroanatomical structures which serve as substrate to talent.

The study

By way of example, let us turn now to the most complete study I have carried out with Loriana Novoa and Deborah Fein: a study that uses the two approaches that can be used with healthy live individuals.

CJ, our subject, was selected via advertising for subjects in language departments of local universities and consulting with numerous colleagues. We required a subject who had learned several languages post-pubertally (and only one pre-pubertally), quickly and to native-like proficiency. Very few names were suggested; CJ was selected from amongst this group because he would be available for testing over the course of a semester. We interviewed native speakers of different languages that CJ speaks and asked them to evaluate CJ's abilities, accent and fluency. They confirm CJ's reports of his native-like abilities, including lack of foreign accent, and the ease and speed of his language acquisition.

We first interviewed CJ about his language learning history as well as general background. The interview included questions regarding his developmental milestones and growth, family history, school and academic performance, parental expectations and interactions, and the Geschwind cluster of neuro-immuno-endocrinological factors linked to left-handedness and exceptional abilities (Geschwind & Galaburda, 1985a,b,c). In addition, we asked him whether there was any other information related to his exceptional abilities in language that might help us better understand his talent.

CJ was a 29-year-old left-handed single Caucasian male who, at the time of testing, was a graduate student in education. He was a native speaker of English who grew up in a monolingual home. He does recall hearing some French spoken in one of the communities where he lived while growing up, and Latin was used in the church services he attended regularly in childhood. However, CJ's first true experience with a second language came at the age of 15 with formal instruction of French in high school. Because he excelled in French classes, CJ decided also to study German while in high school. In addition to two years of formal and traditional instruction in German, CJ also studied Spanish and Latin for one semester each during his early high school years.

In college, CJ majored in French language and literature and spent his junior year, at age 20, in France. A brief visit to Germany while studying in France evidently 'restored' the German he had studied during high school and CJ reports that just hearing the language spoken for a short time was enough for him to once again recover his lost fluency.

Upon graduation from college, CJ accepted a government position in Morocco where he reports learning Moroccan Arabic through both formal instruction and informal immersion. Although Moroccan Arabic was evidently more difficult for him than the Romance or Germanic languages as a result of the greater linguistic distance from English, CJ reports learning it with unusual ease relative to his peers. Subsequently, CJ also spent some time in Spain and Italy where he apparently 'picked up' both Spanish and Italian in a 'matter of weeks'. CJ reports that contact with the media and informal gatherings with native speakers were particularly useful and effective means for him to rapidly acquire these languages.

CJ and his identical twin brother are the eldest of four siblings. The twins are the only family members who are not right-handed. CJ himself shows mixed handedness: fine-motor abilities such as writing and drawing are executed with the left hand. By contrast, gross motor abilities and tasks requiring strength, such as batting and bowling, are usually carried out with his right hand.

CJ was somewhat slow in learning to read although his first language acquisition was apparently normal. Once the basic reading skills were mastered, however, he had no difficulty maintaining an adequate level of performance. To the time of his testing he reported that his reading is slow and somewhat laborious, regardless of the language and/or material involved. Otherwise, CJ considers that he was essentially a good student throughout his school years and was generally quite good in subjects such as mathematics, sciences, graphic arts and music. On the other hand, he reported poor performance in athletics and considered himself extremely inadequate in skills relating to directionality and spatial orientation, such as reading maps or finding his way.

Of the information available to CJ and his mother, CJ reports a number of positive items in relation to the Geschwind cluster. In addition to the left-handedness and the fact that he is a twin, CJ also reports having allergies and hives. CJ also reports that it is possible that a maternal grandfather was diagnosed as schizophrenic. In addition, CJ recognised pre-pubertally that he is homosexual and believes this to be particularly significant in regard to understanding his language acquisition talent. CJ explains that he realised from a very young age that he 'was different' and therefore he chose to be distinctive in particular and specific ways. Doing well in language learning as opposed to athletics, by his analysis, distinguished him markedly from other high school males. Of course Geschwind's explanation would be different: that foetal hormonal levels affected the developing endocrinological system as well as the cortical language areas, thus explaining both his special talent and his sexual preference. Finally it should be noted that CJ's twin brother is also left-handed; he is not reported to have done either notably poorly or notably well at learning languages, although CJ suggests that this may be due partly to lack of opportunity; his brother is a priest.

CJ was given a series of neuropsychological tests to assess his general intellectual functioning and examine some specific cognitive functions that might be expected to be associated with exceptional second language aptitude. Although we focused primarily on tests measuring *memory* and *language abilities* which might be particularly pertinent to second language acquisition, other areas of assessment included *abstract reasoning, visual–spatial functioning, mental control* and *response set*, and *sensory–motor abilities*.

General cognitive functioning

In many respects CJ's functioning was in the average/high average range. On the Weschler Adult Intelligent Scale-Revised, CJ scored a normal verbal IQ of 105, a normal Performance IQ of 110, for a normal full scale IQ of 107. Thus there was no marked verbal/performance discrepancy and his performance was not out of the ordinary.

It is interesting that CJ did not do particularly well on abstracting common properties of two words. His answers tended to be either concrete (a table and a chair both 'have legs') or to be somewhat idiosyncratic, or attentive to form rather than meaning (a poem and a statue both 'have lines' and work and play have 'four letters'). Similarly, on a multiple-choice proverb interpretation test (Gorham Proverbs) CJ's performance was average. He missed the point of some proverbs, while on some he chose a rather concrete interpretation of the proverb rather than an abstract restatement. Likewise on the arithmetic subtest, CJ's performance was average; he did not know the correct procedures for doing the more difficult problems, and was slightly impulsive and sloppy in his calculations on some of the easier items.

Interestingly, CJ's two best performances on the WAIS-R were on tests plausibly closely linked to language acquisition. One high score was on the test they call vocabulary, in which he was asked to define words of increasing difficulty. Not only did he know most of the difficult words, but he was easily able to give accurate one-word synonyms for many of the harder words, such as 'burden' for 'encumber', 'foreboding' for 'ominous', and 'palpable' for 'tangible'. The other WAIS-R subtest on which CJ performed very well was Digit Symbol. On this subtest the subject is asked to place symbols in blank spaces below a series of digits, using a code at the top of the page as a guide. Individuals tend to score better if they are in fact learning the code, rather than merely continually referring to it. That CJ did learn the code was demonstrated by using Edith Kaplan's modification of the test, in which the subject is asked to recall the digit–symbol pairings from memory immediately after the test is given. CJ recalled all nine pairs without error, a superior performance, and retained all nine perfectly after a twenty minute delay. This subtest, which requires acquisition, or at least use, of a code transforming a *known* series of symbols to a previously *unknown* series, bears an obvious relationship to new language acquisition.

CJ also performed very well on two other tests of higher cognitive functioning. On Ravens Progressive Matrices, which requires the subject to decide which of six choices correctly completes a pattern with a piece missing, CJ scored at the 95th percentile. On the Shipley–Hartford abstraction subtest the subject must figure out what relations obtain among a series of letters, numbers or words and then complete the pattern (e.g. surgeon 1234567.....snore 17635.....rogue-----). On this subtest CJ did almost as well as he did on the Shipley vocabulary subtest; he scored at about the 93rd percentile on the two subtests combined. Again, his few errors on the abstraction subtest seemed as much due to impulsiveness as to inability to figure out the rule. Thus, on these two tests (Ravens and Shipley) in which a rather abstract pattern must be apprehended and completed by the subject, CJ performed very well.

Thus, CJ's overall intellectual functioning, as measured by traditional IQ tests, is not out of the ordinary. In particular, he does not use words or even proverbs in a very abstract or sophisticated way. However, there are some areas of outstanding ability or skill. These include vocabulary, acquisition of a new code, and the ability to perceive and complete formal patterns. This facility with patterns obtains in both verbal and visual realms, despite his otherwise relatively poor performance in visual–spatial tasks.

Specific language aptitude

We also administered the Modern Language Aptitude Test as a further measure of his second language abilities. Consistent with his performance on the WAIS-R Digit Symbol, CJ performed at or almost at ceiling on the three subtests requiring learning a new code system, whether it was English numbers to new words, English words to nonsense words, in The Paired Associates task, or a new phonetic transcription system. He also scored near ceiling on the Spelling Cues task that required him to retrieve a word based on only the consonants of that word. However, he was only at the 50th percentile on the subtest called Words and Sentences. On this subtest he was required to judge which two words serve the same functions in two English sentences. Thus, what might be termed his *conscious* appreciation of grammatical structure was only average.

CJ was asked to provide a written description of a standard picture stimulus. He provided an adequate description of the story with nothing remarkable in it. Thus, as on his general cognitive test, CJ's strengths appear to be in the acquisition of new codes, rather than in the higher conceptual manipulation of verbal material.

Visual–spatial functions

It has been suggested by Schneiderman & Desmarais (1988) that exceptional second language aptitude may be associated with a compromised visual–spatial system. They suggest that mild to moderate deficits in visual–spatial functions may be a frequent concomitant of second language aptitude. CJ's strengths certainly did not lie in the visual–spatial area, but his skills on these tests were generally within the average range. He did score at the low end of the average range of the Hooper Test of Visual Organisation which requires the subject mentally to assemble and name a cut-up drawing of an object. He had difficulty with the mental rotations involved, and was frequently observed to rotate the book. He did tend to fail items on this task which require the most appreciation of information about configuration, and if a small part of the picture looked like a thing in itself, he was sometimes pulled to give this as a response.

CJ was also asked to visualise the alphabet and name every capital letter that has a curve in it, and then to think through the alphabet and name every letter that rhymes with 'tree'. For normal right-handed males, the second of these tasks is generally considered to be more reliant on left hemisphere functioning, while naming curved letters is more dependent on right hemisphere functioning. CJ did not show any dissociation between these two tasks. His quick time and few errors on both were normal and did not differ from each other, suggesting no strong bias toward either left or right hemisphere processing styles.

Musical ability

In the popular lore, it has sometimes been suggested that a 'good ear' for language is also reflected in a 'good ear' for music. CJ was given the Seashore Test of Musical Ability. The three subtests given were immediate memory for tonal sequences, rhythmic sequences and pitch discrimination. CJ performed somewhat better on the tonal memory (61st percentile) than he did on rhythm (28th percentile) and pitch (40th percentile) but all scores were in the average range.

Memory

It has also been suggested that second language acquisition may reflect underlying strengths in verbal memory, or in a strong general memory. Indeed, CJ's verbal memoral was clearly outstanding. As mentioned above, he incidentally learned the entire digit symbol code in the WAIS-R, and retained it perfectly after 20 minutes. On the Rey Auditory Verbal Learning Test, CJ showed an average learning curve for his age, but retained this unrelated list of words virtually perfectly after 20 minutes. He showed a high average (84th percentile) performance on paired associates on the Weschler Memory Scale and even retained most of this list after a two-week interval. His outstanding performance, however, was on retention of prose passages, both immediately and on delay. His performance was above the 99th percentile on this task. On the other hand, his memory for digits was not out of the ordinary (6 forward and 7 backward), with the slightly lower digits forwards score probably due simply to fatigue or impulsiveness. Likewise, on visual recall of complex figures his performance was average.

Personality

Personality or cultural factors have also been considered to play a role in second language acquisition. Schneiderman & Desmarais (1988) discuss in some detail the notion that a willingness to adopt the identity or be taken for someone in another culture may significantly influence the readiness with which foreign accent and grammar are picked up. With regard to accent, in particular, where CJ is also outstanding, they suggest that not only must one be willing to sound like someone from another culture, but one must be willing to give up the protection that being foreign confers, since native speakers may make allowances for grammatical errors when the speaker is obviously not a native speaker, and thus the person is protected from sounding foolish. The 'risk taking' of a certain sort, or failure to be strongly identified in a conservative fashion with a 'mainstream' member of one's own culture, may indeed apply to CJ. As mentioned at several points above, CJ's responses were very quick, costing him somewhat in accuracy. Furthermore, he sees himself as something of a maverick, and had not settled down to any steady occupation when we last heard from him. His pride in his sexual orientation bespeaks a certain risk-taking attitude as well.

Personality testing revealed little of significance. On the Rorschach test, he mentioned little in the way of human content or human movement, potentially contradicting the theory of Guiora *et al.* (1972) that individuals who are more empathic have better accents in foreign language learning.

Summary and discussion

To summarise clearly, generally superior cognitive functioning is not necessary for exceptional L2 acquisition. CJ's IQ scores, plus his ability to manipulate abstract verbal concepts and his general fund of information, were at average levels. His musical ability was also average, as was his ability to solve visual problems, such as reproducing block patterns. He also complained of lack of ability to read maps and learn new routes, and he had some difficulty in performing mental rotation problems. Furthermore, no marked discrepancy was seen in overall problem-solving style—his cognitive approach was not in any obvious way favouring a 'left hemisphere' as compared to a 'right hemisphere' style.

CJ's memory was *not* exceptional across the board for all material—visual memory for figures was merely average. However, his verbal memory was exceptional both for English passages, and for acquiring new verbal codes. Furthermore, his performance was quite good on tasks requiring the perception and completion of formal patterns, whether the stimulus was abstract visual symbols or the relationships between series of words (as long as the relationship was formal and not semantic).

To the extent that one can argue from a single case, CJ's pattern of strengths and weaknesses is consistent with some theories of L2 acquisition and contradicts others. CJ provides a counterexample, of course, for the lay belief that good L2 abilities are related somehow to a 'musical ear'. Contrary to what some may expect, exceptional IQ is not a *sine qua non* for good L2 acquisition, nor does Guiora's notion that superior capacity for empathy is required for native-like accent in an L2 receive support from CJ's case. However, CJ's personality characteristics might be taken to support the idea discussed by Schneiderman & Desmarais that high motivation, non-conformist self-concept, and willingness to take risks may be associated with L2 facility, especially in accent.

It is not immediately obvious that ability for prose recall in L1 would necessarily be linked with L2 talent. CJ's exceptional verbal memory, in contrast to his visual memory and his overall average intellectual ability, would at least raise the possibility that exceptional verbal memory would be found strongly linked to L2 talent in other individuals as well. Clearly, exceptional memory for other types of material is *not* necessary, since CJ's memory for digits, visual–spatial and musical material was not remarkable.

It is a provocative but not unexpected finding that CJ performed particularly well on the two tests requiring appreciation and completion of formal patterns. It is plausible that an ability to extract patterns from complex input contributes to appreciating patterns in foreign language input.

Although CJ does not show any frank visual–spatial deficits on neuropsychological testing, his visual–spatial skills are clearly inferior to his verbal abilities, and he reports subjective difficulty with various visual–spatial skills such as map-reading and finding his way around. This may be taken as weak support for the Schneiderman & Desmarais (1986) hypothesis that L2 talent is associated with visual–spatial deficits. One theoretical possibility is that CJ's exceptional ability rests on a more bilateral organisation for language than right-handed males as a group show. As with females, who may generally show such a pattern (Obler & Novoa, 1988), verbal skills appear to benefit from bilateral organisation, while for the same individuals visual–spatial abilities seem to suffer.

As mentioned above, there are several items in the Geschwind–Galaburda cluster in CJ's history (mixed handedness, homosexuality, allergies, twinning, and the possibility of schizophrenia in a grandparent). Indeed all three talented L2 learners who have been studied thus far (Novoa *et al.*, in press; Schneidermann & Desmarais, 1986) all have a striking number of the factors named by Geschwind and Galaburda as having a high correlation with anomalous language dominance (Geschwind & Galaburda, 1985a,b,c). All have a history of allergies or asthma, and two are left-handed, among other factors. Additionally, a pilot study by Klein & Pierpont (pers. comm.) found that subjects falling at either end of the L2 ability scale were positive for Geschwind cluster factors, and the poor second language learner studied by Humes-Bartlo in a case study has a positive family history for language disorders, left-handedness, allergies, early stuttering, homosexuality and asthma (Humes-Bartlo, pers. comm.).

The talents discussed by Geschwind and Galaburda (mathematical, artistic, architectural, engineering, musical and athletic) can all be considered to rest more heavily on right hemisphere processing. Geschwind and Galaburda do allude to the possibility that such individuals 'may have elevated skills related to unaffected regions on the left' (1985a: 432), but they do not specify what such left hemisphere talents might be. We suggest that CJ, with his slowed development and persistent mild difficulty with reading, contrasting with his exceptional L2 acquisition ability, constitutes an example of such a case.

What about extremely poor second language learners? They might *also* be expected to participate in the Geschwind and Galaburda clusters, but in their case we would expect that unusual cellular distribution had resulted in poor organisation for some language related abilities, and perhaps strong performance in other cognitive realms outside the language area.

I have had the opportunity to interview a Sociology Ph.D., the president of a foundation, who would seem to qualify as an extremely poor L2 learner. He had a history of extremely low grades and difficulty in language courses in high school and college, despite the fact that he reports he was always a hard worker and spent long hours at language study. So painful was L2 learning that he took only the required courses, with tutoring during the extra semesters it required for him to pass. Only with accent did he perform well, which actually serves to his disadvantage when he is travelling since people expect him to understand more than he can when they hear his good accent in those few phrases he can produce. This subject, KS, had a curious range of language abilities. He had an extensive vocabulary in English, his L1. Moreover, he employed this vocabulary quite fluently, yet reported greater than he felt average difficulty in recalling people's names. He had been slow to learn reading and remained a poor reader. Yet clearly his talents lie in other areas—not the ones I would have ideally liked since they would support the Geschwind & Galaburda hypothesis most strongly—*not* music or art or mathematics, that is. Rather he had always had extremely good interpersonal skills, and motor–visual skills as evidenced by his advanced mastery of sailing. These abilities are not generally as highly valued as school skills in our society, but Gardner has included them as two of his intelligences—interpersonal intelligence, and kinesthetic intelligence.

Humes-Bartlo's recent study (in press) provides an example of the group approach of studying a group of the particularly poor L2 learners. She selected 46 native Spanish-speaking students in grades 3 to 5 who were in or had been in bilingual classes in New York City. To identify particularly good and particularly poor L2 learners, she measured the number of years taken to pass the Language Assessment Battery (LAB). Students with low IQ or poor *Spanish* performance on the Peabody vocabulary test were excluded from her study so that talent or lack of it could be examined with no suspicion that overall low IQ or general language deficit could account for the poor L2 learners.

Let us consider the extreme learners in her population, outliers on her multifactorial scale: four slow learners who took markedly more than three years to pass the LAB, and six fast learners who took less than three years. The most important of her findings for the purposes of this chapter are (1) the *better* performance of the *slowest* learners on the arithmetic and visual–spatial tests, and (2) the higher scores of the fast learners on several of the verbal tasks in *Spanish*, the L1. This suggests not only that the slowest L2 learners, despite *normal* IQ scores and *normal* Spanish vocabulary, may nevertheless be mildly deficient in first language abilities as well as L2 abilities. Additionally, the data about their better performance on mathematical and visual–spatial tasks conforms to Geschwind's predictions that some brain cells 'destined' for language areas may have been diverted elsewhere, in this case to areas responsible for mathematical or perhaps visual–spatial function. However, contrary to our expectations, the extreme subjects in her *fast* learners as a group showed strong *left* laterality for language, whereas the extremes in her *slow* learners showed bilateral organisation.

In a number of areas, then, it appears that we are approaching a neuropsychological understanding of the abilities consistent with or dissociated from talented L2 acquisition abilities. Verbal memory and coding ability, for example, are seen to be linked to talented L2 acquisition; high IQ, musical and visual–spatial abilities are independent. With respect to laterality, however, our gross but easiest-to-study measure of brain organisation for language, we are left with an apparent contradiction. Bilateral organisation for language is seen in the group of *poor* learners but *not* the group of fast learners in the Humes-Bartlo sample, but is also shown by all three well-studied exceptionally talented adults. Geschwind's theory would predict all these findings except the high left dominance in the Humes-Bartlo fast learners. Normally lateralisation has been associated with left dominance for language. Any clustering of special abilities and/or disabilities could understandably relate to bilateral organisation for language. My current best guess is that the Humes-Bartlo 'fast' population is too large to be comparable to the exceptionally talented individuals studied in case studies; proportionally it constitutes 13% of her population and so includes only one or two of the people who will turn out to be as good L3 acquirers as adults as CJ or the two studied by Schneiderman & Desmarais. Indeed when one looks further at the Humes-Bartlo data, it appears that of the six exceptionally good learners at the high end of her multifactorial scale, five showed the high left dominance manifested by the group, but the sixth, who was *the* individual at the extreme end of the scale, showed bilateral organisation for language. I conclude then, albeit tentatively until we have time to work further with these data, that even within normal learners and speakers of L1 there will be a continuum of base language abilities; normal left cerebral dominance will enable many to learn and acquire second language *well*, while truly exceptional ability will be limited to those with a certain exceptional sort of bilateral organisation.

Acknowledgements

The research and thinking in this chapter have developed through collaboration with a number of colleagues and students whose contributions I acknowledge here: Dr Deborah Fein, Dr Eta Schneiderman, Meg Humes-Bartlo and Dr Loriana Novoa.

Portions of this chapter reporting the case of CJ appear in somewhat more detail in Novoa *et al.* (1988).

References

ALBERT, M. and OBLER, L. K., 1978, *The Bilingual Brain*. New York: Academic Press.

BAKAN, P., 1969, Hypnotizability, lateralization of eye movements, and functional brain asymmetry, *Perceptual and Motor Skills*, 28, 927–32.

CARROLL, J. B., 1983, Psychometric theory and language testing. In J. OLLER (ed.), *Issues in Language Testing Research*. Rowley, MA: Newbury House.

DAY, R., 1979, Verbal fluency and the language bound effect. In C. J. FILLMORE, D. KEMPLER & W. S.-Y. WANG (eds), *Individual Differences in Language Ability and Language Behavior*. New York: Academic Press.

DIAMOND, M. C. and SCHEIBEL, A. B., 1985, Research on the structure of Einstein's brain. In W. REICH, The stuff of genius, *The New York Times Magazine*, July 28, 24–5.

DIAZ, R., 1985, Bilingual cognitive development: addressing three gaps in current research, *Child Development*, 56, 1376–88.

GALABURDA, A., 1983, Definition of the anatomical phenotype. In C. LUDLOW & J. COOPER (eds), *Genetic Aspects of Speech and Language Disorder*. New York: Academic Press.

GALABURDA, A. M. and KEMPER, T. L., 1979, Cytoarchitectonic abnormalities in developmental dyslexia: A case study, *Annals of Neurology*, 6, 94–100.

GALABURDA, A., SANIDES, F. and GESHWIND, W., 1978, Human brain: cytoarchitectonic left-right asymmetries in the temporal speech region, *Archives of Neurology*, 35, 812–17.

GARDNER, H., 1983, *Frames of Mind: A Theory of Multiple Intelligences*. New York: Basic Books.

GARDNER, R. C., 1960, Motivational variables in second-language acquisition. Ph.D. dissertation, McGill University. Cited in R. C. GARDNER & W. E. LAMBERT, 1972, *Attitudes and Motivation in Second Language Learning*. Rowley, MA: Newbury House.

GARDNER, R. C. and LAMBERT, W. E., 1972, Language aptitude, intelligence, and second-language achievement. In R. C. GARDNER & W. E. LAMBERT, *Attitudes and Motivation in Second Language Learning*. Rowley, MA: Newbury House.

GESCHWIND, N., 1983, Genetics: fate, chance and environmental control. In C. LUDLOW & J. COOPER (eds), *Genetic Aspects of Speech and Language Disorder*. New York: Academic Press.

GESCHWIND, N. and BEHAN, P., 1982, Left handedness: association with immune disease, migraine, and developmental learning disorders, *Proceedings of the National Academy of Sciences*, 79, 5097–100.

GESCHWIND, N. and GALABURDA, A. M., 1985a, Cerebral lateralization. Biological mechanisms, associations, and pathology: Part I, *Archives of Neurology*, 42, 428–59.

——, 1985b, Cerebral lateralization. Biological mechanisms, associations, and pathology: Part II, *Archives of Neurology*, 42, 521–52.

——, 1985c, Cerebral lateralization. Biological mechanisms, associations, and pathology: Part III, *Archives of Neurology*, 42, 634–54.

GESCHWIND, N. and LEVITSKY, W., 1968, Human brain: left–right asymmetries in temporal speech region, *Science*, 161, 186–7.

GUIORA, A., BRANNON, R. and DULL, C., 1972, Empathy and second language learning, *Language Learning*, 22, 111–30.

HARTNETT, D., 1976, 'The relationship of cognitive style and hemispheric preference to deductive and inductive second language learning'. Presented at Conference on Human Brain Function, UCLA.

HUMES-BARTLO, M. (in press), Variation in children's ability to learn a second language. In K. HYLTENSTAM & L. K. OBLER (eds), *Bilingualism Across the Lifespan*. Cambridge: Cambridge University Press.

JUDD, T. 1988, The varieties of musical talent. In L. K. OBLER & D. FEIN (eds), *The Exceptional Brain: The Neuropsychology of Talent and Special Abilities*. New York: Guilford.

NOVOA, L., OBLER, L. and FEIN, D. A. (in press), A neuropsychological approach to talented second language acquisition—a case study. In L. K. OBLER & D. FEIN (eds), *The Exceptional Brain: The Neuropsychology of Talent and Special Abilities*. New York: Guilford.

OBLER, L. K. and NOVOA, L., 1988, Gender similarities and differences in brain lateralization. *Genes and Gender V.*

OBLER, L. and FEIN, D. 1988, *The Exceptional Brain: The Neuropsychology of Talent and Special Abilities*. New York: Guilford.

OJEMANN, G., 1983, Brain organization for language from the perspective of electrical stimulation mapping, *Behavioral and Brain Sciences*, 6, 189–230.

PETERS, A., 1981, Language learning strategies: does the whole equal the sum of the parts? In K. DILLER (ed.), *Individual Differences and Universals in Language Learning Aptitude*. Rowley, MA: Newbury House.

PIENEMANN, M., 1980, The second language acquisition of immigrant children. In S. FELIX (ed.), *Second Language Development: Trends and Issues*. Tübingen: Gunter Narr.

PIKE, E. V., 1959, A test for predicting phonetic ability, *Language Learning*, 9, 35–41.

POLITZER, R. L. and WEISS, L., 1969, An experiment in improving achievement in foreign language learning through learning of selected skills associated with language aptitude. Stanford University, ERIC reproduction document no. ED 046261.

SCHNEIDERMAN, E. and DESMARAIS, C., 1986, The talented language learner: some preliminary findings. Paper presented at Language Acquisition Research Symposium, Utrecht.

——, 1988, A neuropsychological substrate for talent in second language acquisition. In L. K. OBLER & D. FEIN (eds), *The Exceptional Brain: The Neuropsychology of Talent and Special Abilities*. New York: Guilford.

SCHWEIGER, A. 1988, A portrait of the artist as a brain-damaged patient. In L. K. OBLER & D. FEIN (eds), *The Exceptional Brain: The Neurospsychology of Talent and Special Abilities*. New York: Guilford.

SELIGER, H., KRASHEN, S. and LADEFOGED, P., 1975, Maturational constraints in the acquisition of a native-like accent in second language learning, *Language Sciences*, 36, 20–2.

SELINKER, L., 1972, Interlanguage, *International Review of Applied Linguistics*, 10, 209–31.

SMITH, S., 1983, *The Great Mental Calculators: The Psychology, Methods, and Lives of Calculating Prodigies Past and Present*. New York: Columbia University Press.

——, 1988, Calculating prodigies. In L. K. OBLER & D. FEIN (eds), *The Exceptional Brain: The Neuropsychology of Talent and Special Abilities*. New York: Guilford.

SNOW, C. and HOEFNAGEL-HOHLE, M., 1979, Individual differences in second language ability: A factor analytic study, *Language and Speech*, 22(2), 151–62.

VIHMAN, M., 1982, The acquisition of morphology by a bilingual child: A whole word approach, *Applied Linguistics*, 3(2), 141–60.

WHITAKER, H. and SELNES, O., 1979, Anatomic variations in the cortex: Individual differences and the problem of the localization of language functions, *Annals of the New York Academy of Sciences*, 280, 845–55.

WONG-FILLMORE, L., 1979, Individual differences in second language acquisition. In C. J. FILLMORE, D., KEMPLER, & W. S.-Y. WANG (eds), *Individual Differences in Language Ability and Language Behavior*. New York: Academic Press.

10 Immigrant children who have failed to acquire native English

GEORGETTE IOUP
University of New Orleans

Introduction

It is widely assumed that children will have no difficulty acquiring language, whether it is their first or second. Everyone knows of families who have lived abroad for a short time and returned with their children sounding, for example, like Germans or Swedes, or of immigrant families in this country where the parents still speak only their native tongue, while the children have developed fluent native English. Many of us have anecdotes from our own family history of relatives who entered school knowing no English, but emerged with native speaker competence.

Such assumptions about the child's second language learning ability are not restricted to the casual observer alone. They have been made implicitly or explicitly in most of the current research on second language acquisition. One of the earliest researchers to undertake an in-depth comparative study of children acquiring a second language was Wong-Fillmore (1979). She followed throughout a one year period the course of acquisition of five Spanish speaking children aged 5–7, who were just beginning to learn English. She observed a considerable amount of variation among the children both in the strategies used to communicate and in the levels of attainment after one year of exposure to English. In spite of the individual differences that Wong-Fillmore detailed, she predicted that all the children would eventually achieve the same level of proficiency, even if it took some of them several years longer.

There are many studies which compare the eventual attainment of child and adult learners. One of the most extensive is that of Oyama (1976). Oyama finds that those who begin learning English before age 11 perform similarly to native speakers on her tasks. She concludes that the notion of a critical or sensitive period which predicts success for only those learners who undertake language acquisition before puberty is indeed valid. Other studies of age differences focus only on whether older learners can learn as well as children. None of them question the assumption that child acquirers will become indistinguishable from native speakers (see the many studies reported in Krashen *et al.*, 1982). Even the research by Snow & Hoefnagel-Hohle (1978), which goes to great length to argue that adults are actually better language learners than children, assumes that the children will eventually attain native proficiency while the adults will not; the difference in success is attributed to motivational variables.

More recent research on age and second language acquisition investigates the role of the innate system of cognitive structures referred to as Universal Grammar. While most researchers acknowledge that an innate system of language specific principles is responsible for a large part of first language acquisition, there is considerable discussion about the role of Universal Grammar in second language acquisition (see Flynn, 1983; Felix, 1985; White, 1985; Hilles, 1986; Zobl, 1986; Rutherford, 1986; Bley-Vroman, 1988; and Bley-Vroman *et al.*, 1988). Interestingly enough, most of the research concerns only whether or not adults learning a second language still have access to the principles of Universal Grammar. There is an implicit assumption in all the research that Universal Grammar is still available to child second language learners. This is considered to be one of the facts which accounts for the successful acquisition of a second language by children.

In spite of all the research over the past 15 years which pictures child L2 acquisition as natural and as unproblematic as child first language acquisition, teachers are witnessing something different in the second language classroom. In college programmes across the country we are now seeing, for example, many of the Southeast Asians who immigrated as young children 10 to 12 years ago with English acquisition which is by no means complete and native-like. In the ESL programme at the University of New Orleans (UNO) we have students who immigrated with their families as young children and were immediately immersed into the New Orleans school system. They have completed grade school through high school and are now entering the university. Their English still has quite pronounced non-native characteristics. They exhibit the same problems encountered by L2 learners who began English after puberty. The discovery that these students had immigrated as young children and spent 10 to 12 years in an American school system without acquiring native-like speech shattered all my stereotypes about second language acquisition by children. Therefore, I decided to study these learners in greater depth to learn more about their acquisition history and their current knowledge of grammar.

Subjects

Six students from our ESL programme were selected for study, five whose native language is Vietnamese and one whose native language is Chinese. All of them were between the ages of six and nine when they immigrated to the US. They are now 18 to 21 years old. Two of the subjects are male (Dao and Thanh) and four are female (Man, Nuyet, Tuyet and Jeanne). All of them scored low enough on the UNO placement exam—consisting of (1) the Michigan Test of Aural Comprehension (MTAC), (2) the Michigan Test of English Language Proficiency (MTELP) and (3) a written composition—to require them to take 15 hours of intensive ESL instruction a week. Most of them to date have had to repeat their ESL courses several times. They all reported that they had little, if any, formal ESL instruction before coming to UNO. Table 1 presents their scores on the UNO proficiency exam. At the time of testing Man and Jeanne had completed two semesters in the ESL programme. The other four subjects had completed one semester.

Each subject was asked to fill out a questionnaire providing demographic information and information on their language learning history. All the subjects had entered grade school in immersion situations without ESL instruction. Four of the Vietnamese subjects attended schools with a large

TABLE 1. *Performance on the UNO Proficiency Exam**

| | Michigan | | Composition |
	MTAC (90 items)	MTELP (100 items)	
Dao	87	60	65
Man	87	73	83
Thanh	90	75	68
Nuyet	81	77	84
Tuyet	90	82	77
Jeanne	87	88	81

*All scores equated to a scale of 100.

Vietnamese population. One of them reported that he associated mainly with Vietnamese friends both during and after school. The other three stated that they spent most of their time with English speaking friends during school hours. One Vietnamese subject attended a school with few other Vietnamese students. All of his friends were English speaking. The Chinese subject had no Chinese speaking classmates at her schools. There is no Chinese immigrant community in New Orleans. Several of the subjects reported that they worked at after school jobs which required a knowledge of English. All of them watched one or more hours of television a day.

Universal grammar

As stated above, a central concern in current research is the role of Universal Grammar (UG) in second language acquisition. But studies to date have only investigated whether Universal Grammar is still accessible to the adult learner. It is assumed that to the extent that Universal Grammar guides the course of first language acquisition, it is equally available to children learning a second language. I was interested in seeing whether my subjects had, in fact, mastered aspects of English grammar which have been shown to derive from the principles of Universal Grammar. The constraints on WH-movement in English follow from two of these principles: Subjacency and the Empty Category Principle. They account for why (1b) and (2b), for example, are grammatical while (3b) and (4b) are not:

(1a) Mary met someone last night.
(1b) Who did Mary meet ø last night?
(2a) Mary believes that Bill said that John met someone last night.
(2b) Who does Mary believe that Bill said that John met ø last night?
(3a) Mary heard the news that John met someone last night.
(3b) *Who did Mary hear the news that John met ø last night?
(4a) Mary wonders who did what last night.
(4b) *What does Mary wonder who did ø last night?

Chinese and Vietnamese do not exhibit syntactic WH-movement. Thus the constraints on English WH-movement which stem from universal principles could not be acquired through transfer, nor are they likely to have been taught explicitly in any language class. If subjects now have knowledge of these constraints, they must have had access to Universal Grammar at the time these facts of English were inductively incorporated into their interlanguage system.[1]

In a recent study investigating the accessibility of Universal Grammar to adult learners, Bley-Vroman *et al.* (1988) developed a questionnaire to elicit knowledge of the constraints on WH-movement. The questionnaire required subjects to decide whether a given sentence was *possible* or *impossible* in English. The test contained 32 sentences, each exhibiting a type of WH-movement to clause initial position. (The complete list of sentences tested is given in Appendix A.) It was first tested on 34 native speaking controls who performed at a level near or exceeding 90% correct on almost all sentences.[2] The native speakers' average score was 92% correct. It was then tested on 92 Korean adult learners. The average correct for the non-native subjects was 75%, which is significantly worse than the native speakers, but significantly better than chance. I administered this questionnaire to the six subjects of this study. The results are presented in Table 2. Correlations of performance on the test of Universal Grammar with proficiency scores are given in Tables 3 and 4.

Table 2 indicates that there is a wide range of variability in subjects' performance on the test of UG. Dao scores at about chance level while Nuyet and Tuyet perform like native speakers. It is easy to find an explanation for Dao's poor performance. He is more comfortable speaking Vietnamese than English, which he tries to avoid as much as possible. Dao lives in a large Vietnamese community which provides for his needs. Thanh, in comparison, performs much better than Dao. He is the only subject who does not live near a Vietnamese ethnic community. Yet he still does not perform at native speaker level on either the test of Universal Grammar or

TABLE 2. *Performance on the Test of Universal Grammar (UG)*

	% correct
Native speakers	92[*]
Adult learners	75[*]
Dao	59
Man	78
Jeanne	81
Thanh	84
Nuyet	91
Tuyet	94

[*] From Bley-Vroman *et al.* (in press)

TABLE 3. *Rank Order Correlation of proficiency scores with UG*

	Michigan		Composition
MTAC		MTELP	
− 0.06		0.74*	0.58

$*\ p \leqslant 0.05$

TABLE 4. *Rank Order Correlation of subparts of the MTELP with UG*

Grammar	Vocabulary	Reading
0.85*	0.37	0.38

$*\ p \leqslant 0.05$

the proficiency exam. In addition, he speaks English with a marked Vietnamese accent. Interestingly, he reports that his older brother has tested on proficiency exams at a native speaker level in English. There is no apparent explanation for Thanh's unsuccessful acquisition. Nuyet and Tuyet both score like native speakers on the test of Universal Grammar. Also, their pronunciation of English is accent free. In addition, they are thoroughly American in their dress and style. They associate with Americans more than Vietnamese. Yet neither has acquired the language particular rules of English—that is, rules which are specific to English that do not follow from the principles of Universal Grammar. Because they have not mastered these rules, they do not speak and write like native speakers. An examination of their writing reveals that they do not adhere to some of the most common language particular rules of English, such as the plural morpheme, correct verb formation, and common derivational morphology. I have no explanation for why these two learners have been able to acquire aspects of English which derive from language universals, but have not been able to acquire certain language particular aspects of English.

Comparison of a successful and unsuccessful learner

To see if there is some underlying neuropsychological explanation for the lack of success in these young learners, I selected one of them for further study. I chose Jeanne since her native language is Chinese and, given the immigrant structure of New Orleans, there is no Chinese community for her to interact in. Her only Chinese speaking resource is her immediate family. Listening to her profile, one would predict that she would be a successful language learner. Jeanne immigrated to the US at the age of nine. Before coming, she attended several years of primary school in Taiwan where she learned to read and write in Chinese. She is now 19 years old and a sophomore in college. She has two younger sisters with whom she communicates in English. With her parents she speaks Chinese, though it is often mixed with English. She reports that her two sisters are much more proficient in English than she is.

In New Orleans Jeanne attended both public and parochial schools. She is a good student and was often placed in honours sections—even in English (although she reports that they did very little writing in these classes). She likes to read and reads both Chinese and English literature. She is good at music and mathematics. Her major at the university is commercial art. She reports that she is a terrible speller and not good at remembering names. Learning new vocabulary is also difficult for her.

At the University of New Orleans Jeanne first entered the intensive ESL programme. After one semester she progressed to the first level of the non-intensive programme. This she had to repeat three times before she finally passed to the next non-intensive level, which she has also had to repeat. Typical of the sentences she produces in writing is the following, taken from one of her compositions: *'Because of many influences and education are for the making money'*. In spite of her incomplete acquisition of English syntax and semantics, Jeanne's pronunciation of English is completely native-like. Listening to her speak, one would assume that she had close to native proficiency.

In order to better interpret her cognitive profile, I selected a successful language learner for comparison. I was looking for someone who was not only considerably better in English than Jeanne, but also someone who had begun English as an adult. Minh fitted that description. Minh is a male Vietnamese ESL student who began learning English as an adult and who was classified on the basis of his proficiency scores, as well as by his teacher, as a good language learner. But, listening to his profile, one would predict that Minh would not be very proficient in English. Minh was 35 years old at the time of testing. He had been in the US for only five years. He did not begin the serious acquisition of English until he came to the States at age 30, although he had had a small amount of English in high school in Vietnam. He currently lives in New Orleans with his Vietnamese wife and baby. His wife is also just now learning English. Minh reports that the language he generally speaks is Vietnamese, but he seeks out every possible opportunity to use English. He and his wife will frequently practice English together. When he hears or reads literate English, he concentrates on the form of the sentences as much as on the content.

Minh studied French for seven years in high school. He immigrated to Italy at the age of 19 where he lived for ten years. While there he completed medical school. Vietnamese and Italian are his best languages. He reports that he is good at maths and science, is not very good at art, but can play the harmonica by ear. He likes to read, is a very good speller and learns new vocabulary easily. At the time of testing, he had had only two semesters of formal ESL instruction—one at the local community college when he first arrived, and one he was just completing at the University of New Orleans where he was placed in the most advanced level and was one of the best students. He has since entered medical school in New Orleans. His English pronunciation has a marked Vietnamese accent. In fact, if one heard both Jeanne and Minh speak, one would assume that Minh was the learner having problems in English, and that Jeanne had close to native proficiency.

Other aspects of grammar

Before undertaking any cognitive testing, I wished to compare their knowledge of English in greater depth. On the UNO proficiency exam Minh scored close to native speaker level. However, on the test of knowledge of universal grammatical constraints, Minh and Jeanne perform similary (see Table 5). Two other aspects of English required investigation. One is knowledge of the semantic structure of the language which is responsible for certain distributions in English, such as the fact that a relative clause containing *any* may modify a head NP determined by *every*, but not by *some*, as shown in (5) and (6).

(5)   Everyone who lost anything must fill out a report.
(6)   *Some child who showed any flu symptoms became ill.

The second is knowledge of facts of English which are specific to it. Some of these facts follow from idiom behaviour as illustrated in the following paradigm, where (7) is an example of a flexible idiom which allows particle movement, and (8) is an example of a fixed idiom which does not.

(7)   Her father laid the law down before she was twelve.
(8)   ?He blew some steam off after he got home.

Others follow from rule-governed behaviour particular to English, illustrated in the following sentences.

(9)   He found a cloth with which to wipe it.
(10) *That's the fork which to eat it with.
(11) The slowly running water quickly filled the tub.
(12) *The responding quickly policeman rescued the child.

In English one cannot strand the preposition in an infinitival relative construction, but must front it with the relative pronoun. This accounts for the grammaticality differences in (9) and (10) above. Sentences (11) and (12) exhibit a contrast in verb/modifier behaviour. When the verbal precedes the noun, its adverb must precede it—exactly opposite the position it assumes when the verbal follows the noun. All the structures selected for test follow from obscure facts of English that are not likely to have been taught.

    I constructed tests of grammatical intuitions in a format similar to the test of Universal Grammar. One test contained 12 randomised sentences pertaining to semantic structure. The other contained 24 randomised sentences following from language particular facts of English. (See Appendices B and C for a complete list of the sentences tested.) My subjects' performance on these tests is given in Table 5. As we can see, in all areas except idiom behaviour, where they both do poorly, Minh performs considerably better than Jeanne. And this is after only five years of residence as an adult in an English speaking environment. What is more surprising is that Jeanne does so poorly.

TABLE 5. *Comparison of the successful and unsuccessful learner on language tests*

	(% correct)	
	Unsuccessful (Jeanne)	Successful (Minh)
Universal Grammar	81	84
Semantic structure	58	83
Particular grammar		
Rule governed constructs	63	81
Idiom behaviour	37	37
Proficiency Exam		
Composition	78	90
MTAC	90	92
MTELP	86	94

Neuropsychological profile

In order to see whether there is a general cognitive profile which characterises her unsuccessful language learning, I administered a series of neuropsychological tests to both Jeanne and Minh. In choosing tests, I drew upon a study by Novoa *et al.* (1988) which described the cognitive functioning of an exceptionally good language learner (see also this volume, chapter 9). On certain neuropsychological tests their subject performed at or near ceiling. These tests were thought to require cognitive abilities necessary for good language learning. The tests on which their subject excelled were the following:

Ravens Progressive Matrices—a general non-verbal intelligence measure requiring subjects to decide which choice completes an abstract pattern with a missing part;

Modern Language Aptitude Test (MLAT)—consisting of five subtests;

Logical Memory subtest of the Weschler Memory Scale—requiring the retention of a paragraph;

All vocabulary tests;

Digit Symbol subtest of the WAIS-R—where subjects match abstract symbols to digits using a given code. Their subject performed extremely well on a modification of the Digit Symbol requiring immediate recall of the code and recall following a 20 minute delay.

Novoa *et al.* concluded from their subject's performance on the test battery that the cognitive skills responsible for his superior language learning ability were a superb verbal memory and the ability to perceive and manipulate formal patterns.

Since the above tests were the ones which distinguished their good language learner, I decided to use them on my two subjects. In addition, I selected two other nonverbal tests of general intelligence, the Thurston–Jeffrey tests of Gestalt Completion and Concealed Figures. The Gestalt Completion test requires subjects to identify a picture from incomplete material, while the Concealed Figures test asks them to locate simple geometric figures embedded in more complex ones. Both tests require subjects to perceive or manipulate patterns, skills central to language acquisition. As my two subjects were not native speakers of English, I could not administer the normal tests of verbal memory. Even so, I tried the Weschler test of Logical Memory, but neither subject did very well. The one verbal memory test which does not depend on proficiency in English is the

TABLE 6. *Comparison of the successful and unsuccessful learner on neuropsychological tests*

	(% correct)	
	Unsuccessful (Jeanne)	Successful (Minh)
Concealed Figures (T–J)	96	93
Gestalt Completion (T–J)	73	58
Ravens Progressive Matrices	82	80
Digit Symbol (WAIS-R)	71	61
Digit Symbol—immed. recall	100	100
Digit Symbol—20 min. recall	78	100
Logical Memory (Weschler)	44	49
MLAT—Vocabulary subtest	79	100

Vocabulary subtest of the MLAT, which is essentially a paired associates test. I used this as the measure of their verbal memory aptitude.

The results of Jeanne and Minh's performance on the cognitive tests are given in Table 6. We can see that Jeanne performs similarly to or slightly better than Minh on all tests except the verbal memory tests. Her weak performance on tests of verbal memory is consistent with her self-reports of poor spelling and vocabulary retention. However, there does not seem to be any other cognitive factor which I could isolate as responsible for her poor second language acquisition. Jeanne appears to be an extremely intelligent individual who performs well on all cognitive tasks, except second language learning. Therefore, I would have to conclude from this research that there could be a degree of talent in language learning ability not related to other cognitive talents.

Conclusion

The question still unanswered is why Jeanne's innate language acquisition mechanism which allowed her to acquire Chinese as a first language did not facilitate the native-like acquisition of her second language before puberty. It is even more mysterious, since her innate mechanism was functioning sufficiently to allow the native acquisition of English phonology. In fact, most researchers have argued that the ability to acquire a phonology diminishes before the ability to acquire syntax and semantics (cf. Seliger, 1978). Following this reasoning, one would assume that the ability to acquire the phonology would imply the ability to acquire the syntax and semantics.

Two facts are certain concerning Jeanne's acquisition of English. First, she has not achieved native fluency in either syntax or semantics despite the fact that she began acquiring English well before puberty. And second, there is no apparent affective or sociolinguistic explanation for this failure. One goal of future research should be to identify how widespread this failure to acquire is. Many learners, on casual observation, appear to have achieved native competence because they have acquired the phonology and in addition use simple, error-free sentences in their speech. It is only when they are required to respond to more complicated syntactic and semantic demands, that one discovers their true linguistic level. Therefore, to document the extent of this phenomenon, we must examine their knowledge of English in greater depth. Certainly, discovering more about this group of learners will give us a clearer picture of the maturational constraints on second language acquisition.

Appendix A: Sentences used to test knowledge of universal grammar

GRAMMATICAL

UNGRAMMATICAL

Subjacency

1. WH-islands

* What does Mary want to know whether John has already sold ϕ?

* What does Tom wonder where Nancy has put ϕ?

* Where did Bill want to know who put the book ϕ?

2. Complex NPs

   a. Factives

What did John think that the teacher had said ϕ?

* What did John believe the claim that Carol had bought ϕ?

What did John realise he could not sell ϕ?

* What did John hear the news that the mayor would do ϕ?

   b. Relative Clauses

* Who did John buy the house that ϕ had recommended to him?

* Where did Bill visit a friend who had just arrived from ϕ?

GRAMMATICAL	UNGRAMMATICAL
	* What did the police arrest the men who were carrying φ?

3. Coordination

* What did John find the ball and φ?
* What does John like to eat tomatoes and φ?

ECP

1. Subject/Object Asymmetries
   a. *Superiority*
   I can't remember who φ did what.   * She forgot what who said φ.

   b. *That-trace filter*
   What did Frank say that Judy would like to read φ?

   * What did John say that φ would fall on the floor, if we're not careful?

   Who did Ellen say Max thought φ would pass the test?

   c. *Sentential subject islands*
   What kind of book is it necessary to read φ?

   * What sort of food is to digest φ easy?

2. PP/adverb islands
   Which bed does John like to sleep in φ?

   * What time will Mary arrive before φ?
   * What did Albert put money in the box during φ?
   * What does John eat hamburgers because he likes φ?

3. Specified Subject Constraint
   What did Mike see pictures of φ?   * What did Mary hear Bill's stories about φ?

Control Sentences

1. Who/Whom
   Who does John want to see φ?
   Who should I give the bracelet to φ?

2. Long Movements
   What did John think Carol wanted her mother to give the postman φ?
   Which apple did Mary say it would be easy for us to cut φ?
   Which information would it be possible for Mary to persuade Susan to tell the reporters φ?

3. P-Stranding
   Where is the person that I want you to talk to φ?
   What did Sally ask her younger brother to look at φ?

Appendix B: Sentences used to test semantic structure

Predicate Contrasts with Declarative and Interrogative Complements
1.   Alice wondered who Jennifer had phoned.
2.   *Who did Sally wonder that Wanda had seen?
3.   *Carol believed what Sarah had taken to the cleaners.
4.   Who did Joan believe that Marsha had met at the party?
5.   Amy realised who Linda had written to.
6.   Who did Mark realise that Tom had spoken to yesterday?

Permissibility of *any* with Quantified Heads
7.   No one who came late was given anything to eat.
8.   No suitcase which contained anything of value was lost.
9.   *Every shop which was broken into was missing anything.
10. Everyone who lost anything must fill out a report.
11. *Some book which was returned had any fines against it.
12. *Some child who showed any flu symptoms became ill.

Appendix C: Sentences used to test English-specific grammar

Contrasts of Fixed and Flexible Idioms
1.   Her father laid down the law to her.
2.   He blew off some steam at the party.
3.   Her father laid the law down before she was twelve.
4.   *He blew some steam off after he got home.
5.   His laying down of the law doesn't make him an authority.
6.   *Your blowing off of some steam surprised us.
7.   The law was laid down by her father early in her life.
8.   *Some steam was blown off at the party.

Rule Governed Contrasts Particular to English
1.   Put down the paper.
2.   *Look up it.
3.   Send me the results.
4.   *Give him it.
5.   The lawyer, arguing persuasively, convinced the jury not to free him.
6.   *The man, convincingly speaking, was able to raise $30,000.
7.   The slowly running water quickly filled the tub.
8.   *The responding quickly policeman rescued the child.
9.   A man proud of his family spends time with his children.
10. *An interested person in learning doesn't avoid difficult courses.
11. Here are the tools for you to work with.
12. *There's a basket in which for you to put it.
13. He found a cloth with which to wipe it.
14. *That's the fork which to eat it with.
15. Mary was avoiding washing the car.
16. *John was continuing seeing horror movies.

Notes to Chapter 10

1. While it is the case that Chinese and Vietnamese have no syntactic WH-movement, both languages manifest WH-movement at the level of logical form (LF). Transfer from the native language is inapplicable only with respect to syntactic WH-movement, those movements restricted by Subjacency. Knowledge of the constraints on WH-movements due to the Empty Category Principle (ECP) could, in fact, be transferred from the first language. However, in the testing described below, there was no significant difference in the acceptability judgements of the deviant sentences following from each of the two principles. In fact, one deviant sentence ruled out on the basis of the ECP was judged acceptable by all subjects:

    * What sort of food is to digest ϕ easy?

2. Native subjects fell below 90% on four test sentences. For a description of the sentences and an explanation of the variance in their performance see Bley-Vroman *et al.* (1988).

References

BLEY-VROMAN, R., 1988, The fundamental character of foreign language learning. In W. RUTHERFORD & M. SHARWOOD SMITH (eds), *Grammar and Second Language Teaching*. New York: Newbury Press.

BLEY-VROMAN, B., FELIX, S. and IOUP, G., 1988, The accessibility of Universal Grammar in adult language learning, *Second Language Research*, 4(1), 1–32.

FELIX, S. 1985, More evidence on competing cognitive systems, *Second Language Research*, 1, 47–72.

FLYNN, S., 1983, Differences between first and second language acquisition: setting the parameters of Universal Grammar. In D. ROGERS & J. SLOBODA (eds), *Symbolic Skills*. New York: Plenum Press.

HILLES, S., 1986, Interlanguage and the pro-drop parameter, *Second Language Research*, 2, 33–52.

KRASHEN, S., SCARCELLA, R. and LONG, M. (eds), 1982, *Child–Adult Differences in Second Language Acquisition*. Rowley, MA: Newbury House.

NOVOA, L., FEIN, D. and OBLER, L., 1988, Talent in foreign languages: A case study. In L. OBLER & D. FEIN (eds), *The Exceptional Brain: Neuropsychology of Talent and Special Abilities*. New York: Guilford Press.

OYAMA, S., 1976, A sensitive period for the acquisition of a non-native phonological system, *Journal of Psycholinguistic Research*, 5, 261–85.

RUTHERFORD, W., 1986, Grammatical theory and L2 acquisition: a brief overview, *Second Language Research*, 2, 1–15.

SELIGER, H., 1978, Implications of a multiple critical periods hypothesis for second language learning. In W. RITCHIE (ed.), *Second Language Acquisition Research*. New York: Academic Press.

SNOW, C. and HOEFNAGEL-HOHLE, M., 1978, The critical period for language acquisition: Evidence from second language learning, *Child Development*, 49, 1114–28.

WHITE, L., 1985, The acquisition of parameterized grammars: Subjacency in second language acquisition, *Second Language Research*, 1, 1–17.

WONG-FILLMORE, L., 1979, Individual differences in second language acquisition. In C. FILLMORE, D. KEMPLER & W. WANG (eds), *Individual Differences in Language Ability and Language Behavior*. New York: Academic Press.

ZOBL, H., 1986, A functional approach to the attainability of typological targets in L2 acquisition, *Second Language Research*, 2, 16–32.

11 Maturational changes of language acquisitional abilities

HENNING WODE
University of Kiel

Introduction

The issue of maturational changes is familiar enough from such areas as biology or conceptual development. It is less obvious, however, whether such changes can be shown to occur also with respect to those abilities that govern the acquisition and development of the more formal properties of linguistic systems. Previous attempts to focus on such phenomena, such as Lenneberg's (1967) critical period hypothesis, are no longer tenable (cf. reviews like Krashen, 1973 or Wode, 1981). Lenneberg suggested that around puberty changes occur in the brain so that after that age, i.e. beginning around 12;0–14;0 people can no longer learn human languages the way young children do. Lenneberg assumed, in particular, that the development of the lateralisation of brain functions was completed by that time. Subsequent research has revealed numerous flaws in Lenneberg's assumptions. Krashen (1973) re-analysed Lenneberg's data on aphasic patients and showed that this evidence was compatible with the view that lateralisation was completed by age 5;0. In addition, I pointed out in Wode (1981) that there are many developmental structures which occur across all age groups. This means that the abilities underlying these structures cannot be assumed to have changed over time. However, it is suggested below that recent advances in language acquisition research call for a reconsideration of the maturational issue, because such changes may occur elsewhere and at different times than those suggested by Lenneberg.

The universal approach to language acquisition

The central issue for any theory of language acquisition is to determine the nature of the language learning mechanism(s). The crucial point is not to find out how children learn one language, but how people in general learn languages, for example, in different external settings, or at different points during their lifetime. Do people activate totally different learning mechanisms depending on the learning situation, for example, whether they are tutored or not, or whether it is their first, second or third language? Or do human beings have only one single language learning mechanism which is flexible enough to cope with differences in external settings? The research of the last two decades on L1 and L2 acquisition, foreign language teaching, or on the re-learning of languages clearly indicates that the first alternative, i.e. assuming a number of totally unrelated learning systems, must be ruled out. Of course, it is not at all difficult to cite some differences between younger and older learners, between first or second language learners, or when learners are faced with different tasks. However, none of these differences is of the sort to require the assumption that these differences are due to totally independent learning mechanisms.

One requirement that such an assumption would have to meet is that there is at least one property that categorically differentiates different acquisitional types, say L1 and L2. To the best of my knowledge no such property has been identified so far. Even age will not do in this respect. Of course, if one compares adult L2 acquisition to child L1 acquisition then the age difference is so obvious that age may conveniently be taken as a property that sets these two types of acquisition apart. However, age is a continuous variable. The question, therefore, is which age range is to be chosen as the criterion. This issue cannot be decided arbitrarily, as in McLaughlin (1978:9) who—arbitrarily—defines L2 acquisition as learning an additional language after the age of 3;0. What is needed is a functional solution in the sense that the learner's development, as reflected in his/her linguistic behaviour, must provide the type of evidence where a given property occurs categorically only with one group of subjects and not with another.

Since no such categorical differences have been noted so far, it follows that a theory of language acquisition should be based on the assumption that there is only one language learning mechanism. However, since there are differences in the linguistic behaviour of different age groups, another assumption has to be made, namely, that at least some of the learning abilities change as a function of age.

In sum, a theory of language acquisition must be universal in two respects: it must be applicable to all types of language acquisition, and it must apply to all age groups, which, in turn, means that it must make proper provision for at least some of the learning abilities to change as a function of age. (For further details on this universal approach see Wode, 1981.)

This chapter deals primarily with the acquisition of phonology from such a universal point of view. The emphasis is on showing that some phonological learning abilities do change and mature during a speaker's lifetime. At present it cannot be decided whether this maturational process is entirely due to biological maturation or whether it is determined by external stimulation.

A hypothesis on the coding of mental representations of the phonological components of lexical items

The hypothesis explored in this chapter relates to how the phonological components of lexical items are coded in memory. The claim is that at the time a child begins to learn his/her first language(s) this information is not coded in terms of segments as with fully matured speakers, at least not to the same extent.

Ferguson & Farwell (1975) have suggested that the acquisition of phonology at first is based on the whole word, rather than on segments as suggested by traditional phonemic analysis and as applied to L1 child phonology, for example, by Jakobson (1941) and the many studies based on the same assumption (e.g. Grégoire, 1937, 1947; Ohnesorg, 1948; Pačesová, 1968; Olmstedt, 1971; Ingram, 1976; Leopold, 1939).[1]

In this chapter I attempt to carry Ferguson's and Farwell's suggestions further by asking how children code the phonological component of lexical items in memory. In particular, the issue is to determine to what extent and at what age children can be assumed to have the ability to mentally represent phonological information of lexical items in terms of segments. It is suggested that the presently available data require the assumption that children when beginning to learn their first language(s) do not have the ability to represent phonological information in terms of segments to the same extent as more mature speakers. We do not yet have sufficient data to rule out completely a stronger hypothesis, namely, that at first children do not have any segments at all. In any case, it takes some time for the child's representations to develop to the point where they are coded in terms of segments to the same extent as with mature speakers. At present, the data discussed below suggest that the outlines of this development tend to be completed at least by age 3;4 and that this may happen as early as around 2;0.

The main thrust of the arguments presented below is to show that the development and availability of segment-based coding procedures is a prerequisite for several well-known characteristics of phonological acquisition; for example, phonological processes of early L1 child phonology, phonological transfer in L2 acquisition, the lack of phonological transfer in early child L1 bilingualism and the burst in the rate of L1 lexical acquisition after the first 50 words.

Some evidence

Phonological transfer as evidence for segments

There are numerous observations, notably of slips of the tongue (e.g. Fromkin, 1973), which suggest that the notion of segment is not only a descriptive device but that segments are psychologically real in the sense that phonological information about lexical items is coded in memory in terms of segments. From the point of view of the universal approach suggested in this chapter, perhaps the most telling evidence is the occurrence and the nature of phonological transfer in the non-L1 types of language acquisition. Consider, for example, some of the notorious transfer errors that Germans tend to produce in trying to learn English.

As is well known, Germans have great difficulties in producing the final voiced plosives and fricatives of English. They tend to be devoiced. Words like *rise* or *ride* will sound like 'rice' and 'write'. Note that what gets devoiced is the final segment and not the initial or medial one. In order for speakers to be able to hit the proper segment of the L2 target, they need to have a mental representation of segments in order for their total planning or processing procedures to be organisable in such a way that the devoicing occurs at the proper spot, i.e. in the final segment and not, say, in the initial or medial one. Of course, the ability to mentally represent segments is not restricted to final segments. This is obvious because of another error notoriously committed by German learners of English. The English vowel [æ] as in *bat* tends to be substituted by a closer vowel [ɛ] so that English *bat* sounds like *bet*. The same argument applies here. For learners to systematically restrict the error to the medial vowel requires the assumption that these learners must have at their disposal a mental representation of segments.

From a developmental point of view it is important to identify the age ranges at which phonological transfer can be observed with young learners. The earliest age reported on is close to 3;0. For example, the data available in the Kiel corpus on L2 German/L1 English include a boy who came to Germany at the age of 2;8 and who was first investigated at 3;4, i.e. 9 months after his first contact with German. At that time the boy's pronunciation was remarkably close to that of his L1 German speaking monolingual age group. However, there were a number of transfer peculiarities, all of them familiar from English learners of German older than 3;4. Such errors include: the unrounding of rounded front vowels, e.g. [ε] in place of lax /œ/ in *Löffel* (spoon); velarisation of final /-l/ as [ɫ] in *Löffel*, replacement of front rounded vowels by back vowels, e.g. lax [u] for lax /y/ as in *Brücke* (bridge) or *fünf* (five), [ɔ] for lax /œ/ in *Löffel* (spoon), tense [o] for tense /ɸ/ as in *schön* (beautiful, nice); or diphthongisation of the German monophthongs /e o/ via [εɪ ou]. We do not know whether the boy's record at 3;4 illustrates his initial state of affairs or the end of what may have been a much more prevalent characteristic of his L2 phonology. In any event, this type of evidence clearly shows that segments must be available at least around age 3;4. Other types of evidence reviewed below suggest that the ability to represent segments may develop as early as around 2;0.

L1 phonological processes as evidence for segments

That L1 children at first do not reproduce the phonetic/phonological features of the target words in exactly the sequence as required by the target is probably one of the most reliably documented findings for early L1 phonology. For example, when English children produce [gɔgi] instead of *doggie* /dɔgi/, or when German children pronounce *Decke* (blanket) as [kɛkə] instead of /dɛkə/, the velar feature is fronted (e.g. Ingram, 1976; Smith, 1973; Pačesová, 1968; Leopold, 1939). With respect to the segment issue of interest here, two points should be noted. First, the phonological processes are highly systematic: they are not restricted to exceptional individuals, but occur with all children. Second, the displaced features are not moved around lexical items in random ways but are shifted only to specific segments. In the case of the two words above, note, for instance, that the velar feature in the German [kɛkə] instead of /dɛkə/ is moved to the initial plosive and not to the vowel, which would result in a back vowel. Nor do the displaced features tend to straddle several segments in the target word. This means that for these early L1 phonological processes to operate the way they do requires the existence of segments either in the mental representation of lexical items or as psychologically real units within the total processing operations.

Phonological evidence not consistent with segments: holistic coding

Ferguson & Farwell (1975) have pointed out two important characteristics of L1 children's very early utterances. First, they do contain phonological features of the respective target items, but not necessarily in the same order as in the target. Word final features may appear at the beginning in the child's version or at other places which do not agree with the sequencing in the target. Second, the sequencing of features in the child's productions is not always consistent across several tokens of the same item. Ferguson & Farwell (1975:423) report a particularly bewildering example from a child, K. The following forms were recorded for K's new word *pen* in a 30 minute session in the order below:

(1) [mã] (imitation)
(2) [yÃ] (imitation)
(3) [dɛ^{dn}]
(4) [hɪn]
(5) [^{m}bõ]
(6) [p^{h}ɪn]
(7) [t^{h}nt^{h}nt^{h}n]
(8) [ba^{h}]
(9) [d^{h}au]
(10) [buã][2]

Ferguson & Farwell point out that the child's difficulty is not in identifying the phonetic/phonological features of the target. One way or another, they are reflected in the child's ten attempts. The difficulty for the child is to reproduce them in the proper sequence as required by the target. For example, the nasal feature occurs at the end of the target *pen*. In the child's reproductions nasality surfaces initially, medially and/or finally. This evidence strongly suggests that what the child lacked was the ability to process phonetic features on the basis of segments. This means the unit to which the phonetic features are allocated is the lexical item, as suggested by Ferguson

& Farwell (1975) and as explained above. However, within the lexical item there is no sequencing of the features, such that they are assigned to specific segments of the lexical item. This type of coding is here called *holistic*. No matter whether holistic coding pertains only to some lexical items or to the entire vocabulary, since older children and adults code on the basis of segments, it follows that it develops subsequent to some initial state. Whether this ability relates to the mental representations proper, or whether it is part of the retrieval or production processes, is a different matter, which, at the present time, is very difficult to solve.

Phonological transfer in L1 bilinguals

If the above hypothesis is correct, bilingual children should at first not show evidence of phonological transfer of the sort familiar from L2 acquisition. Unfortunately, to the best of my knowledge, there have not been any large-scale investigations to determine the extent of phonological transfer and the point in the development of bilingual children when transfer first occurs. However, two sources of data are helpful: personal reports by parents and the available literature on the acquisition of phonology by bilingual children (e.g. Ronjat, 1913; Pavlovitch, 1920; Leopold, 1939).

The informal reports I have had from parents all agree that with bilingual children there is at first no phonological transfer from one language to the other. The available studies, e.g. those mentioned above, are compatible with the parental reports in that there is no mention of phonological transfer. Given the interest in, and the attention devoted to, phonetic details in these studies, one can be sure that the lack of mention of transfer is not due to oversight. There simply was no transfer. The observations concerning early bilinguals contrast with the fact that at later stages bilingual children have no difficulty at all in transferring phonological properties from one language to the other, for example, in mimicking the respective accents. These observations agree with the hypothesis of this chapter. Just like monolingual children, bilingual children at first lack the ability for segment-based coding essential for phonological transfer to occur. A telling instance is reported by Leopold (1939). His daughter grew up bilingual with German and English. At one time she had both the German and the English word for 'ball'. The German word is *Ball*. One difference between English and German relates to the final /-l/. The German /l/ is 'clear', i.e. alveolar, the English is 'dark', i.e. retroflex or velar. In L1 acquisition final clear /l/'s tend at first to be reproduced by children in terms of an i-like vowel; dark /l/'s in terms of a u-type vowel. Leopold's daughter had the German word at 1;5, the English word at 1;9. The German word tended to be pronounced [baɪ], the English [bau]. Although the German word was acquired four months before the English version the child at no time transferred the German i-like quality to her English word *ball*.

The implication of the observations concerning bilinguals and young L2 learners is that although segment-based coding is a necessary prerequisite for transfer, it is, apparently, not a sufficient one. Additional prerequisites need to develop. Future research will have to identify them.[3]

L1 lexical acquisition: the first fifty words

It appears that the hypothesis explored here, although dealing with phonological acquisition, can also be related to, and gain support from, a well-known characteristic of L1 vocabulary development. This consideration is extremely important because it highlights how developments in one area may set the stage for developments in other areas.

Many reports show that the rate of vocabulary acquisition for L1 children changes drastically after they have acquired a vocabulary of about fifty words (e.g. Nelson, 1973; McCarthy, 1954). L1 children may spend several weeks before they progress from, e.g. the third to the fourth or the tenth to the eleventh word. However, once the vocabulary gets to the size of about 50 words the number of words acquired per time unit, say per day or week, increases dramatically. This burst is reported to occur any time between 1;4 and 2;0 (e.g. Nelson, 1973).

The question is, why this sudden burst? Is it because caretakers suddenly decide to teach their children? Or do they move them into environments where the input is richer? These explanations must be ruled out, because parents, in general, do not do this sort of thing. The hypothesis concerning the ability of segment-based coding abilities offers a different and more convincing explanation, namely, in terms of a reorganisation of the storing or processing principles operative in human memory.

Storing and processing mechanisms that do not allow for phonological information to be organised in terms of segments are much less economical than those that do. In terms of building a vocabulary, holistic procedures allow for little more than compiling unordered lists. In terms of recognition, such lists allow only for fairly clumsy retrieval procedures. These operations become increasingly inefficient as the number of items to be checked through increases. Coding based on segments allows for much more economical and systematic processing procedures. It appears, therefore, that what causes the sudden burst in the rate of acquisition of vocabulary in L1 learners is the emergence of new organisational principles for coding linguistic information. The change towards segment-based coding makes the dramatic increase in vocabulary acquisition possible. That is to say, what seems to be at the bottom of the notorious burst around the first fifty words is not conceptual growth, increases in word knowledge, or advances in logical thinking. It is hypothesised that it is a change in the way linguistic information is coded in memory that allows the child to better exploit the richness of his/her own non-linguistic development.

Some conclusions

It is important to note the speculative nature of this chapter. First, a most serious gap undoubtedly relates to the data that bear on the issue of holistic coding. To be sure, there is no lack of material on phonological processes based on segments, because this is the period of development that most L1 research has traditionally been focused on (e.g. Jakobson, 1941; Pačesová, 1968; Macken, 1979; see also reviews like Ingram, 1976; Menn, 1983). In fact, one major assumption underlying this work has been that for children's productions to be regarded as language, the structure of their words must be such that they can be related to target items on the basis of segments. The research by Ferguson & Farwell (1975) and Waterson (1970, 1971) as well as the hypothesis explored here suggests that this assumption is not only unwarranted but that it may be barring future progress. We urgently need large-scale studies that focus on, and that do not discard as non-speech, such evidence as the examples of 'pen' above. It is data of this kind that are needed to evaluate or make more precise the hypothesis of this chapter or to help us devise better alternatives. For example: are early child productions totally holistic or do children already have some kind of basic segments like syllable onset and syllable nucleus? Does the phenomenon identified in this chapter as holistic coding relate to the mental representations proper or to some stages in the total processing operations involved in learning or producing target items? Is holistic coding limited to specific, perhaps phonologically complex target items? Or to what extent is there individual variation between children? To what extent can the children reported on by Ferguson & Farwell (1975) and Waterson (1970, 1971) be regarded as normal learners, or is this chapter overshooting the mark because the hypotheses put forward above are based on exceptional, perhaps deviant, learners?

Another extremely important issue is whether and to what extent the development of the coding abilities is determined by external stimulation or biological growth. The case of Genie (Curtiss, 1977) provides some hints. Recall that Genie was a little over 13 years old when she was discovered. At that time she could not speak English, although she may have heard a few words before her parents shut her off from any contact whatever. The available reports on how Genie learned English after her discovery are unanimous in not reporting any data that would suggest that Genie either went through a stage of holistic coding or that she made any use of phonological processes characteristic of early L1 child phonology. It is impossible to explain these observations by the richness of external stimulation. At best one could claim that the initial exposure to English, short as it was, may have been sufficient to trigger the process of development of the phonological coding abilities. However, it may be more appropriate not to rule out completely the possibility that the growth of the coding abilities for phonological representations may not entirely be due to external stimulation. Surely, there must be a strong biological bias, if not some totally autonomous development.

In spite of the research gaps and uncertainties alluded to above, I regard two points as undisputed. First, the maturational issue is anything but settled and it should remain on our research agenda. Second, this issue can only be approached in a sensible way by adopting a universal approach, i.e. by not restricting the domain of a language learning theory to one acquisitional type, such as L1 acquisition or adult L2 acquisition. The most insightful way of pursuing the maturational issue appears to be to redefine the domain of a language learning theory in such a way that it relates to people's language learning ability in general.

Notes to Chapter 11

1. Among other things, Ferguson & Farwell (1975:425) point out that the range of phonological variation found with children in their first 50 words cannot be described in a systematic way on the basis of segments. For example, in one word a child may alternate between, say, [b : w : p] *baby*, but have only [b ~ ß] in *bye-bye* and [b] in *bang*.

2. Ferguson and Farwell do not give the exact date of the interview. However, judging from their table 1 and what they report about the intervals at which the children were recorded, K must have been approximately 1;3 at the time the ten versions of *pen* were recorded.

3. For more details on the phonological data concerning transfer and phonological processes in monolinguals and bilinguals, see Wode, 1987.

References

CURTISS, S., 1977, *Genie: A Psycholinguistic Study of a Modern Day 'Wild Child'*. New York: Academic Press.

FERGUSON, C. A. and FARWELL, C. B., 1975, Words and sounds in early language acquisition, *Language*, 51, 419–39.

FROMKIN, V. A., 1973, *Speech Errors as Linguistic Evidence*. The Hague: Mouton.

GRÉGOIRE, A., 1937, *L'apprenttissage du langage I. Les deux premières années suivantes*. Paris, Liège: Droz.

——, 1947, *L'apprenttissage du Language II. La troisème année et les années suivantes*. Paris, Liège: Droz.

INGRAM, D., 1976, *Phonological Disability in Children*. London: Edward Arnold.

JAKOBSON, R., 1941, *Kindersprache, Aphasie und allgemeine Lautgesetze*. Uppsala: Almqvist & Wiksell.

KRASHEN, S. D., 1973, Lateralization, language learning, and the critical period: Some new evidence, *Language Learning*, 23, 63–74.

LENNEBERG, E. H., 1967, *Biological Foundations of Language*. New York: Wiley.

LEOPOLD, W. F., 1939, *Speech Development of a Bilingual Child. A Linguist's Record*, Vol. I. Evanston, Ill: Northwestern University Press.

MACKEN, M. A., 1979, The developmental reorganisation of phonology: A hierarchy of basic units of acquisition, *Lingua*, 49, 11–49.

MCCARTHY, 1954, Language development in children. In L. CHARMICHAEL (ed.), *Manual of Child Psychology*. New York: Wiley.

MCLAUGHLIN, B., 1978, *Second Language Acquisition in Childhood*. Hillsdale, NJ: Lawrence Erlbaum.

MENN, L., 1983, Development of articulatory, phonetic, and phonological capabilities. In B. BUTTERWORTH (ed.), *Language Production II: Development, Writing, and Other Language Processes*. New York: Academic Press.

NELSON, K., 1973, *Structure and Strategy in Learning to Talk*. Monographs of the Society for Research in Child Development 38. Chicago, Ill: Society for Research in Child Development.

OHNESORG, K., 1948, *Foneticka Studie Edětské Řeci*. Prague: Univerzity Karlovy.

OLMSTEDT, D. L., 1971, *Out of the Mouth of Babes. Early Stages in Language Learning*. The Hague: Mouton.

PAČESOVÀ, J., 1968, *The Development of Vocabulary in the Child*. Brno: Universität J.E. Purkynè.

PAVLOVITCH, M., 1920, *Le Langage Enfantin: Acquisition du Serbe et du Français par un Enfant Serbe*. Paris: Champion.

RONJAT, J., 1913, *Le Développement du Langage Observé Chez un Enfant Bilingue*. Paris: Champion.

SMITH, N. V., 1973, *The Acquisition of Phonology*. Cambridge: Cambridge University Press.

WATERSON, N., 1970, Some speech forms of an English child: A phonological study, *Transactions of the Philological Society*, 1–24.

——, 1971, Child phonology: A prosodic view, *Journal of Linguistics*, 7, 179–211.

WODE, H., 1981, *Learning a Second Language. An Integrated View of Language Acquisition*. Tübingen: Gunter Narr.

——, 1987, The rise of phonological coding abilities for the mental representation of lexical items. In H. BLUHME & G. HAMMARSTRÖM (eds), *Descriptio Linguistica. Proceedings of the First Conference on Descriptive and Structural Linguistics*. Tübingen: Gunter Narr.

Section Five:
Attrition

12 Variation in the use of referential forms within the context of foreign language loss

AHMED FAKHRI
University of Toledo

Introduction

One of the most striking features of interlanguages (ILs) is their variability, and many attempts have been made to describe and explain such variability.[1] In particular, IL variability has been viewed as resulting from situational factors on the one hand, and linguistic factors on the other (Ellis, 1985).

With respect to situational factors, many second language researchers, following Labov's work on variation in native speech, showed that language learners' performance varies consistently with the particular task used to elicit interlanguage data (LoCoco, 1976; Dickerson & Dickerson, 1977; Tarone, 1979). Tarone (1982) views such variation in terms of a continuum of interlanguage styles and claims that style-shifting along this continuum is the result of the amount of attention the learner pays to his or her linguistic output.

On the other hand, linguistic factors may also explain variation in interlanguage. The learner may use a particular target language form in one type of obligatory linguistic context but not in another (Dickerson, 1975).

Purpose

This chapter deals with the second type of IL variation (i.e. variation resulting from linguistic context) in foreign language loss. The purpose of the study was to investigate change in the use of referential forms (i.e. full NPs and pronouns) in the written narrative discourse of learners of French as a foreign language who had interrupted their study of the target language. It was predicted that the interruption of language instruction would result in an increase of the use of full NPs and avoidance of pronominalisation to refer to participants in narrative discourse. Some justification for this prediction is in order.

In narrative discourse, one of the important tasks of the narrator is to keep reference to the participants straight. To achieve this goal, the narrator has available various means of encoding referents, ranging from grammaticalised and less salient linguistic elements to heavier and more salient ones. Examples of less salient forms are pronoun clitics and agreement markings on the verb. More salient forms include full noun phrases. These referential devices can be represented on a grammaticalisation scale, the lightest forms (e.g. clitics) being the most grammaticalised (Givón, 1984).

The prediction made above, then, would amount to saying that as a result of the interruption of language instruction, learners would rely more on the use of heavy referential forms (i.e. full NPs) and avoid weaker forms of reference (i.e. pronouns). This prediction seems plausible if we assume that the loser's interlanguage would behave like other exceptional language systems such as pidgins and creoles, child language, and dying languages (Obler & Menn, 1983). In fact, studies of such language systems showed that they exhibited a higher frequency of salient forms to encode meaning when compared to the language of adult monolinguals (Valdman & Phillips, 1977; Trudgill, 1976; Bellugi, 1967). I believe that the encoding of referents by means of full noun phrases, when weaker and more grammaticalised forms such as clitics would suffice, is a similar phenomenon.

Method

Design and subjects

The type of design adopted in this study is a combination of the longitudinal and cross-sectional approaches used in language acquisition studies. The cross-sectional comparisons involved three groups of subjects who took the same language course but varied in terms of the recency of their exposure to the target language: Groups 1 ($n = 17$) and 2 ($n = 17$) had received no language instruction for twelve and eight months, respectively, when the study began. Group 3 ($n = 16$), the control group, had just finished their language course. Longitudinal data were obtained by retesting group 3 a second time after three months and ten days with no language instruction. The following diagram illustrates the comparisons involved:

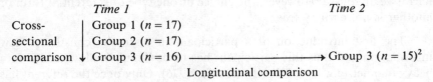

| | *Time 1* | *Time 2* |

Cross-sectional comparison ↓ Group 1 ($n = 17$), Group 2 ($n = 17$), Group 3 ($n = 16$) ——————→ Group 3 ($n = 15$)[2]

Longitudinal comparison

The subjects were American undergraduate students at the University of Michigan who had completed *French 232*, the last one-semester course in a four-course sequence, in order to fulfil the foreign language requirement. In order to ensure maximum equivalence between the groups with respect to language ability, only students with grades between 2.70 and 3.30 (out of 4) on the Michigan point system were selected for the study. The average grade for each group was 3.00 (see Fakhri, 1985, for more details).

Instrument

The subjects were shown a short film (approximately six minutes long) and then given 30 minutes to report in writing what happened in it. The film, known as the *Pear Film*, was a 16 mm colour and sound film produced under the direction of Wallace Chafe of the University of California at Berkeley (see Chafe, 1980). The following is a summary of the film:

> The opening scene shows a man picking pears on a ladder in a tree. He comes down, puts the pears in three baskets under the tree and climbs the ladder again. Another man, with a goat on a leash, passes by. Then a boy on a bicycle comes by and stops near the baskets. He lifts one of the baskets, puts it on his bicycle and drives off. After a while, a girl on a bicycle passes him. The boy turns to look at her and his bicycle hits a rock and falls over. Then three boys come by and help him pick up the pears and put the basket back on the bicycle. The boy gives them some pears. The three boys continue to walk, eating their pears. Meanwhile, the pear picker comes down the ladder, and notices that one of the baskets is missing. The three boys pass by the picker, who watches them as they walk away, still eating their pears.

Measurements

In order to quantify the types of referential forms in the subjects' narratives, it is necessary to develop some understanding of the expected distribution of such forms in narrative discourse. It was mentioned earlier that the narrator has available different means of encoding participants in narrative discourse. However, the choice of one type of referential form or another is not entirely free.

The first introduction of a participant in discourse constitutes new information and thus this participant has to be linguistically encoded in a heavy manner (e.g. as a full NP) (Chafe, 1976). Only once the referent has been clearly established can more attenuated forms of reference be used. However, other factors may force the narrator to use heavy referential forms even for a previously established referent. Givón (1984) identified two such factors. The first one is the gap separating two mentions of the same referent. The larger this gap is, the more likely is the decay of the referent. Consequently, the length of this gap may require the narrator to re-establish the referent through heavier encoding. The second factor is the potential interference from other referents. Although the gap separating two mentions of the same referent may be relatively short, the presence of other referents in the discourse stretch between the two mentions may make appropriate reference difficult. This is especially true when the various referents in the discourse environment under consideration share the same semantic features (see Givón, 1984, for further details). In brief, then, the choice of one referential form rather than another is determined by the gap separating two successive mentions of the same referent, or referential distance in Givón's terms, and by the presence of other intervening referents.

The first measurement of the types of referential forms will be based on the shortest gap between two mentions of the same referent in terms of the number of clause boundaries (Givón, 1984; Clancy, 1980). In other words, we will examine the types of forms used by the subjects to refer to a participant mentioned one clause earlier, and this for two reasons. First, as shown in Table 1, the great majority of anaphoric instances in the subjects'

TABLE 1. *Frequency of instances of reference after n clause boundaries*

| Group | Number of intervening clause boundaries | | | | Total |
	1	2	3	4/more	
1	352 (67%)	87 (16%)	36 (7%)	53 (10%)	528
2	335 (69%)	74 (15%)	28 (6%)	51 (10%)	488
3T1	299 (66%)	75 (17%)	28 (6%)	50 (11%)	452
3T2	240 (69%)	50 (14%)	25 (7%)	35 (10%)	350

narratives occur after one clause boundary. Thus the results will be more reliable since the observations will be based on a fairly large number of cases of anaphora.

Second, the effect of a one-clause gap on the choice of referential forms is clear: heavy encoding of the same referent after one clause boundary through a full NP is highly unlikely and could be safely interpreted as avoidance of pronominalisation on the part of the subjects. Now our initial prediction can be specified in the following manner: the attrition groups would use full noun phrases to achieve reference after one clause boundary more frequently than the control group (i.e. group 3 at time 1). The frequency of such noun phrases is calculated as a proportion of the total number of referential forms used after one clause boundary.

The second measurement is the frequency of potential pronominalisation. Potential pronominalisation refers to instances where the subjects could have used pronouns instead of full noun phrases without any risk of ambiguity of reference. This measurement will enable us to show that the attrition groups used full noun phrases even in environments where there was no interference from other referents. The frequency of potential pronominalisation is calculated as a proportion of the total number of instances of pronominalisation, potential and actual, as shown in the following formula:

proportion of potential pronominalisation =

$$\frac{\text{number of instances of potential pronominalisation}}{\text{number of pronouns} + \text{number of instances of potential pronominalisation}}$$

Since the identification of instances of potential pronominalisation involves some judgement, this task was carried out by me and double-checked by a native speaker of French. In the event of a discrepancy in the scores assigned by the two judges to a particular narrative, the average of the two scores was used.

Statistical procedures

Since the observed values are proportions, the arc sine transformation was applied to the observations in order to stabilise the variance (Neter & Wasserman, 1974:507). The values of the transformed observations were obtained from the statistical tables provided in Owen (1962:293ff.). These values were used to compute the relevant statistics.

In the cross-sectional phase of the study, a series of one-way Analysis of Variance tests were used to compare group means. The Tukey procedure was used for pairwise comparisons (Neter & Wasserman, 1974:474). In the longitudinal phase, the comparison between the mean scores of group 3 at times 1 and 2 was done by means of one-tailed matched t-tests.

Results

Table 2 gives the mean proportions of full NPs after one clause boundary and the mean proportions of potential pronominalisation. The results showed that the mean scores obtained by group 3 at time 1 and time 2 were virtually identical and, thus, no statistical analysis was necessary. The results of the cross-sectional phase suggested that the attrition groups (i.e. groups 1 and 2) used more full NPs after one clause boundary and exhibited a higher frequency of potential pronominalisation than the control group (i.e. group 3 at time 1). However, the analysis of variance (Tables 3 and 4) showed that the differences between the groups were not significant ($p < 0.10$).

These results suggest, at best, a slight tendency in the direction of the

TABLE 2. *Mean proportions of full NPs after one clause boundary and mean proportions of potential pronominalisation*

Measurements	Cross-sectional phase			Longitudinal phase (Group 3)	
	Group 1	Group 2	Group 3T1	Time 1	Time 2
Full NPs	0.30	0.22	0.17	0.17	0.18
Potential pronominalisation	0.23	0.18	0.12	0.12	0.13

TABLE 3. *ANOVA for proportion of full NPs after one clause boundary*

Source of variance	SS	d.f.	MS	F
Between groups	0.78	2	0.39	3.250*
Within groups	5.79	47	0.12	
Total	6.57	49		

* $p < 0.10$

TABLE 4. *ANOVA for potential pronominal-isation*

Source of variance	SS	d.f.	MS	F
Between groups	0.63	2	0.31	3.10*
Within groups	4.87	47	0.10	
Total	5.50	49		

* $p < 0.10$

prediction that the attrition groups would rely on heavy encoding of participants more frequently than the control group. However, a re-analysis of the data, taking into consideration aspects of linguistic variation, provides a more accurate picture of the evolution of the subjects' interlanguage. In the following we will consider two linguistic variables not dealt with in the initial analysis: the thematic persistence of participants and the grammatical function of referential forms.

The thematic persistence of participants

The thematic persistence of a participant refers to the uninterrupted presence of a participant as the sole theme in a sequence of clauses. Typically, at the beginning of the subjects' narratives, the focus is on one character at a time. First, the pear picker is introduced and his actions described; then the same strategy is employed to introduce the man with the goat and the bicycle boy. This strategy is motivated by the fact that in the film itself the focus is on one character at a time, and by the absence of interaction between the characters. To illustrate this point, I will examine the chain of reference to the various characters in the narrative of one of the subjects from group 1, which is typical of all the narratives in this respect. In order to do this, each character will be assigned a letter:

P   the pear picker
M   the man with the goat
B   the bicycle boy
G   the girl
A   the three boys
C   one of the three boys

The chain of reference to the characters in the clauses of the narrative is as follows (the dashes represent clause boundaries):

First part of the narrative:

P–P–P–P–M–M–P–P–P–B–B–B–B–B–B–B–B–B–B–P–P–

Second part:

B–BG–B–B–G–A–A–B–A–B–A–AB–A–C–C–B–BC–B–
AP–P–PA–P–A.

Before the episode where the bicycle boy meets the girl (hereafter called the first part of the narrative), the mention of a particular character is fairly continuous. For example, in ten successive clauses, the only character referred to is the bicycle boy. From that episode on (hereafter called the second part of the narrative) no single participant is persistent to any significant degree. Instead, the narrator had to switch more frequently from one character to another. Thus we would predict that referential choice in the second part of the narrative would be more problematic for the subjects and, consequently, the differences between the groups would be more prominent.

In order to test this prediction, the measurements used earlier were applied to the second part of the narratives only. Table 5 gives the mean proportions of full NPs after one clause boundary and the mean proportions of potential pronominalisation in the second part of the narratives. The analysis of variance (Tables 6 and 7) showed that the difference between the groups in the cross-sectional phase is significant both for full NPs after one clause boundary and for potential pronominalisation ($p < 0.05$ and $p < 0.01$, respectively). The Tukey procedure for pairwise comparisons showed that the difference between group 1 and group 3 at time 1 is significant at the 0.05 level for full NPs after one clause boundary and at the 0.01 level for potential pronominalisation.

In the longitudinal phase, the one-tailed matched t-test showed that the

TABLE 5. *Mean proportions of full NPs after one clause boundary and mean proportions of potential pronominalisation in the second part of the narratives*

Measurements	Cross-sectional phase			Longitudinal phase (Group 3)	
	Group 1	Group 2	Group 3T1	Time 1	Time 2
Full NPs	0.35	0.27	0.19	0.18	0.25
Potential pronominalisation	0.26	0.19	0.12	0.11	0.18

TABLE 6. *ANOVA for full NPs after one clause bound-ary in the second part of the narratives*

Source of variance	SS	d.f.	MS	F
Between groups	1.09	2	0.55	4.231[*]
Within groups	6.04	47	0.13	
Total	7.13	49		

[*] $p < 0.05$

TABLE 7. *ANOVA for potential pronominalisation in the second part of the narratives*

Source of variance	SS	d.f.	MS	F
Between groups	1.17	2	0.585	5.571[*]
Within groups	4.96	47	0.105	
Total	6.13	49		

[*] $p < 0.01$

difference between the means obtained by group 3 at time 1 and at time 2 is significant for potential pronominalisation ($p < 0.05$), but only approaches significance for full NPs after one clause boundary ($p < 0.10$).

It is clear, then, that only once we considered the linguistic environment where the subjects had to handle the encoding of different participants at the same time did the differences between the groups show up.

The grammatical function of referential forms

It was suspected that the frequency of avoidance of pronominalisation would vary depending on the grammatical function of the NPs considered. Specifically, it was hypothesised that the differences between the groups with respect to potential pronominalisation would be more prominent when we consider direct or indirect object NPs rather than NPs which function as subjects or objects of prepositions. This can be accounted for in the following manner. Pronominalisation involving direct and indirect objects is more intricate since it requires the preverbal placement of the object clitic, which would result in a marked and opaque word order in French, SOV, the normal word order being SVO.

TABLE 8. *Potential pronominalisation and grammatical functions*

	Direct and indirect objects			Subjects and objects of a preposition		
	Number of clitics used	Number of instances of potential pronominalisation	Total	Number of pronouns used	Number of instances of potential pronominalisation	Total
Group 1	45 (62%)	27 (38%)	72	256 (83%)	54 (17%)	310
Group 2	40 (66%)	21 (34%)	61	257 (86%)	43 (14%)	300
Group 3 (T1)	52 (84%)	10 (16%)	62	250 (90%)	27 (10%)	277
Group 3 (T2)	30 (65%)	16 (35%)	46	208 (91%)	20 (9%)	228

Unfortunately, quite a few narratives did not include a sufficient number of instances of the different grammatical functions, especially direct and indirect objects. Consequently, statistical comparisons between the groups were deemed inappropriate.[3] However, the global frequencies of potential pronominalisation for each group are quite revealing. The data in Table 8 indicate that the attrition groups failed to pronominalise at least twice as frequently (38%, 34% and 35%) as the control group (16%) when the NP is a direct or an indirect object. In the case of subjects and objects of prepositions, the differences between the control group and the attrition groups are not as large (10% for the control group, and 17%, 14% and 9% for the attrition groups).

Discussion

The above analysis suggests that consideration of linguistic variation is essential for understanding interlanguage change within the context of language loss. The prediction that the attrition subjects would rely on heavy encoding of participants in narrative discourse and avoid pronominalisation was borne out only when we considered particular linguistic environments. Specifically, the attrition groups' IL exhibited an important increase in the use of full NPs and avoidance of pronominalisation in the following instances:

1. when no single participant was continuously present in the discourse and the subjects had to handle the encoding of different participants at the same time;
2. when the referential form functioned as a direct or an indirect object.

The avoidance of pronominalisation by the attrition subjects may be explained in terms of a communication strategy whose purpose is to avoid ambiguity of reference. It is safer to use full NPs to achieve reference to participants, especially in stretches of discourse where more than one participant is involved. This explanation seems plausible when we consider that French has a complex system of pronominal forms which carry grammatical gender (*le* 'him' vs. *la* 'her'), number (*le* 'him' vs. *les* 'them'), case (*le* 'him' vs. *lui* 'to him') and person (*te* 'you' vs. *le* 'him') and which have to occur pre-verbally in a particular order (indirect objects except *lui* 'to him' and *leur* 'to them' precede direct object clitics; see Grevisse, 1959, for further details).

The theoretical implication of these findings is that the deterioration of a particular linguistic subsystem (in this case, rules of anaphora) will be manifested first in some linguistic environments and eventually spread to other environments. This conclusion seems to suggest that language loss is the mirror image of language acquisition. In fact, it has been documented that the acquisition of a particular form may be influenced by the linguistic context in the sense that the learner may show mastery of that form in a certain linguistic environment but fail to do so in other environments. Only later will she or he use that form correctly in every linguistic environment (Dickerson, 1975). Thus the present study tends to support the regression hypothesis which was proposed to account for second language loss in other works such as Cohen (1975) and Berko-Gleason (1982).

Notes to Chapter 12

1. This chapter is based on parts of my dissertation, which was supported by a grant from The Rackham School of Graduate Studies at the University of Michigan. I would like to thank the members of my doctoral committee: Alton Becker, Susan Gass, M. Peter Hagiwara, Deborah Keller-Cohen and Larry Selinker. I am also grateful to Dennis Preston for helpful comments on this paper. Any errors are my own.

2. Notice that at time 2 the number of subjects in group 3 is 15 rather than the original 16. This is because one of the subjects in that group was not available for re-testing.

3. Notice that the average numbers of 'obligatory contexts' for direct and indirect objects range between 3 and 4, which is too low for computing meaningful percentages of potential pronominalisation for each subject.

References

BELLUGI, U., 1967, 'The acquisition of negation.' PhD dissertation, Harvard.
BERKO-GLEASON, J., 1982, Insights from child language acquisition for second language loss. In W. LAMBERT & B. FREED (eds), *The Loss of Language Skills*. Rowley, MA: Newbury House.
CHAFE, W., 1976, Givenness, contrastiveness, definiteness, subjects, topics and point of view. In C. LI (ed.), *Subject and Topic*. New York: Academic Press.
——, 1980, *The Pear Stories: Cognitive, Cultural and Linguistic Aspects of Narrative Production*. Norwood, NJ: Ablex.
CLANCY, P., 1980, Referential choice in English and Japanese narrative discourse. In W. CHAFE (ed.), *The Pear Stories: Cognitive, Cultural and Linguistic Aspects of Narrative Production*. Norwood, NJ: Ablex.
COHEN, A., 1975, Forgetting a second language, *Language Learning*, 25(1), 127–38.
DICKERSON, L., 1975, The learner's interlanguage as a system of variable rules, *TESOL Quarterly*, 9(4), 401–7.
DICKERSON, L. and DICKERSON, W., 1977, Interlanguage phonology: Current research and future directions. In S. P. CORDER & E. ROULET (eds), *The Notion*

of Simplification in Interlanguage and Pidgins and their Relation to Second Language Pedagogy. Geneva: Droz.

ELLIS, R., 1985, *Understanding Second Language Acquisition.* Oxford: Oxford University Press.

FAKHRI, A., 1985, 'Linguistic outcomes of foreign language loss: Short term changes in the interlanguage of American learners of French.' Ph.D. dissertation, University of Michigan.

GIVÓN, T., 1984, *Topic Continuity in Discourse: A Quantitative Cross-Language Study.* Amsterdam: John Benjamins.

GREVISSE, M., 1959, *Le Bon Usage.* Paris: Librairie Orientaliste.

LoCoco, V., 1976, A comparison of three methods for the collection of second language data: Free composition, translation, and picture description, *Working Papers in Bilingualism,* 8, 59–86.

NETER, J. and WASSERMAN, W., 1974, *Applied Linear Statistical Models.* Homewood, IL: Richard D. Irwin.

OBLER, L. and MENN, L. (eds), 1983, *Exceptional Language and Linguistics.* New York: Academic Press.

OWEN, D., 1962, *Handbook of Statistical Tables.* Reading, MA: Addison-Wesley.

TARONE, E., 1979, Interlanguage as chameleon, *Language Learning,* 29, 181–91.

——, 1982, Systematicity and attention in interlanguage, *Language Learning,* 32(1), 69–84.

TRUDGILL, P., 1976, Creolization in reverse: Reduction and simplification in the Albanian dialects of Greece, *Transactions of the Philological Society,* 35–50.

VALDMAN, A. and PHILLIPS, J., 1977, Pidginization, creolization, and the elaboration of learner systems, *Studies in Second Language Acquisition,* 1(1), 21–40.

13 Morphological interaction between L1 and L2 in language attrition

D. KAUFMAN
M. ARONOFF
SUNY at Stony Brook

Introduction

Previous studies of attrition in individuals who have experienced dramatic reduction in exposure to their dominant language have shown attrition to involve regression, interference and loss of specificity in the lexicon (Berman & Olshtain, 1983; Olshtain & Barzilay, in press; Sharwood-Smith, 1983). Attrition research is in its infancy and the purpose of this chapter is to provide further insight into the field. In this chapter we will show that typological differences between L1 and L2 have an effect on attrition, and that attrition is not simply a loss of one language but an interplay between two. In particular, we will show that differences in the attrition patterns of Hebrew nouns and verbs on the part of a young native speaker of Hebrew placed in an English dominant environment are directly attributable to morphological differences between the languages. Hebrew verb morphology is very different from English verb morphology, while their nominal morphologies are not so far apart.

This chapter focuses on the structural metamorphoses of the L1 verbal and nominal systems and on the role of L2 in the changes that have occurred in L1. These are studied through instances of *code-blending*, where morphemes from one language are combined with morphemes of another language within a single word while the phonological features of the respective source languages are retained (Kaufman & Sridhar, 1986).

In previous work (Berman, 1979; Swain, 1972), code-blending has been dismissed as an insignificant and infrequent phenomenon. In this chapter, we will show how code-blending has been very robust in the child's utterances, and has provided access to the developmental sequence of simultaneous acquisition and loss of productive morphological systems in the young child. The typological differences between the languages have resulted in data that allow firm conclusions about stages in the child's morphological productivity in each of the languages.

The study is based on daily notes and bi-weekly recordings of primarily naturalistic observations as well as occasional elicitation activities and probes designed to ascertain the child's competence in L1 and L2. The data were collected primarily in the home environment, where the use of L1 dominated.

Our subject, Michal, is a native speaker of Hebrew, who at 2;6 came to the United States, and by 2;8 was immersed in an English dominant environment at the preschool, for 7 hours a day 5 days a week. Hebrew was exclusively spoken to her by her parents and sisters (7 and 11 years old). The study began upon the child's arrival in the United States and to date has covered a period of over two years. At the outset of the study the child's language exhibits good command of the linguistic features of L1 that are typically acquired by children of her age as discussed in Berman (1985). Some examples of utterances that illustrate the child's command of the noun and verb morphology are:

(1) 2;8   *ani   e-efox   axšav   daf*
          I   1.FUT-turn   now   page
          I will turn the page now

(2) 2;9   *ani roc-a   l-akri   sipur-im, lo i-kre-ti*
          I   want-fs to-read(benef) story-mp, no benef-read-1s.PAST
          sipur
          story
          I want to read stories, I did not read a story

(3) 2;10 *lo   aav-ti   et   ha-salat*
          no   like-1s.PAST   OM   the-salad
          I didn't like the salad

This chapter focuses on the morphological disintegration and reconstruction of L1 as attested in the data at around the age of 3;4. The earlier stages of attrition are discussed at greater length in Kaufman & Aronoff (in press). In order to obtain objective appraisals of the child's growing competence in L2 (English), standardised probes were administered at age 3;4 (10 months after arrival in the United States). These included the PPVT (Peabody

Picture Vocabulary Test), selected items of the PLAI (Preschool Language Assessment Instrument), selected subtests of the ITPA (Illinois Test of Psycholinguistic Abilities) and SOLST (Stephens Oral Language Screening Test). These have indicated that after 10 months in the United States the child had reached linguistic competence equivalent to monolingual English speakers of the same age group. Our focus here is on the child's use of Hebrew within this developing English system.

The nominal and verbal systems of Hebrew and English

The hallmark of Semitic languages is their root and pattern (or template) morphology. For example, the consonantal root k-t-v may appear in a variety of different patterns: *katav* 'wrote', *nixtav* 'was written', *(h)ixtiv* 'dictated', *(h)itkatev* 'corresponded', *mixtav* 'letter', *maxteva* 'desk'. Modern Hebrew has seven verbal templates and any verb that is used in the language, including all borrowings, must adhere to one of these templates (Bolozky, 1978). The templates are of the forms CaCaC, niCCaC, CiCeC, CuCaC, hiCCiC, hoCCaC and hitCaCeC. Roots of three consonants are the most frequent, and may appear in any template. Roots of four or more consonants appear only in the two most productive templates, CiCeC and hitCaCeC, with the latter usually being intransitive (McCarthy, 1984). The Hebrew verb for telephone, for example, is *tilfen*. English, of course, has no such verbal system. It is affixal, mostly suffixing, and the most productive affixes have no phonological effects on their bases.

What is less known is that the nominal system of Hebrew and all Semitic languages differs from the verbal system. There are templates, but they are much more varied and less productive. There are, in addition, purely affixal noun forming patterns, where the base sometimes remains unaltered, just as in English, and finally, borrowed nouns are left intact; the Hebrew noun for telephone is *telefon*. Modern Hebrew noun morphology is thus much closer to English than is the verb morphology. The relation between the two languages is schematised in Table 1.

We will show that this relation is evidenced in attrition. With nouns, where root and pattern morphology is less pervasive, L1 nouns lose their L1 morphology and are used as if they were L2 words, that is, L2 morphological markers are affixed to L1 nouns. With verbs, however, the child does not simply lose the L1 system, but rather creates a novel template for L1 verbs in an L2 context. The resulting verbal system is thus an accommodation between L1 and L2. The rest of this chapter is organised as follows. First we discuss nouns; at an early stage, the child mixes L2 nouns

TABLE 1. *Reorganisation of L1 morphology to accommodate L2*

	Hebrew (L1)	English (L2)	Child's L1 + L2
Nouns:	· C/T	C	C
Verbs:	T	C	T/C

C = concatenative; T = template
Nouns: L2 morphology replaces L1 morphology.
Verbs: L2 morphology is added to a reconstructed L1 morphology.

in an L1 context without modifying them; at a later stage, as evidenced from both plurals, noun compounds and lexical innovations, L1 morphology is lost and L1 nouns are treated morphologically in the same way as L2 nouns, although they retain L1 phonology. Second, we discuss verbs, which pattern differently: at an early stage, not only L1 verbs but even L2 verbs are found in L1 templates; at a later stage, the child uses her own idiosyncratic template to mix L1 verbs in L2. Verbs thus contrast with nouns at both ends of the attrition process.

The child's nominal system

The early stage—L2 in L1

Attrition in its early stages affected the lexicon. L2 nouns were increasingly inserted in an L1 syntactical environment from the age of 2;9, three months after initial contact with L2. An analysis of the L2 nominal insertions in the data reveals that three types of insertions prevail. First are L2 words for new concepts that had never been acquired in L1. This category includes L2 culture-loaded words such as *cereal, pumpkin, lunch-box*. Second are L2 words for school-related concepts that had been known in L1 but for which new L2 words are learned and reinforced at school, such as words for geometrical shapes and colours. Third are L2 words for common, and frequently used, concepts for which L1 words had previously been used. It is early loss of words of the third type that is most puzzling in the study of attrition. Some examples of these are:

(4) 2;9 *ima*   *t-oxl-i*   *et*   *ha*-apple   *šel-i*.
         mommy   2.FUT-eat-2fs   OM   the-apple   of-me
         Mommy, eat my apple.

(5) 3;0 *simi-i*   *et*   *ha-tik*   *al*   *ha*-back   *šel-i*.
         put.IMPER-fs   OM   the-bag   on   the-back   of-me
         Put the bag on my back.

(6) 3;0 *at*   *zoxer-et*   *et ha-yalda ba*-book   *ha-hu*?
         you   remember.PRES-fs   OM the-girl in.the-book   the-that?
         Do you remember the girl in that book?

The Hebrew words *tapuax* 'apple' (example 4) and *sefer* 'book' (example 6) were among the child's early acquisitions in L1 and it therefore seemed puzzling that when asked for the L1 equivalent of these words the child became, as time progressed, hesitant and unsure, needed prompting, and in a growing number of instances was unable to produce the L1 word. One explanation for this phenomenon may lie in the fact that early acquisition of these L2 nouns and increased exposure to them in the school setting meant that they were more readily available for production. It should be pointed out that no difficulty was demonstrated in the comprehension of these words. The nominal insertions were prefixed by the definite marker of L1, *ha*, which is a bound morpheme in Hebrew and is obligatory in these contexts.

The late stage—L1 in L2

Plural nouns

Attrition of the L1 nominal system is dramatically attested in the increasing misuse of the L1 plural markers, which undergo gradual disintegration of form and gender distinctions. Noun plurals in Hebrew are generally formed by adding -*im* and -*ot* to masculine and feminine nouns respectively. The plural morphemes are stressed and are therefore perceptually salient and are acquired early by children. Gender in animate nouns is semantically motivated, whereas in inaminate nouns it is semantically empty. Levy (1983) studied the pattern of acquisition of noun plurals in 2–3-year-olds and found initial indiscriminate use of the unmarked masculine form, followed by gradual introduction of the feminine plural morpheme based on phonological clues inherent in the singular noun. Typical feminine endings -*a*, -*et*, -*it*, -*at*, respectively, were used as clues in the gradual productive use of the feminine plural morpheme -*ot*.

Prior to the onset of attrition, the child in the present study had acquired the plural system of Hebrew to a level described in studies of 2–3-year-old native speakers of Hebrew (Berman, 1981, 1985; Levy, 1983). Thus, all the plural forms that are attested in the data at the early stage

(2;8–3;3) are in fact normatively correct, and the errors made in her subsequent speech, therefore, are of particular interest for the investigation of attrition. Analysis of these errors reveals two simultaneous factors: first, manifestations of regression to earlier developmental speech patterns found in L1 acquisition, and second, the impressive role of L2 morphology in reshaping L1 words.

Regression to earlier developmental patterns includes predominant though not exclusive use of the unmarked masculine morpheme -*im* on most nouns, including those with typical feminine endings on singular nouns, for example: *xulca*/*xulca-im*, 'shirt/shirts', *calaxat*/*calaxat-im*, 'plate/plates'. The semantically unmarked masculine morpheme is very productive at this stage of attrition as shown in these examples:

(7)   3;5   You have *sear-im*
          You have hair-mp

(8)   3;8   *agala-z-im*
          stroller-z(Eng pl)-mp

The word *sear*, 'hair' is usually used in the plural *sear-ot*. Hence re-analysis of the word and the choice of the masculine morpheme attests to its greater productivity. The word *agala* has the typical feminine ending -*a*, which is the first to be acquired as a phonological clue for the use of the feminine morpheme in the plural (Levy, 1983). Here it serves instead as a phonological clue for the English plural allophone /z/, which, in turn, is further supplemented by the Hebrew masculine plural morpheme.

Another regressive pattern (attested in examples 9 and 10) involves loss of sensitivity to the morphophonological rules of vowel reduction, vowel change and obligatory stress movement associated with the plural form. Plural formation in nouns of certain patterns requires penultimate stem-vowel reduction where CVCVC becomes CCVC-*ím* as in *pérax*/*praxím*, 'flower' (example 9). The form CéCeC (Berman, 1978) becomes CCaC-*ím* as in *séfer*/*sfarím*, 'book' (example 10) involving vowel reduction as well as stem-final vowel lowering. The form CiCCá becomes CCaC-*ót* involving a vowel reduction as well as a stem change as in *simlá*/*smalót*, 'dress/dresses'. In all these examples a stress shift to the plural morpheme occurs in normative use.

(9)   2;11   *pérax*   *prax-ím*
            flower   flower-mpl
      3;8   *pérax-im*
      4;3   Look at the *pérax*-s, aren't they pretty?
                        flower-z(Eng pl)

(10) 2;8   *séfer*   *sfar-ím*
            book   book-mpl
      3;7   *séfer-im*
      4;1   What *séfer*-z are there?
            book-s(Eng pl)

Developmental errors in the young language acquirer result in part from regularisation across noun patterns. Berman (1985) shows how the canonical alternation *tikra/tikrot*, 'ceiling/ceilings', leads to incorrect *ricpa/ricpot* 'floor/floors' and *simla/simlot* 'dress/dresses'. In the case of language attrition where exposure to L1 is reduced dramatically, paradigmatic overgeneralisation is inhibited and the pattern selected in pluralisation instead reflects a strategy of opting for least change in the stem. Hence *simla* becomes *simla-ot* rather than *siml-ot* as would be predicted from paradigmatic overgeneralisation.

The strategy of opting for least change may be motivated, first by regression to earlier developmental forms that display no change in the form of the stem, and second, by the influence of L2 plural formation rules which, in the case of English, require addition of the phonologically appropriate plural allophone to a stem which is generally unchanged in vowel pattern or stress. Our data seem to suggest that in the earlier stages of attrition of the nominal system, regression played a more prominent role, whereas in the later stages, L2 morphological rules played an increasingly crucial role in shaping the child's plural forms as L2 was becoming more dominant.

Errors made between 3;5 and 3;8 attest to the increasing functional role of L2 as a plural marker. Although the L1 masculine and feminine plural markers are still present, their use is redundant and is probably formulaic and unanalysed. This is evident in examples such as (12) where the correct plural form is used (compare with the singular form *magevet* in example 11) but where the use of the L2 plural marker shows that the form *magavot* is used as a formulaic expression. In example 13 the word *garbonim* is treated as ending in [z], thus the child totally ignores the L1 plural marker, and the appropriate L2 plural allophone is added.

(11) 3;5   I need a *magevet* for my eyes
(12) 3;5   Don't forget to take *magav-ot*-s
            Don't forget to take towel-fp-s

(13) 3;9   *garbon-im*-z-iz
            tight-mp-z-iz

(14) 3;6   I like *cimuk-im*-z
            I like raisin-mp-z

Other examples seem to suggest that although the L1 plural marker is present in form, it no longer serves a function, and it is the L2 plural marker that is required for number marking (example 14). This may explain the emergence (at 3;9, 15 months after exposure to L2) of the stable plural form

TABLE 2. *Progression of attrition in pluralisation*

Singular	Plural Early Stage 2;8–3;3	Plural Intermediate Stage 3;4–3;8	Plural Late Stage 3;9–4;4	Gloss
agala	(agalot)	agalazim	–	stroller
agas	agasim	agasim/agasiz	agasiz	pear
agvaniya	agvaniyot	agvaniyot/agvaniyaz	agvaniyaz	tomato
banana	bananot	bananos/ bananim/bananaot	bananaz	banana
bul	(bulim)	–	bulz	stamp
calaxat	calaxot	calaxatim	calaxats	plate
cimuk	cimukim	cimukim/cimukimz	cimukimz	raisin
cipor	ciporim	ciporim/ciporz	–	bird
ec	ecim	–	eciz	tree
–	garbonim	garbonimz/garbonimziz	garbonimz	tights
gezer	(gzarim)	–	gezerz	carrot
kapit	kapiyot	kapiyots	kapits	spoon
kis	kisim	–	kisiz	pocket
kos	kosot	–	kosiz	glass
magevet	magavot	magavots	–	towel
mapit	mapiyot	mapiyot/mapitot	mapiyots/mapits	napkin
mazleg	mazlegot	–	mazlegz	fork
parpar	(parparim)	parparz	–	butterfly
peca	(pca'im)	–	pecaz	wound
perax	praxim	peraxim	peraxs	flower
pilpel	(pilpelim)	–	pilpelz	pepper
sakin	sakinim	–	sakinz	knife
šaon	(še'onim)	šaonz	–	watch
sefer	sfarim	seferim	seferz	book
simla	(smalot)	simlaot	–	dress
smixa	smixot	smixots	–	blanket
tapuax	tapuxim	tapuaxim	tapuaxs	apple
ugiya	ugiyot	ugiyaz	ugiyaz	cookie
xor	(xorim)	–	xorz	hole
xulca	(xulcot)	xulca'im	xulcaz	shirt
xut	(xutim)	–	xuts	thread

The parenthesised normative forms are not attested in the data.

of the L1 noun in which the L1 plural marker is systematically dropped and the L2 plural marker is code-blended with the L1 singular noun.

It is important to note that the L1 noun has retained its phonetic form and the choice of the code-blended L2 plural allophone is motivated by L2 phonological rules. Code-blending in the child's speech is not a product of input and it therefore highlights much linguistic information about acquisition and attrition. Hybrids like *perax*-s, *ec*-iz, *xor*-z (see Table 2), provide important evidence for the acquisition/attrition process. First, L2 morphological rules dominate plural formation. Second, no attempt has been made by the child to assimilate L1 phonemes which do not exist in L2, in order to approximate L2 phonemes. L1 words retain their phonetic form and the choice of L2 plural allophones to be code-blended is determined by the phonetic properties of the L1 phonemes. Third, the sounds uvular *x, r, c* are not found in English, and the correct choice of allophone is based solely on the phonetic properties of these sounds. This gives further support to Halle's proposition (1978) that native speakers of English base their choice of the plural marker on innate knowledge of the feature composition of speech sounds. In this way the English plural formation rule may apply to any foreign word retaining its phonetic form. (Halle (1978) cites the plural of 'Bach'—[baxs]—as an example.) Fourth, the code-blended hybrids which contain phonemes that are not found in English further indicate that attrition in its present state has had little effect on L1 phonetic form, although it has had a significant impact on the syntax and morphophonological rules of L1.

In sum, disintegration of the L1 number marking has occurred from about 3;4 (10 months after initial exposure to L2). Attrition becomes evident first, in regression to earlier developmental forms and second, in the increasing dominance of the L2 plural formation rules that are imposing new forms on the L1 words (see Intermediate Stage in Table 2). The emergence of a single code-blended form (see Late Stage in Table 2) attests to the rejection of the L1 plural marker in favour of the now dominant L2 marker.

Hybrid lexical innovations

The growing dominance of L2 morphosyntactic rules in L1 attrition is further attested in the child's use of compounding. Children's lexical innovations created to fill lexical gaps provide insight into the word formation processes they use (Clark, 1982). In English, once the structural devices of suffixation and compounding are acquired, children freely produce numerous innovations. In Hebrew, innovations are created by combining the stem with an affixal pattern (Clark & Berman, 1984; Berman & Sagi, 1982). Compounding in Hebrew is restricted to noun–noun and adjective–noun combinations, and its productive use occurs with older children 5–6 years old, or even later, in cases where the compounds involve morphological and phonological changes in the head noun (Berman, 1985; Clark & Berman, 1987). Instances of noun compounds, however, do appear in younger children, although these are restricted to formulaic compounds like *bet sefer*, 'school', *beged yam*, 'bathing suit'.

The lexical innovations with which we are concerned here are of three types: first, hybrid noun compounds where words from L1 and L2 are juxtaposed to create an innovative noun compound (examples 15, 16); second, two L1 nouns compounded in L2 syntactical pattern (example 17); and third, code-blends involving L1 words combined with L2 suffix (examples 18, 19, 20).

(15) 3;11 it's almost *šeleg* time
                        snow

(16) 4;0   I'm *ašpa* man
                      garbage

(17) 4;0   another *banana af*
                        banana nose

(18) 3;7   I need to wash my hand it's *sabon*-y
                                             soap-y

(19) 4;3   **Child:** Mommy when can I ride my bike?
            Parent: *kše'iye*   *yoter xam*
                        when be.FUT more hot
            Child: *xam*-er?
                        hot-er

(20) 3;10 this is the *pilpel inagev*-er
                          pepper wipe-r

In the noun compounds the stress is on the first member of the compound in all instances, following the English and not the Hebrew pattern. Note that *banana* (example 17) is Hebrew, as evidenced by the use of [a] rather than [ae]. The morphosyntactic environment is that of L2 in all these examples. The child is using words retained from L1 to create a compound which is syntactically acceptable in L2. In examples 15 and 16, L1 nouns are used as modifiers to the L2 head nouns. The nouns 'time' and 'man' appear in many noun compounds used by preschool age children (Clark, 1982).

In example 17, the child is referring to the nose of the snowman (made of a banana). In Hebrew, head nouns precede modifiers, which would generate *af banana*, although the standard form in this case would be the use of a noun phrase instead of a compound. In this example, the L1 nouns have been arranged to accommodate L2 compounding rules.

The impact of L2 morphology and syntax is further illustrated in example 18. Although the word 'soap' is known to, and has been previously used by the child, an L1 word is selected here and is transformed into an adjective by the addition of '-y' to obey L2 morphosyntactic constraints.

The comparative in Hebrew is always formed with the word *yoter*, inserted before, or less often, after the adjective. In example 19, despite the input from L1 the child is employing L2 rules which require the adjective to be marked with '-er' to indicate a comparative. The L1 input, in this case, has prompted the use of the adjective *xam* but L2 syntax dictates the appropriate morphological marking.

Example 20 uniquely combines elements of the second and third types of innovations. It involves the juxtaposition of an L1 noun as the modifier and a head noun composed of a Hebrew verb used in the child's idiosyncratic form of the verb (discussed below), combined with the L2 agentive 'er' which transforms it into a noun. It should be noted that formal categorisation into classes of nouns and verbs appears to have remained intact. Nominal and verbal insertions as well as innovative hybrids all attest to correct categorisation of L1 words, even though their use is within L2 morphological and syntactical environment. The data presented here show that organisational categories are indeed part of a child's early grammar (Maratsos, 1982), and the child is sensitive to their existence and usage. For the study of attrition it is significant that these categories are retained even after other elements of the language have been lost.

In sum, the lexical innovations have revealed how L1 words which remain in the lexicon are used within an L2 morphosyntactic environment. A growing command of and dependence on the morphosyntactic rules of L2 is evident. These rules are so powerful that they even minimise the effect of direct input, and they completely dominate the child's utterances.

The child's verbal system

The early stage—L2 in L1

Early L2 verbal insertions in the L1 context attest to the child's knowledge of the derivational and inflectional Semitic verb morphology.

The L2 verbs are treated as L1 two- and three-consonantal verbs and are set in an L1 verb template.

(21) 3;0 *im   ze   it-laxlex   ani a*-kliyn   *ot- jam*.
          if   this   3s.FUT-get.dirty   I   1s.FUT-clean OM-them
          If this gets dirty, I'll clean them.

(22) 3;0 *ani   bala-ti   et   ze   xazak*.
          I   blow.PAST-1s   OM   this   hard
          (English verb 'blow' inflected as a Hebrew verb)
          I blew this out (candles) hard.

In example 21 an uninflected form of the verb 'clean' is blended with the L1 bound morpheme of the first person singular future prefix *a*. In example 22 the English verb 'blow' is treated as a two-consonantal Hebrew verb CVCV like the verb *bala*, 'swallow', and is inflected accordingly. The L1 verb morphology requires the incorporation of any borrowed L2 verb within the L1 verb template system. This is a more complex process than is required for the incorporation of nouns, and indeed the data show that L1 verbal insertions appeared later and were far fewer than L1 nominal insertions.

The late stage—the idiosyncratic L1 template

Unlike L1 nominal insertions which were borrowed as whole units and inserted into L2 morphosyntactic contexts, verbal insertions displayed an interesting phenomenon. Following a period where utterances displayed a variety of verbal forms that contained traces of the L1 verbal, derivational, and inflectional morphology, a single template emerged and was over-regularised across all L1 verbs. This template, *iCaCeC*, which is similar to but not identical to an actual L1 form, becomes very productive in the child's speech and attests to her knowledge of the obligatory template system of the Semitic verbal system. (For a detailed examination of the emergence of this idiosyncratic template see Kaufman & Aronoff (in press).) Almost all the L1 verbs which are used in the child's speech about ten months after initial contact with L2 are used in this template and accommodate L2 morphosyntactic rules. L2 verbal inflections are code-blended with these reconstructed verbs to indicate person and tense. No gender distinctions are made because these are non-existent in L2. Some examples follow.

(23) 3;6 Are we gonna come back after we *isader* the things?
          'arrange'

(24)   3;7   I just need to *isaben* my legs.   'soap'

(25)   3;9   I need to *ixaded* my pencil. I know some that can't *ixaded*.
              'sharpen'

(26)   4;0   Mom, Dad is *ixamem*-ing my bread.   'warm'

(27)   4;1   We get up when it *icalcel*-z.   'ring'

(28)   4;2   Where is the coat you *ixabes*-ed?   'wash'

Conclusion

We have shown that the attrition patterns of L1 nouns and verbs are quite different from one another in this case and we have traced this difference to the interaction between the morphological systems of L1 and L2. This finding only highlights the fact that L1 attrition does not take place in a vacuum but rather in a context of simultaneous acquisition of L2. The result is not simply a loss of L1 but also its accommodation to L2. The implications for future research are clear: attrition must not be studied in isolation but should be examined in the context of the language that is being acquired. The structural differences between the two languages will, of necessity, affect the attrition patterns.

Acknowledgement

We would like to thank Marsha Laufer for administering and analysing the results of the PPVT, PLAI, ITPA and SOLST to determine Michal's competence in L2. We would also like to thank Ellen Broselow, Bob Hoberman, Kamal Sridhar, Elite Olshtain, and especially Ruth Berman for their comments on an earlier version of this chapter.

References

BERMAN, R. A., 1978, *Modern Hebrew Structure*. Tel Aviv, Israel: University Publishing Projects.
——, 1979, The re-emergence of a bilingual: A case study of a Hebrew–English speaking child, *Working Papers in Bilingualism*, 19, 157–79.
——, 1981, Children's regularizations of plural forms, *Papers and Reports on Child Language Development*, 20, 34–43.
——, 1985, The acquisition of Hebrew. In D. I. SLOBIN (ed.), *The Crosslinguistic Study of Language Acquisition*. Hillsdale, NJ: Lawrence Erlbaum.

BERMAN, R. A. and OLSHTAIN, E., 1983, Features of first language transfer in second language attrition, *Applied Linguistics*, 4(3), 222–34.

BERMAN, R. and SAGI, Y., 1982, Al darxey tetsurat hamilim vexidushan hagil hatsair (Word formation processes and lexical innovations of young children), *Hebrew Computational Linguistics Bulletin*, 18, 31–62.

BOLOZKY, S., 1978, Word formation strategies in the Hebrew verb system: Denominative verbs, *Afroasiatic Linguistics*, 5(3), 111–36.

CLARK, E. V., 1982, The young word maker: A case study of innovation in the child's lexicon. In E. WANNER & L. GLEITMAN (eds), *Language Acquisition: the State of the Art*. New York: Cambridge University Press.

CLARK, E. V. and BERMAN, R. A., 1984, Structure and use in the acquisition of word formation, *Language*, 60, 542–90.

——, 1987, Types of linguistic knowledge: Interpreting and producing compound nouns, *Journal of Child Language*, 14, 547–68.

HALLE, M., 1978, Knowledge unlearned and untaught: What speakers know about the sounds of their language. In M. HALLE, J. BRESNAN & G. A. MILLER (eds), *Linguistic Theory and Psychological Reality*. Cambridge, MA: MIT Press.

KAUFMAN, D. and ARONOFF, M., (in press), Morphological disintegration and reconstruction in first language attrition. In H. W. SELIGER & R. VAGO (eds), *First Language Attrition: Structural and Theoretical Perspectives*. New York: Cambridge University Press.

KAUFMAN, D. and SRIDHAR, S. N., 1986, 'The process of becoming a bilingual: Simultaneous language loss and language acquisition.' Paper presented at LSA/AAAL Annual Conference, New York.

LEVY, Y., 1983, The acquisition of Hebrew plurals: The case of the missing gender category, *Journal of Child Language*, 10, 107–21.

MARATSOS, M., 1982, The child's construction of grammatical categories. In E. WANNER & L. GLEITMAN (eds), *Language Acquisition, the State of the Art*. New York: Cambridge University Press.

MCCARTHY, J. J., 1984, Prosodic organization in morphology. In M. ARONOFF & R. T. OEHRLE (eds), *Language Sound Structure*. Cambridge, MA: MIT Press.

OLSHTAIN, E. and BARZILAY, M., (in press), Attrition of English in adult native speakers of American English living in a Hebrew speaking environment in Israel. In H. W. SELIGER & R. VAGO (eds), *First Language Attrition: Structural and Theoretical Perspectives*. New York: Cambridge University Press.

SHARWOOD-SMITH, M., 1983, On first language loss in the second language acquirer: Problems of transfer. In S. GASS & L. SELINKER (eds), *Language Transfer in Language Learning*. Rowley, MA: Newbury House.

SWAIN, M. K., 1972, 'Bilingualism as a first language.' Ph.D. Dissertation, University of California, Irvine.

Section Six:
Linguistic Foundations

14 Variable rules as prototype schemas

H. D. ADAMSON
University of Arizona and University of Pennsylvania

The general topic with which this chapter deals is the theory of marked-ness. [1] The idea of markedness is that some linguistic structures are in some sense 'more natural' or 'easier' than others. As Ferguson (1984:243) puts it, 'The terms "less marked" and "unmarked" are now commonly used to mean "to be expected", "normal", "natural" in human languages'. Perhaps the most influential markedness theory is Stampe's (1969) theory of natural phonology, which applies to sequences of phones. Stampe argues that due to the structure of the human vocal tract, certain sound sequences are easier to produce than others, and therefore are produced first by children. For example, a voiced consonant is more natural intervocalically than a voiceless consonant, and a voiceless consonant is more natural word finally than a voiced consonant. The natural sequences are 'unmarked', and the less natural sequences are 'marked'. According to Stampe, a child must learn to suppress unmarked tendencies when acquiring the phonology of a language.

The idea of markedness has been carried over into syntax and semantics by several scholars, including Traugott (1977) and Slobin (1985). Slobin claims that due to the structure of the human perceptual and cognitive apparatus, certain morphological and syntactic patterns are more natural, or less marked, than others and that these patterns emerge first in all varieties of child language. He calls the system of combinatorial principles, or grammar, which underlies the early structures 'Basic Child Grammar'. Like the system of natural phonology, Basic Child Grammar produces unmarked linguistic patterns, which are gradually replaced by more marked patterns. Slobin (1985:1160) states, '[Semantic and formal] entities are arrayed in an ACCESSIBILITY HIERARCHY according to which some notions and forms are likely to emerge earlier ... than others'.

(Emphasis in the original.) And, 'Children move from a *universal* grammar to the divergent grammar of individual languages'. (Emphasis in the original.) In Slobin's theory, children's early utterances linguistically encode notions that are part of what he calls 'prototypical scenes'. One such scene is the 'manipulative activity scene', in which 'prototypical direct manipulation' occurs when an agent causes a physical and perceptible change in a patient by means of direct body contact.

Data supporting Slobin's theory come from studies of how the accusative marker is acquired. These studies show that accusative markers are first used to mark objects that have been changed by an agent by means of some action. For example, Gvozdev (quoted in Slobin, 1985:1176) noted that in his son's acquisition of Russian, the accusative inflection was apparently first limited to the direct objects of verbs involving direct, physical action on things—such as *give*, *carry*, *put* and *throw*. Thus, at first the accusative inflection marked the prototypical object of the manipulative scene, rather than the more abstract grammatical category Direct Object. Later, of course, the accusative inflection came to mark this latter category. In terms of markedness theory, one could say that from a learner's point of view the sequence in example (1) is less marked than the sequence in example (2), because (1) contains an agent subject, an action verb, and an object that is physically affected by the subject:

(1)   Sam kicked the rock.
(2)   Sam saw the rock.

How do children expand very limited initial categories like Object Affected by an Action Verb to more general and abstract categories like Direct Object? This question was explored in an experimental study in first language acquisition by de Villiers (1980). De Villiers trained 37 children between the ages of 2;10 and 4;10 from a variety of socioeconomic levels to produce passive and cleft sentences. Only the passive experiment is described here, but the results of the cleft sentence experiment were essentially the same. The children, who did not produce passives in their speech, were shown pictures of an animal performing some action that involved an agent and a direct object, such as a frog lifting a rabbit or a tiger smelling a flower. One group of children was trained by imitating the passive sentence which described the picture, for example: 'The frog is being lifted by the rabbit'. On randomly placed trial tests the children were asked to describe the picture, thus possibly eliciting the passive structure. A second group of children was trained by asking them to describe the pictures and then expanding their sentences into passives. These children also were tested by asking them to describe a picture. The pictures were designed to elicit passives that fell into three different groups. Type A passives involved an action verb affecting an animate, logical direct object. Type B passives involved an action verb and an inanimate direct object. Type C passives involved a nonaction verb and an inanimate object.

De Villiers (1980:26) believed that it would be easier for children to learn type A passives than type B, and easier to learn type B passives than type C. (Her reasons for this belief will be explained in a moment.) Therefore, de Villiers made two predictions about the outcome of her experiment: (1) children trained on type A events would produce more passives than children trained on type B or type C events; (2) children would produce more type A passives regardless of their training. Both predictions proved correct. All groups of children produced more type A passives than other types, and more type B passives than type C passives. The fact that types A and B outranked type C indicates that the children preferred a pattern involving an action verb. The fact that type A outranked types B and C indicates that the children preferred a pattern involving an animate surface subject. This fact also indicates that the favouring effect of the animate surface subject was stronger than the favouring effect of the action verb.

Why did de Villiers predict that type A passives would be the easiest to learn? At first glance this prediction seems at odds with Slobin's theory, since Slobin predicts that the most easily learned *active* construction involves an agent (and therefore animate) surface subject, and an action verb, whereas de Villiers predicts that this combination of surface subject and verb constitutes the most easily learned *passive* construction. The apparent contrad˙ction is resolved when we consider the stage of development each theory describes. Slobin refers to an earlier stage of linguistic development than de Villiers. De Villiers notes (1980:25), 'It is a reasonable conjecture that by the age of three or four years, children have rules in their speech that would require postulating knowledge of abstract grammatical relations such as subject and object'. Thus, de Villiers' subjects were beyond the stage of encoding a basic scene in a string of words, and were well along toward developing abstract grammatical categories such as Subject and Verb. However, it is possible that the origins of these abstract categories can be found in the original manipulative scene. In this scene, the prototype verb is an action verb and the prototype subject is an animate subject. It is possible, then, that for de Villiers' subjects, the grammatical categories Subject and Verb were still mentally organised around these original members, just as, according to Bowerman (1977) the meanings of lexical items cluster around a prototype which is generally the first referent for which the word is used. Thus, de Villiers believed that the action verbs were less marked, and therefore cognitively more accessible, than other kinds of verbs, and that the same was true of animate subjects. It follows that children should be better able to construct a new linguistic pattern using these less marked members of an emerging grammatical category. As we have seen, the results of de Villiers' experiment support this hypothesis.

De Villiers' theory implies that in language acquisition the members of a grammatical category such as Verb do not all have an equal status. Some members are better examples of, or more central to, the category than others. For example, action verbs like *hit* are 'verbier' than experiential verbs like *see* or stative verbs like *know*. Similar claims are found in two related areas of language scholarship: prototype theory in psychology and variation theory in linguistics, and I now briefly review relevant research in these two fields.

Prototype theory is an important theory of human categorisation within psychology. Its chief theoretician is the psychologist Eleanor Rosch, who proposed the theory as an alternative to the classical theory of categories, which dates from Aristotle. According to the classical theory, the members of any conceptual category such as Bird or Mammal share essential or defining features. The defining features of Mammal might be: 'gives live birth' or 'suckles young'. As we know, Aristotle identified the defining features of Human Being as 'bipedal' and 'without feathers'. However, Rosch (1978), following Wittgenstein (1953), proposed an alternative to the classical theory. She claimed that members of the same conceptual category need not have any features in common. Rather, the members of the category need only have some of the features of a central or prototypical member of that category. Rosch noted that this arrangement is like a family resemblance. For example, two sisters may have no features in common, but they may still be recognised as members of the same family because they each have different features of their mother, who would be the central or prototypical member.

Rosch based her theory on a number of well-known experiments which showed that the classical theory did not square with the facts of human categorisation. The classical theory predicts that no member of a conceptual category will have a special cognitive status. If category membership depends only on possessing certain essential features, all entities that possess those features will be cognitively equal. However, Rosch found that people often consider some members of a category more typical, or central to the category, than other members. Thus, people consider robins and sparrows typical birds, but not chickens and penguins. In one experiment, Rosch asked her subjects to mark on a scale of one to seven how good an example of a category various members were. How good an example of

Bird is a chicken? Rosch found that her subjects' judgements of typicality correlated strongly. In another experiment, she asked subjects to press a button to indicate true or false in response to statements like 'a dog is a pet'. She found that the subjects' reaction times were much faster for central or prototypical members of categories than for peripheral members. This variation in reaction time, which reflects an uncertainty in judgement, is called a 'prototype effect'. Prototype effects occur when people have to categorise an entity which varies from a prototypical member of that category. We will encounter prototype effects in grammaticality judgements below.

Rosch's experimental results led her to conclude that conceptual categories like Bird and Pet are not mentally organised according to the principles of set theory, as in the classical account where all members of a category share essential features, but are organised around a prototypical member. Entities can be members of a conceptual category to the degree that they share the features of the prototypical member of that category. Stated in terms of prototype theory, then, de Villiers' theory makes the following cognitive claims: (1) for children action verbs are prototypical verbs, and animate subjects are prototypical subjects; (2) these prototypical members enter more easily into cognitive operations, such as constructing new sentence patterns, than do peripheral members.

We now turn to the relationship between de Villiers' theory and variation theory. De Villiers relates her work to that of John Robert Ross, who, in a series of papers starting in the mid 1970s, developed a non-categorical theory of grammar. While Ross is not a central figure in variation theory, his ideas have often been presented in variationist forums, such as the N-WAVE conference, and, as I will show, his conception of grammatical rules is more compatible with the variable rules proposed by Labov (1972) than with the categorical and optional rules proposed by Chomsky (1965).

Ross's (1973, 1979) theory of adult grammar is similar to de Villiers' theory of child grammar. He claims that grammatical categories have a prototype structure, so that some members of the category are more central than other members, and that central members are better able to enter into various grammatical constructions. Furthermore, he claims that the distinction between central and peripheral members can be semantic. [2] Ross's evidence for these claims is shown in Table 1, which is called a *squish*. [3] It is an implicational hierarchy where various candidates for the category Noun Phrase (NP) are aligned along the horizontal axis and various grammatical constructions are aligned along the vertical axis. The left-most variety of NPs—animate NPs—are the most 'nouny' because they can be used in all

TABLE 1. *A Noun Phrase squish (from Ross, 1973)*

	Animates	Forces of nature concretes	Events	Abstracts	TACK	HEADWAY	IT (BE MUGGY)	IT (S)	IT (rain)	THERE	T ABS	HEED
TAG FORMATION	OK	OK	OK	OK	OK	OK	OK	OK	OK	OK	?.	?.
Head of relative clauses	OK	OK	OK	OK	OK	OK	DNA	DNA	DNA	DNA	[?*]	[?:]
Inside derived nominals	OK	OK	OK	OK	[?]	?	?	?	??	[?]	??	?*
Get passives	OK	OK	OK	OK	OK	?	[*]	?	[*]	[?*]	??	??
TO BE DELETION	OK	OK	OK	OK	[?]	[??]	?	[OK]	??	??	?*	[*]
CONJUNCTION REDUCTION	OK	OK	OK	OK	OK	[OK]	?	[*]	??	*	*	[?*]
Acc-ing	OK	OK	OK	OK	OK	?	??	??	?*	[OK]	[?*]	?*
...'s	OK	OK	OK	OK	?	?	??	??	?*	*	[*]	*
PRONOMINALISATION	OK	OK	OK	OK	?	?*	DNA	DNA	DNA	DNA	*	*
EQUI	OK	OK	[?]	OK	?	?*	[?]	*	[??]	*	*	*
TOUGH MOVEMENT TOPICAL- ISATION AND SWOOPING	OK	OK	OK	OK	[OK]	[?]	*	*	*	*	*	*
NP SHIFT	OK	OK	OK	OK	??	?*	DNA	DNA	DNA	DNA	[?*]	*
RIGHT NODE RAISING	OK	OK	OK	OK	??	?*	DNA	DNA	DNA	DNA	*	*
LEFT and RIGHT DISLOCATION	OK	OK	OK	OK	??	*	*	*	*	*	*	*
BEING DELETION	OK	OK	OK	?	??	*	*	*	*	*	*	*
What's ... doing X	OK	?.	??	??	??	[?*]	*	*	[?]	*	*	*
Think of ... as X	OK	?.	??	??	?*	[*]	[?*]	[??]	*	*	*	*
Double RAISING	OK	?.	??	??	?*	*	*	[??]	*	[?*]	*	*
PROMOTION and subject of be prevented	OK	?.	?*	*	*	*	*	*	*	*	*	*

Note: DNA = does not apply. Cells that interfere with horizontal good behaviour contain parallel lines. Cells that interfere with vertical good behaviour contain parallel lines.

the grammatical constructions listed. Moving to the right along the horizontal axis, the varieties of NP become less 'nouny' because they can be used in fewer of the constructions. I will not give examples of all the possible NPs and grammatical constructions found in Table 1, but consider how well animate NPs in column 1, abstract NPs in column 2, and existential *there* in column 10 can participate in the double raising construction. Animate NPs are acceptable in double raising constructions, as in example 3:

(3)   John is likely to be shown to have cheated.

Inanimate, concrete NPs are less acceptable, as in (4):

(4)   ?The toaster is likely to be shown to have exploded.

Existential *there*, which is usually classified as an NP, is unacceptable, as in (5):

(5)   ?*There is likely to be shown to be no way out of this mess.

Comparing Ross's theory and Rosch's theory, we see that the premises are identical: membership in a category can be by degrees rather than all or none, and the boundaries of a category can be fuzzy rather than absolute. A second important observation is that grammatical categories can have a prototype structure, not just in the developing grammar of children, but in the adult grammar as well.

Ever since Ross began circulating his ideas, it has been clear that they are more compatible with the theory of variable rules proposed by Labov (1972) than with the theory of categorical rules proposed by Chomsky (1965). In T–G grammar, phrase structure and transformational rules specify grammatical categories, such as NP and Verb, which are absolute; these categories have no internal structure and no degrees of membership. But variable rules take the form of a weighted feature bundle in which properties of a category can be specified and weighted according to how much their presence favours the application of the rule. In de Villiers' experiment the feature [+ animate] on the subject noun phrase and the feature [+ action] on the verb favoured the production of the passive structure. A variable phrase structure rule to describe her subjects' performance could be written as:

(6)   S$_{PASSIVE}$ →
       NP   (is) (being) VERB   (by) NP
       [+ patient]   ⟨B[+ action] ⟩   [+ agent]
       ⟨A [+ animate] ⟩

Variable rule (6) says that the passive construction taught by de Villiers is more likely to be produced when the surface subject is animate and the verb is an action verb. The angle brackets around the features [+ animate] and [+ action] indicate that these favouring features are optional, not required. The A (alpha) in front of [+ animate] indicates that this feature (or *variable constraint*) favours the application of the rule more strongly than does the feature [+ action], which is marked with a B (beta).

To summarise the argument so far, Slobin believes that at first, children's concepts are structured in terms of prototypical scenes. Although these scenes are learned as wholes, they also have an internal structure which can be specified. Such scenes are emergent—that is, they are perceived and remembered early on because of the way our perceptual and cognitive apparatus interact with physical objects in the world. At a later stage, the child perceives that there are other, less obvious relationships between entities such as the relationship in 'John saw the ball', where the subject is not an agent but an experiencer. Gradually, the child abstracts narrow, semantically defined elements into abstract grammatical categories. Undoubtedly, these categories are defined in part by their privileges of occurrence, as Maratsos & Chalkley (1980) have pointed out. But, as Ross (1973) suggests, a semantic residue remains, and some members of a grammatical category are still more central than others.

I would now like to consider briefly a second example of a prototypical scene that has an associated grammatical construction. Lakoff (1987) has studied deictic locative constructions, such as examples (7) and (8). This construction is based on a prototypical scene that Lakoff calls 'the pointing out scene', where a speaker directs attention to a figure at some distance from the speaker.

(7)   There's Sadie.

(8)   Here comes John with the beer.

The figure in the pointing out scene can be either stationary or moving toward or away from the speaker. The deictic pointing out scene, like the manipulative activity scene, has an internal structure, and its components can be specified and represented in the form of a weighted feature bundle. This weighted feature bundle can be written as a variable rule, which can be viewed as a mental schema for a sentence expressing the pointing out scene. According to Lakoff (and I have greatly simplified his explanation) the unmarked form of the deictic locative construction contains a verb in the present tense, which is either the general locative verb (the verb *be*) or a general motion verb (such as *come* or *go*). We cannot confidently rank these features, since Lakoff did not collect statistical data to determine the acceptability of deviations from the prototype as did de Villiers, but we can list them. An incomplete variable phrase structure rule for the deictic locative construction is shown in (9).

(9)   DEICTIC LOCATIVE →

$$\begin{Bmatrix} here \\ there \end{Bmatrix} \quad \left\langle \begin{array}{c} \text{VERB} \\ [+ \text{ simple pres tense}] \\ \begin{Bmatrix} [+ \text{ general motion}] \\ [+ \text{ general location}] \end{Bmatrix} \end{array} \right\rangle \quad \text{NP} \quad \text{(X)}$$

Rule (9) says that the prototype deictic locative begins with a locative adverb, either *here* or *there*. The second element is a verb which is in the present tense and is either the general locative verb *be*, or a general motion verb such as *come* or *go*. The third element in the construction is an NP which is the sentence subject. The optional fourth element can be a number of things such as a locative phrase or a present participial phrase. Lakoff discusses some elaborate features of this last constituent, which I will not go into here.

(10) and (11) are examples of deictic locatives which fit the prototype form.

(10)   Here comes George.

(11)   There's Marsha, driving her new Yugo.

Some deictic locatives which vary from the prototype (and therefore don't sound as good) and the ways in which they vary are shown in examples (12)–(14). They are listed in their order of acceptability to me.

(12)   There sits John. (Verb is a location verb, but not the general location verb *be*).

(13)   ?Here came John, carrying our lost suitcases. (Verb is in the past tense.)

(14)   *?Here walked John, carrying our lost suitcases. (Verb is in the past tense, and verb is not a general motion verb.)

As an example of prototype research in second language acquisition, I will briefly discuss an experiment performed by Gass (1987), who studied the interpretation of sentences with animate versus inanimate subjects and objects. Gass played 27 English sentences to Italian speakers studying English and 27 corresponding Italian sentences to English speakers studying

Italian. The students were asked to identify the logical subject of each sentence. The test sentences were varied according to four parameters: word order, animacy of the first noun, animacy of the second noun and topicalisation, as shown in Table 2. Since topicalisation did not have a major effect on the results, only the first three of these parameters will be discussed. Some possible examples of the test sentences include:[4]

(15) The camel smells the cigarette.
      (NVN word order, +animate first N; −animate second N; −topicalised)

(16) The dog the stick bites.
      (NNV word order; +animate first N; −animate second N; −topicalised)

(17) As far as the bear goes, looks at the bear, the zebra.
      (VNN word order; +animate first N; +animate second N; +topicalised)

Gass (1987) notes that both Italian and English are SVO languages; however, word order in Italian is much freer than in English, so the Italian equivalents of sentences (16) and (17) are grammatical.

On the basis of an experiment involving first language speakers by Bates *et al.* (1982), Gass predicted that in deciding whether the first NP in a test sentence was the subject, the students would be guided by some prototypical combination of the features in Table 2. In other words, she suggested that her subjects had a prototype schema for expressing the subject–verb relationship. The goal of her experiment was to determine which sentence construction corresponded to this schema, and in what ways other sentence constructions diverged from it. Remarkably, Gass found that both groups of students most often selected the first NP as subject for the same sentence construction, namely a sentence with NVN word order, an animate first NP, and an inanimate second NP. This finding suggests that both groups of learners have the same prototype schema for representing the subject–object relationship: a schema where an animate subject acts on

TABLE 2. *Parameters of the test sentences in Gass (1987)*

Word order	First noun	Second noun	Topicalisation
NVN			
NNV	±animate	±animate	±topicalised
VNN			

an inanimate object. This schema is, of course, remarkably similar to the schema proposed by Slobin for the manipulative activity scene.

As in the examples of prototype research discussed above, Gass' experiment can be expressed in variationist terms. The prototype schema for expressing the subject–object relationship can be represented as a variable rule, in which the constraints are NVN word order, animate first noun, and inanimate second noun. Gass found that for both groups of learners the NVN word order was the strongest constraint, followed by the animate first noun and then by the inanimate second noun. She also found that for word orders other than NVN the weighting of the constraints was different for the two groups of learners. In deciding the subject of sentences with these word orders, the native Italian speakers tended to rely more on animacy cues and the native English speakers more on word order cues. These trends reflect the tendencies of the two native languages. In sum, Gass' findings suggest that in second language acquisition, both cognitive universals (such as the semantic information from the manipulation scene) and patterns from the native language (such as canonical word order) can influence the interpretation of target language sentences.

I will conclude with a few remarks about language teaching and natural language acquisition. De Villiers' experiment is an experiment in teaching, and it cannot be assumed that because her subjects learned type A passives more easily than type B passives that this order will occur in natural acquisition. As a matter of fact, there is evidence that children learn agentless passives before passives with agents, such as types A, B and C. What de Villiers experiment does show is that explicitly teaching grammatical constructions to children can be effective, at least in the short run, and that which kinds of constructions are taught makes a difference. Krashen (1981) has questioned the effectiveness of explicitly teaching specific structures in second language acquisition. He claims that there is a natural order of acquisition for both children and adults (not necessarily the same) which will be followed regardless of explicit instruction. The fact that de Villiers was able to teach the passive structure to children argues against Krashen's claims (although lacking longitudal data, we cannot be sure the teaching was effective).

A more serious challenge to Krashen's position comes from Pienemann (1985), who distinguishes between developmental and variable features of interlanguage. Developmental features are acquired in a natural order, as in Krashen's account, and cannot be learned out of sequence. Variable features, on the other hand, can in principle be learned at any time, and Pienemann claims that with regard to these features 'instruction has a drastic influence on L2 speech production' (Pienemann, 1985:37). In support of this claim, Pienemann cites an experiment in which he taught the German copula to Italian schoolchildren. After the training session the rate of copula usage rose dramatically and remained high during a testing session administered one week after the training session.

The claim of prototype theory, that some members of grammatical categories and some types of grammatical constructions are less marked than others, bears on the issue of teachability in the following way. As noted, de Villiers' subjects who were taught marked passives, that is type C passives, were able to infer that unmarked type A passives were also grammatical, and in fact, produced more type A passives than type C passives. But the reverse pattern did not occur. That is, subjects who were taught unmarked passives did not infer that marked passives were grammatical, and they produced very few such passives. In second language acquisition the learner's ability to infer the existence of unmarked forms on the basis of marked forms has been noticed by several scholars including Lightbown (1985).

Thus, perhaps we should not expect learners to infer marked forms on the basis of unmarked forms. To take an example from the Noun Phrase squish, perhaps we should not expect learners to know that existential *there* can be part of a tag question if they have been taught tag questions with animate NPs. Nor should we expect learners to know that deictic locatives can contain verbs other than *be*, *come* and *go*, if they have been taught using only these verbs. This conclusion is similar to that of Tanaka *et al.* (1987), who studied Japanese students' intuitions of grammaticality involving the verb *make*. They found that their subjects tended to judge prototypical uses of *make*, such as, 'The boys are making wooden swords in the field' to be grammatical, whereas they judged more peripheral uses of *make*, such as 'The boys are making a mess' to be ungrammatical.

In conclusion, I would like to suggest that variation in the speech of language learners, both first and second, can be motivated by the fact that some grammatical categories and constructions can be represented mentally as a prototype structure, and that the tools of variation theory can be useful for investigating such structures.

Notes to Chapter 14

1. I would like to thank the Mellon Foundation for a postdoctoral fellowship at the Linguistics Department, University of Pennsylvania, during which this research was completed. I would also like to thank Shana Poplack and Tony Kroch for

most helpful discussions about variation theory; however, they should not necessarily be held responsible for the ideas expressed here.

2. This account of grammatical categories is similar to that of the functionalist school of linguistics, for example in Givón (1984).

3. At this point in the discussion, we must take heed of de Villiers (1980:20) caveat, 'Linguistics being what it is, the intuitions of Ross and his coworkers will have to be taken in lieu of the tabulated responses of four hundred college sophomores.'

4. Gass (1987) gives examples of the words used in her test sentences, but not the sentences themselves; therefore, these examples are only representative of the sentences she used.

References

BATES, E., MacWHINNEY, B., DEVESCOVI, A. and SMITH, A., 1982, Functional constraints on sentence processing: A cross-linguistic study, *Cognition*, 11, 245–99.

BOWERMAN, M. L., 1977, The acquisition of word meaning: An investigation of some current conflicts. In D. MOREHEAD & A. MOREHEAD (eds), *Directions in Normal and Deficient Language*. Baltimore MD: University Park Press.

CHOMSKY, N., 1965, *Aspects of the Theory of Syntax*. Cambridge, MA: MIT Press.

DE VILLIERS, J., 1980, The process of rule learning in a child's speech: A new look. In K. NELSON (ed.), *Children's Language*, Vol. 2. New York: Gardner.

FERGUSON, C., 1984, Repertoire universals, markedness, and second language acquisition. In W. E. RUTHERFORD (ed.), *Language Universals and Second Language Acquisition*. Amsterdam: John Benjamins.

GASS, S., 1987, The resolution of conflicts among competing systems: A bidirectional perspective, *Applied Psycholinguistics*, 8, 329–50.

GIVÓN, T., 1984, *Syntax: A Functional–Typological Introduction*, Vol. 1. Amsterdam: John Benjamins.

KRASHEN, S., 1981, *Second Language Acquisition and Second Language Learning*. Oxford: Pergamon.

LABOV, W., 1972, *Sociolinguistic Patterns*. Philadelphia: University of Pennsylvania Press.

LAKOFF, G., 1987, *Women, Fire and Dangerous Things*. Chicago: University of Chicago Press.

LIGHTBOWN, P., 1985, Can language acquisition be altered by instruction? In K. HYLTENSTAM & M. PIENEMANN (eds), *Modelling and Assessing Second Language Acquisition*. San Diego: College Hill Press.

MARATSOS, M. and CHALKLEY, M. A., 1980, The internal language of children's syntax: The ontogenesis and representation of syntax. In K. NELSON (ed.), *Children's Language*, Vol. 2. New York: Gardner.

PIENEMANN, M., 1985, Learnability and syllabus construction. In K. HYLTENSTAM & M. PIENEMANN (eds), *Modelling and Assessing Second Language Acquisition*. San Diego: College Hill Press.

ROSCH, E., 1978, Principles of categorization. In E. ROSCH & B. B. LLOYD (eds), *Cognition and Categorisation*. Hillsdale, NJ: Lawrence Erlbaum.

Ross, J. R., 1973, A fake NP squish. In C.-J. N. Bailey & R. W. Shuy (eds), *New Ways of Analysing Variation in English*. Washington, DC: Georgetown University Press.

——, 1979, Where's English? In C. J. Fillmore *et al.* (eds), *Individual Differences in Language Ability and Language Behavior*. New York: Academic Press.

Slobin, D., 1985, Crosslinguistic evidence for the language-making capacity. In D. Slobin (ed.), *The Crosslinguistic Study of Language Acquisition, Vol. 2: Theoretical Issues*. Hillsdale, NJ: Lawrence Erlbaum.

Stampe, D., 1969, The acquisition of phonetic representation. In R. Binnick, A. Davison, G. Green & J. Morgan (eds), *Papers from the Fifth Regional Meeting of the Chicago Linguistics Society*. Chicago Department of Linguistics.

Tanaka, S., Takahashi, T. and Abe, H., 1987, 'Acquisition of the lexeme *make* by Japanese learners of English.' Paper presented at the Seventh Los Angeles Second Language Research Forum.

Traugott, E., 1977, Natural semantax: Its role in the study of second language acquisition. In S. Pit Corder & E. Roulet (eds), *The Notions of Simplification, Interlanguages and Pidjins and their Relation to Second Language Acquisition*. Geneva: Droz.

Wittgenstein, L., 1953, *Philosophical Investigations*. New York: Macmillan.

15   L2 tense variation in Navajo English

H. GUILLERMO BARTELT
California State University, Northridge

In the vastness of the American Southwest, enclaves of native Indian speech communities have survived, and they provide the linguist not only with an easily accessible pool of non-Indo-European languages for verification of synchronic theories but also with a rich laboratory for the study of language contact and human cognition. Interestingly, the spread of English to Southwestern Indian reservations has not resulted in the total anglicisation of Indian communities; instead, English has gone through a process of Indianisation, generating ethnically identifiable nonstandard lects with a great deal of seemingly unsystematic variation. These 'Indian Englishes' are now being nativised by children who often have only a passive understanding of the ancestral substrate. The aim of this chapter is two-fold: first, certain ethnohistorical claims regarding possible pidginisation stages leading up to the nativisation of English by American Indians are briefly reviewed; second, the application of a creolisation model to this type of nativisation is proposed.

Varieties of English spoken by American Indians were initially referred to in Leechman & Hall (1955) as American Indian Pidgin English, a label that intended to imply a relationship between these contact languages and other kinds of Pidgin English throughout the world. This claim that Pidgin English reached American Indians because of European expansionism was elaborated and slightly altered in Dillard (1972). According to Dillard, runaway slaves and freed indentured servants, who often settled among Indians, were responsible for spreading Pidgin English to them, and supposedly, white traders learned from Indians already knowledgeable in it. The clearest case of such African-to-Indian transmission Dillard sees among the Seminoles, who allowed refugee slaves from British colonies to settle in

Florida in the eighteenth century. By the early nineteenth century, white travellers began to take notice of Blacks being well established among the Seminoles. In addition, Dillard points out the diffusion of African patterns of agriculture and music among the Seminoles, and he infers linguistic contributions by English-speaking Blacks to the Seminoles from the records of white travellers who mention Black English and Seminole bilinguals acting as interpreters. Ultimately, this kind of interpretation attempts to connect American Indian Pidgin English historically with African-based pidgins derived from the Portuguese trade pidgins.

However, the evidence from studies on other North American contact situations such as Chinook, Mobilian, Delaware and Eskimo Jargons seems to indicate that the various language hybridisations resulted in very diverse pidgins. Consequently, Dillard's insistence on the spread of some Ur-pidgin from the Mediterranean among Southeastern Indians seems highly improbable. (See, for example, Silverstein, 1972; Haas, 1975; Crawford, 1978; Drechsel, 1979, 1981.)

Among Southwestern Indians, particularly in the Rio Grande Valley, Spanish had served as a lingua franca for at least 200 years before annexation of the territory by the United States. Hispanic communities modified the cultural patterns of the various Southwestern tribes, and a great deal of pidginisation and creolisation of Spanish must have taken place. In any case, there is no evidence that tribes in the Southwest had any knowledge of Dillard's hypothetical American Indian Pidgin English, supposedly spread by runaway slaves or trade patterns between the tribes. In fact, Dubois (1977) has clearly shown by referring to historical sources that for the period 1846–1880 Spanish was the vehicle for communicative interaction between Indians and Anglo-Americans. Though forms of Indianised Spanish may have gone through a process of pidginisation, Dubois was unable to find in her survey of these records any references to speakers of Pidgin English, Black translators living with the Indians, or any other persons who could have served as models for the Indians' acquisition of Pidgin English.

Because of the geographic isolation in the Southwest, and because of the prevalent use of Spanish for communication with Europeans, it seems likely that the first systematic exposure of Southwestern Indians to English in the nineteenth century occurred in the schools. In the 1860s and 1870s education for Southwestern Indian children was in the hands of the various religious denominations who were interested in converting the tribes to Christianity. However, the success of these educational efforts was very limited. Especially among the Navajo and the Hopi, most of these programmes failed simply because of lack of attendance.

It became clear to both church mission boards and to the US Bureau of Indian Affairs that to make the transmission of the English language to Indian children more effective, it was necessary to physically remove them from the influence of their linguistic communities and to place them in boarding schools far from the reservations. The boarding school became an effective device for the teaching of English for two reasons. First, the policy forbidding students the use of their native languages was strictly enforced. Second, the intertribal and multilingual context of the boarding school student population made it necessary to resort to English as a lingua franca outside the classroom in such places as the dormitory and cafeteria and in extra-curricular activities. Spicer (1962:44) describes the boarding school situation in this way:

> Out of touch with parents and other Indian adults, and under the instruction of men and women who were officially and usually personally antagonistic to native Indian ways including language, as well as unequipped for learning the Indian languages, the students in periods of three or four years learned how to speak English and, somewhat less effectively, to read and write it. A sort of boarding school dialect of English developed, recognisable as a 'foreign' version of English ...

The linguistic phenomenon Spicer refers to as 'Boarding School English' or Harvey (1974) calls 'Dormitory English' was surely not a uniform dialect but was probably characterised primarily by individual Indian substrata. However, that would not have ruled out a certain amount of levelling based on general interlingual strategies available to all learners of a second language.

The majority of Southwestern Indians who went to school at all after the turn of the century attended one of the regional government boarding programmes in New Mexico, Arizona or California. Spicer (1962) estimates that after inauguration of those programmes, approximately one tenth of Southwestern Indians became exposed to that type of educational environment where they came in contact with tribesmen from all parts of the Southwest and where they relied largely on a pidginised intertribal English code. Even though the success of these programmes, which offered the equivalent of a grade school education with additional vocational training, might be questionable, the regional boarding schools nevertheless represented a major source of the diffusion of this pidginised English into an area relatively isolated from the superstrate. Until World War II, the presence of English speakers, on the Navajo Reservation at least, was very low and was restricted to government officials, traders, teachers and public health officials, who maintained a rigid social distance.

As a result, Navajo as an L1 not only persisted but also kept in check pidginised forms of English well into the 1950s and 1960s even as off-reservation contact increased (Spolsky & Kari, 1974). However, in the 1970s Navajo children began to prefer the use of the L2 and in many cases even nativised English. What has developed on the Navajo Reservation since then is a monolingual Navajo/monolingual Indian English continuum. This situation differs somewhat from classic pidginisation and creolisation due to the continual presence of the ancestral tongue which provides constant input into the linguistic context. In classic situations, for example, a pidgin becomes most likely a creole if input from the superstrate is limited due to social or geographic isolation; and, consequently, continuity of language transmission is severely affected (Bickerton, 1975). This limited access to the standard forces the pidgin to rely on universal language properties which are further expanded when pidgins are creolised. Certainly, the Southwest has never experienced the social conditions in which continuity of L1 transmission was severely affected as was often the case in former slave societies.

A language qualifies as a creole, according to Bickerton (1981:4), only if it arose out of a pidgin which had not existed for more than a generation and if it arose in a population where not more than 20% were native speakers of the dominant language and where the remaining 80% was composed of diverse language groups. However, it has been noted by critics of this rather narrow definition that such constraints would eliminate a number of languages such as Reunion Creole which have traditionally been regarded as creoles. Countless other contact situations which have produced massive structural changes in various languages would also be ruled out.

Bickerton's restrictive definition is a prerequisite for the emergence of his theoretical bioprogram concept, which defines the basis of human language as an innate blueprint determining a large part of the semantic as well as syntactic categories. Yet, Bickerton (1981) claims that fragments of the bioprogram can also be detected in early L1 acquisition; furthermore, Huebner (1985) claims to have found evidence of its existence in adult L2 acquisition. Specifically, Huebner applied Bickerton's proposed universal features for referentiality to variability over time in L2 referential markers. Huebner's data seem to support Bickerton's claims about the primacy of the specific/nonspecific referent distinction made in the theorised bioprogram.

Thus, it seems likely that fragments of such a cognitive blueprint might surface in various kinds of language contact other than classic creoles.

As mentioned previously, the Southwestern Indian situation differs somewhat from the classic ones stipulated in Bickerton's definition. The persistence of L1 input in the form of transfer is obvious, especially at the phonological, morphological and syntactic levels. For example, the uniform CV structure regardless of L1 constraints, which is often present in pidgins (Kay & Sankoff, 1974), is not found in Navajo English. Instead, a clear picture of phonological transfer emerges. Thus, the absence of glides in Navajo results in monophthongisation in Navajo English, and the absence of six English consonantal phonemes in the Navajo inventory produces a number of interlingual approximations in Navajo English (Bartelt, 1986). Furthermore, certain Navajo verbal morphological features such as subject as well as object pronominal affixes and certain syntactic features such as SOV sentence order are often transferred to Navajo English (Bartelt, 1986). However, accountability of a number of Navajo English morphological characteristics regarding tense and aspect becomes problematic when the analysis relies solely on contrasting superstrate with substrate, but it becomes plausible when such phenomena are related to operations activated by an innate bioprogram.

According to Bickerton's formulations, the bioprogram handles tense and aspect by making distinctions between state/nonstate and punctual/nonpunctual categories. For instance, in Guyanese, Bickerton (1975:29) found that past nonstatives and nonpast statives form a single nonanterior category marked by zero stem forms:

(1)   Me *wake* up them pikni and so, all of them *hold* on 'pon me.

(2)   Mi na *no* wai dem a du dis ting.
       (I don't know why they are doing this.)

On the other hand, past statives are clearly marked:

(3)   Dem *bin* gat wan lil haus.
       (They had a little house.) (Bickerton, 1975:35).

Nonstatives are also marked by the attachment of a nonpunctual marker:

(4)   Mi *a* kom back haptanuun.
       (I am coming back this afternoon.) (Bickerton, 1975:34).

The nonpunctual marker never attaches to statives because they are, by nature, already durative. Since punctual actions are more frequent than nonpunctual ones, principles of markedness require nonpunctuals rather than punctuals to be marked. In addition, discourse constraints define nonpast statives and past nonstatives as a single nonanterior tense because neither antedates the main discourse topic under discussion. The stative/ nonstative distinction is purely a semantic one and depends not on the lexical item but on the nature of the proposition. For example, Bickerton (1975:30) points out that in,

(5)   tu an tu mek fo (two and two make four)

the lexical item *mek* would be considered stative, whereas in,

(6)   dem mek i stap (they made him stop)

the same lexical item would be regarded as nonstative.

Certain characteristics regarding tense and aspect in Southwestern Indian English are not unlike those described in classic creoles. For example, in Navajo English unmarked verb forms referring to past contexts are quite common. Some of those cases such as,

(7)   the next day they all *gather* in the auditorium

could be explained on the basis of the transfer of a Navajo phonological constraint of infrequent occurrence of consonant clusters in word final position. Though that may be a plausible explanation for the omission of past tense markers in regular verb forms, productions such as the following become somewhat problematic if the analysis relies solely on transfer:

(8)   Borrowing money and *give* it to them because they *help* her a lot
        when she *was* sick.

Whereas L1 phonological transfer may be responsible for the zero form in *help*, the same phenomenon in the irregular verb *give* seems to demand a different kind of explanation. Cook's (1982) assertion that Southwestern Indian languages lack tense is not entirely accurate because even though the Navajo verb system is based primarily on modes and aspects, past tense is implicit when the perfective mode is applied. It seems that in productions such as (8), neither L1 nor L2 constraints are relevant and that an application of the categories as specified in the bioprogram might be more appropriate.

A pattern begins to emerge if the stative/nonstative distinction is applied to texts such as (8). The zero form verbs *give* and *help* can be classified semanticaly as nonstatives referring to past time and belonging to the unmarked nonanterior tense. The past form verb *was*, on the other hand, can be classified as a stative in a durative context referring to past time and belonging to the marked anterior tense. Similarly, for Guyanese,

Bickerton (1975:35) reports on the occurrence of zero forms in past nonstatives:

(9)   Well one night more we *hear* drum a knock again.

And he points out the presence of past markers in past statives:

(10)   o gaad man ayu *bin* kyan kilawi lass night.
        (Oh God, man, you could have killed us last night.)

Interestingly, the use of *was* as a past marker in conjunction with infinitive forms of verbs is very common in Navajo English:

(11)   Ron was drive to work.

This use has also been reported in Cook (1982:241) for English varieties of both Navajos and Western Apaches:

(12)   He was go to the trading post.

Even though Cook (1982:241) does not speculate on this pattern, except to state that '*was*, for some linguistic reason, is being used as a past marker', it could be suggested that *was* functions as a marker of past statives much like *bin* takes that role in Anglo-creoles.

Dependent upon the stative/nonstative distinction is the punctual/nonpunctual one. Reflecting continuative, iterative or habitual contexts, nonpunctual aspectual markers attach themselves to nonstatives. In Navajo English, as in many English-based creoles, -*ing*, often without copula, serves as the nonpunctual marker:

(13)   I live by the beliefs that *coming* from both the Navajo culture and
        Christianity.

Such is also the case in Guyanese, according to Bickerton (1975:76):

(14)   de *bilin* di bilding
        (they are building the building)

In both examples the actions appear to be of a habitual or iterative nature without specific reference to time. It could perhaps be argued that the use of *ing* in Navajo English, even though it represents mesolectal morphology, might nevertheless reflect basilectal semantics.

Thus, productions in Navajo English seem to indicate that the zero form with nonstative verbs marks past and with statives marks nonpast, forming a single nonanterior category. In habitual or iterative contexts the nonpunctual marker *ing* attaches itself to nonstative verbs. Similar forms in classic creoles have been viewed as reflections of universal grammatical properties and are regarded in Bickerton's model as manifestations of a theorised bioprogram.

Independent support for this kind of universals-oriented analysis of Navajo English comes from the work of Leap (1976) on another variety of American Indian English, the English of the Tanoan Tiwa-speaking Pueblo of Isleta in New Mexico. For example, Leap discovered in Isletan English the use of uninflected BE, resembling the 'distributive BE' in Black English (Fasold, 1969). After ruling out any possible transfer from Tiwa and dismissing any claims of historical diffusion of Black plantation creole to the Southwest, he proposes the view that any language learned through a 'natural' fashion will exhibit certain similarities regardless of native or first language input. In other words, there are certain 'natural' properties in English, or any other language, which particular speech communities make use of in different ways. In Isletan English, for example, Leap (1976:82) points out that the use of uninflected BE functions as a marker of distributive sense often in iterative contexts:

(15)   I be inside the post office every Thursday at noon.

Leap (1976:98) accounts for this phenomenon by appealing to a concept which he refers to as the principle of natural English properties:

> The principle requires the use of an a-temporal verb in deep structure, which is why a consistent agreement in its tense-aspect properties does not emerge under formal assessment ... The 'natural English' argument implies, of course, that any speaker of English could, save for the interference of standard English constraints, use a distributive BE principle in conversational reference.

In a similar vein, Stout & Erting (1976:119) suggest that uninflected BE in Isletan English is one of many manifestations of:

> general nonstandard features which operate across ethnic and geographic boundaries—features which may be reflections of universal language properties. These 'universals' then interact with specific features from the native languages ... to yield varieties of nonstandard English. These varieties then become associated with ethnically identifiable communities of speakers through a separate process.

In short, natural English properties constitute a kind of inter-speech community overlap. These general constraints are in turn controlled by speakers in terms of their idiosyncratic linguistic backgrounds.

It must be kept in mind that in Isletan English or in Navajo English, as in other language contact continua, nonstandard forms are not static but increasingly co-exist with standard forms in individuals who approach perceived prestige norms as a result of such factors as formal education. However, even the limited presence of the ancestral tongue, though it is often stigmatised, perpetuates a nonstandard English context among reservation residents regardless of levels of education. In addition, it could be argued that in a day and age when Southwestern Indian monolingualism has virtually vanished and even balanced bilingualism is on the decline, reservation varieties of English have actually become the new vehicles for the perpetuation of an Indian cultural identity (Bartelt, 1986). In a sense, Indian English bridges the gap between the often stigmatised L1 and the somewhat alienating effects of the use of standard English. Leap (1974:55), for example, noted that, in Isleta Pueblo, members of the reservation community who have acquired standard English for more effective dealings with the outside find it necessary to resort to the conscious use of diglossia or style-switching in order not to appear to be 'trying to talk like a white man'. Among the Navajos the community variety of English seems to serve also as an internally generated solution to a somewhat problematic cultural identity.

In summary, the first aim of this chapter has been to review some ethnohistorical claims as they have been discussed in the linguistic literature in regard to a monogenetic interpretation of varieties of American Indian English. The conclusion of that review seems to indicate that in view of the influential role of the boarding school system, a polygenetic view of Southwestern Indian English might be more plausible. The second aim has been to suggest that universal properties such as those proposed in Bickerton (1981) may surface in contact situations other than classic creoles and that Bickerton's definition of a creole may be overly constrained. The two requirements which need to be re-examined in Bickerton's model are the existence of a prior pidgin for only one generation and the degree of disruption of language transmission. Thus, while ideal conditions for the creation of a creole have never existed in the American Southwest, it could, nevertheless, be argued that a combination of geographic isolation and social distance based on a history of Anglo-Saxon racism has made standard English not only somewhat inaccessible but also relatively unacceptable for a Southwestern Indian community. In other words, disruption of language transmission can in part be self-imposed, as was clearly demonstrated in Schumann (1976). As a final note, it must be pointed out that much comparative work on varieties of American Indian English other than Navajo, Western Apache and Isleta remains to be completed in order to be able to make a more comprehensive statement about the emergence of universal properties in a picture of seemingly unsystematic variation.

References

BARTELT, G., 1986, Language contact in Arizona: The case of Apachean English, *Anthropos*, 81, 692–5.

BICKERTON, D., 1975, *Dynamics of a Creole System*. New York: CUP.

——, 1981, *Roots of Language*. Ann Arbor: Karoma.

COOK, M. J., 1982, Problems of Southwestern Indian speakers in learning English. In P. TURNER (ed.), *Bilingualism in the Southwest*. Tucson: University of Arizona Press.

CRAWFORD, J. M., 1978, *The Mobilian Trade Language*. Knoxville: University of Tennessee Press.

DILLARD, J. L., 1972, *Black English: Its History and Usage in the United States*. New York: Random House.

DRECHSEL, E. J., 1979, *Mobilian Jargon: Linguistic, Sociocultural, and Historical Aspects of an American Indian Lingua Franca*. Ann Arbor: Univ. Microfilms.

——, 1981, A preliminary sociolinguistic comparison of four indigenous pidgin languages of North America (with notes towards a sociolinguistic typology in American Indian linguistics), *Anthropological Linguistics*, 23, 93–112.

DUBOIS, B. L., 1977, Spanish, English, and the Mescalero Apache (1846–1880). In W. L. LEAP (ed.), *Studies in Southwestern Indian English*. San Antonio: Trinity University Press.

FASOLD, R., 1969, Tense and the verb BE in Black English, *Language*, 45, 763–76.

HAAS, M. R., 1975, What is Mobilian? In J. M. CRAWFORD (ed.), *Studies in Southeastern Indian Languages*. Athens: University of Georgia Press.

HARVEY, G. C., 1974, Dormitory English: Implications for the teacher. In G. BILLS (ed.), *Southwestern Areal Linguistics*. San Diego: Inst. for Cultural Pluralism.

HUEBNER, T., 1985, System and variability in interlanguage syntax, *Language Learning*, 35, 141–63.

KAY, P. and SANKOFF, G., 1974, A language-universals approach to pidgins and creoles. In D. DECAMP & I. HANCOCK (eds), *Pidgins and Creoles: Current Trends and Prospects*. Washington, DC: Georgetown University Press.

LEAP, W., 1974, Ethnics, emics and the new ideology: The identity potential of Indian English. In T. FITZGERALD (ed.), *Social and Cultural Identity*. Athens: University of Georgia Press.

——, 1976, Uninflected BE in Isletan English: A problem in accountability. In W. LEAP (ed.), *Studies in Southwestern Indian English*. San Antonio: Trinity University Press.

LEECHMAN, D. and HALL, R. A.., 1955, American Indian pidgin English: Attestations and grammatical peculiarities, *American Speech*, 30, 163–71.

SCHUMANN, J., 1976, Social distance as a factor in second language acquisition, *Language Learning*, 26, 135–43.

SILVERSTEIN, M., 1972, Chinook Jargon: Language contact and the problem of multilevel generative systems, *Language*, 48, 378–406.

SPICER, E. H., 1962, *Cycles of Conquest*. Tucson: University of Arizona Press.

SPOLSKY, B. and KARI, J., 1974, Apachean language maintenance, *Linguistics*, 128, 91–100.

STOUT, S. and ERTING, C., 1976, Uninflected BE in Isletan English: Implicational scaling and the relationship of Isletan English to other ethnically identifiable varieties of English. In W. LEAP (ed.), *Studies in Southwestern Indian English*. San Antonio: Trinity University Press.

16 Interlanguage, interdialect and typological change

PETER TRUDGILL
University of Essex

This chapter is based on work I have been doing over the past few years on dialect contact, but it branches out also to look at the topic of language contact. It examines the role of accommodation, second dialect acquisition, and second language acquisition, of the sort that occur in contact situations, in producing typological change in language. But it also considers the notion of what is *normal* or usual in language change. And it takes a look, with reference to interlanguage and interdialect, at the notion of *simplification* as this affects language change and learnability.

Dialect contact and rate of change

I will begin my discussion by comparing high-contact dialects with low-contact dialects and its consequences, namely second dialect acquisition and new-dialect formation. I will then move on to the comparison of high-contact and low-contact languages and second language acquisition. In each case I will examine first of all the role of contact in influencing *speed* of change, and then its role in producing particular *types* of change. In each case I will compare high-contact with low-contact situations.

Of course, at the level of dialects of a particular language, it is well known that degree of contact is an important influence on rate of change. It is a principle very familiar to dialectologists and geographical linguists that geographically-peripheral areas tend to be less innovating as compared to varieties spoken in more central areas. For example, the English dialects of the southeast of England are in most, although not all respects, considerably more innovating than those of northeastern England where, for example, monophthongal forms such as *oot* and *hoose* can still be heard, although they disappeared from the south several centuries ago. Similarly, the most conservative dialects of Norwegian are by general consent those found in remote inland valleys, while the most innovating are those in the well-trafficked southern coastal areas. The latter have, for example, lost the marking of the dative case on nouns, while the former have retained it. And very many other examples could be given.

The conservatism of these peripheral or isolated varieties surprises no one, but we should note that it is actually not a simple matter to produce detailed or analytical explanations for why contact does mean change in this way. Explanations, however, have been advanced. In a sociolinguistically sophisticated paper called 'Linguistic change, social network and speaker innovation', Milroy & Milroy (1985) have pointed out that 'linguistic change is *slow* to the extent that the relevant populations are well-established and bound by *strong* [network] ties, whereas it is *rapid* to the extent that *weak* ties exist in populations'.

Type of change: high dialect contact

However, I want now to go on to argue that dialect contact plays a role not only in affecting *rate* of change but also in affecting *type* of change. This is obviously not particularly controversial. Everyone would accept, I assume, that borrowing, for instance, takes place only in contact situations. It is, however, possible to take this issue somewhat further. In my recent book *Dialects in Contact* (Trudgill, 1986), I examined developments which typically occur in situations of high contact between mutually-intelligible varieties, concentrating on dialect-mixture and new-dialect formation. Dialect contact, it appears, leads most usually to what we call *simplification*, *not* reduction, as had been observed by a number of scholars. Jakobson long ago, for instance, noted that dialects which serve a relatively wide socio-spatial function tend to have simpler systems than dialects with a more restricted function (Jakobson, 1929). And Labov has pointed out that, in contact situations, phonological mergers spread at the expense of contrasts. In dialect contact generally, it seems that we most often encounter a process of *koinéisation*, in which *levelling* and *simplification* both play a role. By *levelling* we mean the loss of minority, or marked, variants present in the dialect-mixture in favour of majority, or unmarked, forms also present. By *simplification* is meant, in this case especially, the growth of new or *interdialect* forms that were not actually present in the initial mixture but developed out of interaction between forms that *were* present; these interdialect forms are more regular than their predecessors.

Explanations for why koinéisation takes exactly the form it does are again not necessarily straightforward, but it seems likely that the greater learnability of regular forms is an important factor. The main explanation must be the inability of post-adolescents to acquire new language varieties perfectly, and the particular difficulties caused for them as far as learnability is concerned, by irregularity. Andersen (1986) stresses the role of child language acquisition in imposing order on contact situations which are characterised by 'blurred norms'. We can imagine children, for example, playing an important role in the levelling process by selecting the most common variants. And we can imagine them aiding the simplification process by selecting simpler forms already present in the mixture in preference to more complex forms. But notice that it is most likely to be post-adolescents who provide *new* simpler alternatives in the form of interdialect variants not originally present in the mixture.

Interestingly, koinéisation also seems to be a process that is on the increase in many parts of the world, with increasing urbanisation, in particular, leading to a growth in the number of new, mixed and therefore levelled and simplified dialects.

Type of change: low dialect contact

In any case, we can say that the changes we have labelled koinéisation are those which are normal in high dialect-contact situations. But what of changes that take place in other contexts? What can we expect to happen in low-contact situations? In fact, much less is actually known about the sorts of developments that typically occur in dialects in relative isolation. In low-contact situations we know that the speed of linguistic change will typically be slow. But it is not entirely clear what *types* of linguistic change we can expect to be normal in these contexts. However, there now seems to be the beginnings of an interesting consensus that many of the changes that take place in this sort of situation are of a type that move in the *opposite* direction to those that occur as a result of simplification. Not only is the social context the opposite—low dialect contact versus high dialect contact: but the linguistic consequences are in a sense the opposite also—*complication* as opposed to simplification.

Evidence for this hypothesis is advanced, for example, by Henning Andersen, in a recent important paper. Andersen (1986), suggests that his Slavic language data do indeed point to the reverse of Jakobson's observations that koinés develop simpler systems. Andersen claims in fact that 'dialects that serve predominantly local functions are more prone to elaborate phonetic detail rules than dialects with a wider sphere of use'. He argues that 'there is a connection between the limited socio-spatial function of a dialect, its relative closedness [in a network sense], and its ability to sustain exorbitant phonetic developments.' Andersen also points out that such dialects will 'preserve morphological irregularity with relatively great faithfulness'. A detailed example that Andersen employs to make the point about phonetic elaboration is the following. He points out that in a number of widely dispersed geographically isolated areas of Europe, the same type of unusual phonetic norm elaboration has occurred. The areas are: the upper reaches of several Romansch-speaking Alpine valleys; the upper reaches of a number of Provençal-speaking Alpine valleys; the most peripheral part of Flanders; the sparsely-populated Eifel plateau of Luxembourg; the heart of the Hessian hills in Germany; and the most isolated parts of the Jutland peninsula in Denmark. The unusual phonetic development is the development of parasitic consonants out of diphthongs. Thus, in Waldeck in Hesse, parasitic *k* has developed after *i* and *u* (with *n* instead of *k* before *m* and *n*). Thus *Eis* 'ice' = *iks*; *aus* 'out' = *uks*; *neun* 'nine' = *ninne*; and so on. Andersen claims that it is not a coincidence that this relatively strange phonetic change has occurred in these isolated areas, and not in areas of high contact. In other words, these developments occur only where there is low involvement of accommodation and second dialect acquisition.

Caveat

Note, however, that there is a caveat I feel we should introduce here. I agree entirely with Andersen's argument, but terminology such as 'exorbitant phonetic developments' may be somewhat misleading. The fact is that those of us who ourselves live in high-contact second dialect learning (SDL) situations and therefore speak koinés have to guard against making the too easy assumption that these high SDL-involvement koinés are more 'normal' or worthy of study, rather than simply *normal in a particular social context* with which we happen to be most familiar. Andersen's numerous examples make it plain that the development of parasitic consonants is perfectly normal in isolated social contexts, where little SDL is involved.

Note, too, that there may be a tendency, because of the levelling element of koinéisation, to regard isolated varieties as somewhat bizarre just because they are unusual from the point of view of a particular language. Many scholars of English, for instance, regard the peripheral and conservative dialects of northeast Scotland as somewhat strange because one of the changes they have experienced is that of *hw* becoming *f*, as in *what* = *fit*, *where* = *faur*. Now this *is* odd. But it is only odd amongst dialects of English. A change from *hw* to *f* is not at all strange from a phonetic point of view, or from the point of view of, say, the Polynesian languages.

In any case, we can say that where post-adolescent second dialect acquisition, or accommodation, occurs on a wide scale, koinéisation takes place. The study of koinéisation, then, tells us much about second-dialect learning. On the other hand, it could be argued that for students of language change, and of child language acquisition, and for those concerned with the inherent nature of human language systems themselves, the study of isolated varieties should not be neglected.

Another implication of this must be that, for adults in a language learning situation, some dialects of a language will probably be genuinely easier to learn than others. Most often in SL teaching there are so many other factors to consider that we do not have any choice about which variety we are going to teach the learner, but if we *do* have a choice, we should obviously consider selecting koinés over non-koinés. If I were teaching Norwegian to foreigners, I would certainly select the more highly koinéised Bøkmål rather than the other standard variant, if ease of acquisition were the main criterion.

Language contact

I now want to draw some parallels between what we know about differences between high- and low-contact dialects and differences between high- and low-contact languages. Here, too, it is widely agreed that, other things being equal, languages whose speakers have frequent contact with speakers of other varieties change faster than varieties whose speakers have infrequent external contacts. We can note that, for example, Danish is in most respects considerably more innovating than the more conservative Faroese. That is to say that Danish and Faroese, having descended from a common ancestor, Old Norse, today differ considerably one from the other. This is because of linguistic changes which have taken place in the last 1,000 years or so—but, crucially, far more of these changes have taken place in Danish than in Faroese. And we can surely agree that the Faroes have for the last 1,000 years been a more isolated linguistic community than Denmark.

Type of change: high language contact

If we now turn to the question of how high- and low-contact situations affect the *nature* of change, it is again clear that changes which take place in some high-contact situations have been relatively well studied. Our investigations of lingua francas, pidgins, creoles and other high-contact language varieties involving adult second-language learning have led us in fact to expect, in these situations, developments such as the following: change from analytic to synthetic structure, reduction in redundancy, and increases in regularity. Now notice that many of these changes were originally thought of by some older historical linguistics as being normal in *all* contexts, and of course we cannot rule out the possibility altogether that these changes might sometimes be evolutive. But we also have to consider the strong possibility that the widespread feeling that these changes are 'normal' may have stemmed from the fact that many examples occur in the languages with which the earlier European historical linguists were most familiar—and that this familiarity may have been misleading. As is very well known indeed, changes of this type are attested in the histories of the Indo-European languages of Western Europe, as well as in the Semitic languages and elsewhere. In comparing continental Scandinavian with Old Norse, English with Old English, German with Old High German, French with Latin, we find features such as reduction in overt case-marking and an increase in prepositional usage; reduction in conjugations, declensions and inflections; loss of the dual number; increase in periphrastic verb forms; more restrictions on word order; and so on.

It is, however, much more satisfactory to advance explanations for these phenomena in terms of contact than in terms of internal motivation. All changes of this type can again be described by the technical term of *simplification*. What are the origins of this simplification? The answer to this becomes clear if we ask: simplification for whom? Probably not for the native speaker, or in any serious way for the young child. Rather, it is simplification for the *adult non-native learner*. Hence the link between the imperfect learning by adults that takes place during pidginisation, and the tendency to simplification that occurs in other high-contact varieties.

It is usual for lay people to claim that some languages are easier to learn than others. Linguistics have tended to counter this suggestion by pointing out that it depends what your point of departure is. Spanish may be easier for an English speaker to learn than Tibetan, but for a Burmese speaker it might be the other way round. However, it is fair to suggest that some languages really are, in an absolute sense, easier to learn than others, at least in the initial stages. These are the languages which have experienced relatively high contact, a relatively high degree of imperfect language learning by adults, and therefore a relatively high degree of simplification. If I were given a month to learn a language, I would certainly choose Norwegian or Spanish rather than Faroese or Latin.

It should be made clear at this point, however, that when we talk of high-contact situations, what we say can in fact only be true of certain high-contact situations, namely those where it is principally *post-adolescent second-variety acquisition* that is involved. High-contact situations come in many different forms, and we will not necessarily expect to find simplification in those (very many) contact situations where childhood bilingualism and second-variety acquisition are the norm. In these situations, on the contrary, we are liable, although not certain, to find intensive borrowing and interpenetration of linguistic systems, with possible resulting complication. It is precisely the imperfect language learning abilities of the adult which, we postulate, is the chief mechanism behind simplification.

At the International Historical Linguistics Conference in 1979, I gave a paper which was entitled 'On the rise of the creoloid'. In that paper, I used the term *creoloid* to refer to language varieties which, relative to some earlier stage or to some parent variety, have undergone considerable pidginisation, but without ever passing through the stage of actually being a pidgin. That is, they have undergone the processes of admixture and simplification, but have not experienced the process of reduction, because they have maintained a continuous tradition of native speakers. They are usually, moreover, still mutually intelligible with the source language, if this survives. A good candidate for the label of creoloid, then, is Afrikaans, which looks like a decreolised Dutch-based creole, but really isn't. Relative to Dutch, it demonstrates admixture and simplification, but it is clearly not a Dutch-based creole in the same sense that, say, Sranan is an English-based creole. The paper then went on to argue, as we just have above, that relative simplification, of the type that we see in pidgins, creoles and creoloids, crucially represents simplification for the adult non-native learner, and that adult language acquisition, as we have just noted, occurs more often in high-contact situations than in low-contact situations. Now, given the changes that have taken place in the last several centuries in communications, transportation and perhaps especially in demography, we can probably suggest that high-contact linguistic situations have become much more common in recent times. It will therefore not be surprising if more languages than in earlier ages have undergone greater simplification and ended up looking like creoloids. There may well be, that is, an evolutionary trend in human languages, but this is due to demography rather than anything else. There are simply many more people around now than there were 1,000 years ago, and like koinés, creoloids may be on the increase. This may mean, amongst other things, that more languages are getting easier for post-adolescents to learn.

Types of change: low language contact

If we now turn our attention to *low*-contact languages, we have to note once again that rather less is known of the sorts of changes these varieties undergo. Andersen's observations about isolated dialects, however, give us a certain amount of confidence in predicting that the same sort of relationship will obtain between changes which occur in high- and low-contact situations at this level also. It seems quite possible, that is, that we will find in low-contact languages changes that are the converse of simplification, i.e. complication.

One problem with this is that, unlike the considerable amounts of information that we have on koinés, creoloids and other high-contact varieties, we have very few studies of low-contact varieties *as such*. That is, few studies have attempted to explain the characteristics of low-contact varieties precisely in terms of *low contact*. However, although we are obviously on much less sure ground here than we are with the well-studied creoles and koinés, I want to suggest, with some support from C. J. Bailey in his 1982 book, that changes typical of low-contact social contexts would include phenomena such as movement from analytic to synthetic structure and a general increase in redundancy, such as development of complex forms of grammatical agreement. We might also expect the development of case-endings or verbal person inflections out of independent lexical items, through cliticisation and morphologisation processes. And, recalling that Andersen argues that low-contact dialects are more likely to preserve morphological irregularity, we might even go one stage further and predict an increase in such languages of morphological irregularity. In phonology, we might again look for the reverse of the observations made by scholars such as Jakobson and Labov; that is, we might expect a growth in the number of phonological contrasts. This latter speculation is supported by Bailey (1982) who, citing also a personal communication from Eric Hamp, points out that such developments lead to phenomena in low-contact varieties such as the proliferation of clicks in the Khoisan languages and the proliferation of other 'unusual' consonantal articulations in isolated languages such as Scots Gaelic, Amerindian languages of the Pacific Northwest of the USA, and languages of the Caucasus. Note that, of course, the

Pacific Northwest and the Caucasus are, or were, highly multilingual areas with considerable possibilities for contact. These situations, however, were stable situations and therefore provided good opportunities for borrowing, for the development of child bilingualism, and for lingua francas, with correspondingly low levels of adult language learning. It is also likely that in certain relatively small language communities, it is the tight social networks and the absence of *dialect* contact which are the most significant factors not only in producing slow rates of change but also in producing complication. Even in the case of, say, Danish versus Faroese, it may well be that the fact of high versus low dialect contact is as important, if not more so, than the factor of high versus low language contact. That is, one of the most important factors about isolated language varieties may be not just that they are isolated but that they are demographically *small*.

Caveat

However, this now leads us once again into an area where there may be less consensus. Bailey (1982), for example, has argued that these developments may, while being perfectly normal in themselves, lead to *results* or *states*, in languages such as the Caucasian and the Khoisan, which 'no one would wish to call natural'. He also writes of, for instance, 'incredible consonant clusters' in certain languages and suggests that too many such changes in a language can lead to states that are 'intolerable'. He also indicates that languages need a balance between simplification and complication to keep them 'healthy'. I feel uneasy about this in the same way that I do about the 'exorbitant' phonetic developments.

I would like to suggest that it is surely important to stress that both the changes in isolated languages which lead to these states *and* the states themselves can be regarded as being (at least) entirely *normal*. To suggest that there is something unusual about certain Caucasian consonant systems is obviously correct, but only if one ignores the factor of contact and second language acquisition. We have to be very careful not to fall into the Eurocentric trap of regarding our high-contact world as producing language varieties that are in general more *normal* or interesting than others. We saw above that it is easy to fall into the trap of supposing that there is something bizarre about northeast Scottish dialects of English just because these are the only dialects which have the change of *hw* to *f*. There is a parallel here with the tendency to regard some *languages* as more bizarre than others.

Bickerton has argued for the importance of the study of the development, by children, of creole languages in high-contact situations, as a window into the nature of linguistic competence. I want to suggest, in a kind of mirror-image of his argument, that if we are keen to learn more about the inherent nature of linguistic systems and of their propensity to change, we can also usefully turn out attention to linguistic changes of the type that occur in low-contact varieties—'complication'. And of course this will be easiest to do by researching the most isolated language varieties that it is possible to find.

Of course, we have to acknowledge that there was probably never any such thing as a truly isolated language. But it is surely true that isolated languages—and therefore complication or low-contact type changes—were more common formerly than they are today. Isolated varieties are presumably getting harder to find every year. By way of illustration, a few years ago I was planning to begin some work on the English of the Falkland Islands, only to find that suddenly this variety had become very non-isolated. And even my current work on the English of Tristan da Cunha indicates some influence, by the 1960s, from South African English. This, of course, is simply the other side of the coin of the rise of the creoloids and the koinés. Nevertheless, I want to argue for the importance of the study of low-contact varieties. For one thing, even though there will be fewer changes to study in these languages because of their lower rate of change, they will be of the greatest interest for any scholar adopting, in historical linguistics, the 'use of the present to explain the past' approach. When it comes to contact, the present is *not* like the past, and it is by investigating isolated languages that we are most likely to gain insights into the sorts of linguistic changes that occurred in the remote past.

Even if isolated languages and dialects do have, to those of us of a European-language background, and to those of who speak standard koinés, 'amazingly' large consonantal inventories or 'peculiar' phonetic features, they are of interest precisely because they represent, to the clearest extent, the limits to which languages can go when, as Bailey (1982) says, they are 'left alone'.

Students of second language acquisition have to be interested in koinés, pidgins, creoloids and other varieties which show, in their development, considerable historical simplification. Students of historical linguistics, first language acquisition, and language typology may, on the other hand, find it of considerable benefit to study isolated, non-simplified varieties while there are still such language varieties left to study. If we want to gain a better understanding of the human language faculty and of the full range of possible human languages, we cannot afford to ignore the isolated, the remote, or the marginal.

Acknowledgements

Other versions of this paper were given at the Conference on Social Context and Language Change, Stanford University, California, August 1987, and at the Conference on the Causes of Linguistic Change, Tromsø University, Norway, October 1987. I am grateful to participants at all three conferences for their helpful comments. I am also especially grateful to Donna Christian, Ralph Fasold and Jean Hannah for their comments on earlier drafts.

References

ANDERSEN, H., 1986, Center and periphery: Adoption, diffusion and spread. Paper presented at the International Historical Dialectology Conference, Poznań, Poland.

BAILEY, C. J., 1982, *On the Yin and Yang Nature of Language*. Ann Arbor: Karoma.

GIVÓN, T., 1984, Universals of discourse structure and second language acquisition. In W. RUTHERFORD (ed.), *Language Universals and Second Language Acquisition*. Amsterdam: Benjamin.

JAKOBSON, R., 1929, Remarques sur l'évolution phonologique du russe comparée à celle des autres langue slaves. In *Selected Writings I*. The Hague: Mouton.

MILROY, J. and MILROY, L., 1985, Linguistic change, social network, and speaker innovation, *Journal of Linguistics*, 21, 339–84.

SLOBIN, D., 1973, Cognitive prerequisites for the development of grammar. In C. FERGUSON & D. SLOBIN (eds), *Studies in Child Language Development*. New York: Holt, Reinhard & Winston.

——, 1977, Language change in childhood and history. In J. MACNAMARA (ed.), *Language, Thought and Language Learning*. New York: Academic Press.

TRUDGILL, P., 1983, On the rise of the creoloid. In *On Dialect*. Oxford: Basil Blackwell.

——, 1986, *Dialects in Contact*. Oxford: Basil Blackwell.

Contents of Volume I

Index

Note: Figures in italics refer to tables and diagrams.
Abbreviations: L1 = first language; L2 = second language